# File for Divorce in New Jersey

## Second Edition

F. Clifford Gibbons
Rebecca A DeSimone

Attorneys at Law

SPHINX® PUBLISHING
AN IMPRINT OF SOURCEBOOKS, INC.®
NAPERVILLE, ILLINOIS
www.SphinxLegal.com

Second Edition: 2005

Published by: **Sphinx® Publishing, A Imprint of Sourcebooks, Inc.®**

<u>Naperville Office</u>
P.O. Box 4410
Naperville, Illinois  60567-4410
(630) 961-3900
Fax: 630-961-2168
www.sourcebooks.com
www.SphinxLegal.com

This publication is designed to provide accurate and authoritative information in regard to the subject matter covered. It is sold with the understanding that the publisher is not engaged in rendering legal, accounting, or other professional service. If legal advice or other expert assistance is required, the services of a competent professional person should be sought.

*From a Declaration of Principles Jointly Adopted by a Committee of the
American Bar Association and a Committee of Publishers and Associations*

**This product is not a substitute for legal advice.**

*Disclaimer required by Texas statutes.*

**Library of Congress Cataloging-in-Publication Data**
Gibbons, F. Clifford.
  File for divorce in New Jersey / F. Clifford Gibbons, Rebecca A. Desimone.-- 2nd ed.
       p. cm.
  Rev. ed. of: How to file for divorce in New Jersey. 2003.
  Includes index.
  ISBN 1-57248-512-4 (alk. paper)
  1. Divorce suits--New Jersey--Popular works. I. DeSimone, Rebecca A., 1963- II. Gibbons, F. Clifford. How to file for divorce in New Jersey. III. Title.

KFN1900.Z9G53 2005
346.74901'66--dc22                                                          2005014539

Printed and bound in the United States of America.
BG — 10 9 8 7 6 5 4 3 2 1

# Contents

# Using Self-Help Law Books

Before using a self-help law book, you should realize the advantages and disadvantages of doing your own legal work and understand the challenges and diligence that this requires.

**The Growing Trend**

Rest assured that you will not be the first or only person handling your own legal matter. For example, in some states, more than 75% of the people in divorces and other cases represent themselves. Because of the high cost of legal services, this is a major trend, and many courts are struggling to make it easier for people to represent themselves. However, some courts are not happy with people who do not use attorneys and refuse to help them in any way. For some, the attitude is, "Go to the law library and figure it out for yourself."

We write and publish self-help law books to give people an alternative to the often complicated and confusing legal books found in most law libraries. We have made the explanations of the law as simple and easy to understand as possible. Of course, unlike an attorney advising an individual client, we cannot cover every conceivable possibility.

**Cost/Value Analysis**

Whenever you shop for a product or service, you are faced with various levels of quality and price. In deciding what product or service to buy, you make a cost/value analysis on the basis of your willingness to pay and the quality you desire.

When buying a car, you decide whether you want transportation, comfort, status, or sex appeal. Accordingly, you decide among choices such as a Neon, a Lincoln, a Rolls Royce, or a Porsche. Before making a decision, you usually weigh the merits of each option against the cost.

When you get a headache, you can take a pain reliever (such as aspirin) or visit a medical specialist for a neurological examination. Given this choice, most people, of course, take a pain reliever, since it costs only pennies; whereas a medical examination costs hundreds of dollars and takes a lot of time. This is usually a logical choice because it is rare to need anything more than a pain reliever for a headache. But in some cases, a headache may indicate a brain tumor, and failing to see a specialist right away can result in complications. Should everyone with a headache go to a specialist? Of course not, but people treating their own illnesses must realize that they are betting on the basis of their cost/value analysis of the situation. They are taking the most logical option.

The same cost/value analysis must be made when deciding to do one's own legal work. Many legal situations are very straightforward, requiring a simple form and no complicated analysis. Anyone with a little intelligence and a book of instructions can handle the matter without outside help.

But there is always the chance that complications are involved that only an attorney would notice. To simplify the law into a book like this, several legal cases often must be condensed into a single sentence or paragraph. Otherwise, the book would be several hundred pages long and too complicated for most people. However, this simplification necessarily leaves out many details and nuances that would apply to special or unusual situations. Also, there are many ways to interpret most legal questions. Your case may come before a judge who disagrees with the analysis of our authors.

Therefore, in deciding to use a self-help law book and to do your own legal work, you must realize that you are making a cost/value analysis. You have decided that the money you will save in doing it yourself outweighs the chance that your case will not turn out to your satisfaction. Most people handling their own simple legal matters never have a problem, but occasionally people find that it ended up costing them more to have an attorney straighten out the situation than it would have if they had hired an attorney in the beginning. Keep this in mind while handling your case, and be sure to consult an attorney if you feel you might need further guidance.

**Local Rules**

The next thing to remember is that a book which covers the law for the entire nation, or even for an entire state, cannot possibly include every procedural difference of every jurisdiction. Whenever possible, we provide the exact form needed; however, in some areas, each county, or even each judge, may require unique forms and procedures. In our state books, our forms usually cover the majority of counties in the state or provide examples of the type of form that will be required. In our national books, our forms are sometimes even more general in nature but are designed to give a good idea of the type of form that will be needed in most locations. Nonetheless, keep in mind that your state, county, or judge may have a requirement, or use a form, that is not included in this book.

You should not necessarily expect to be able to get all of the information and resources you need solely from within the pages of this book. This book will serve as your guide, giving you specific information whenever possible and helping you to find out what else you will need to know. This is just like if you decided to build your own backyard deck. You might purchase a book on how to build decks. However, such a book would not include the building codes and permit requirements of every city, town, county, and township in the nation; nor would it include the lumber, nails, saws, hammers, and other materials and tools you would need to actually build the deck. You would use the book as your guide, and then do some work and research involving such matters as whether you need a permit of some kind, what type and grade of wood is available in your area, whether to use hand tools or power tools, and how to use those tools.

Before using the forms in a book like this, you should check with your court clerk to see if there are any local rules of which you should be aware or local forms you will need to use. Often, such forms will require the same information as the forms in the book but are merely laid out differently or use slightly different language. They will sometimes require additional information.

**Changes in the Law**

Besides being subject to local rules and practices, the law is subject to change at any time. The courts and the legislatures of all fifty states are constantly revising the laws. It is possible that while you are reading this book, some aspect of the law is being changed.

In most cases, the change will be of minimal significance. A form will be redesigned, additional information will be required, or a waiting period will be extended. As a result, you might need to revise a form, file an extra form, or wait out a longer time period. These types of changes will not usually affect the outcome of your case. On the other hand, sometimes a major part of the law is changed, the entire law in a particular area is rewritten, or a case that was the basis of a central legal point is overruled. In such instances, your entire ability to pursue your case may be impaired.

# Introduction

Divorce is a difficult, emotional, and uprooting event. For many, divorce can be one of the most devastating events imaginable.

There are as many reasons for couples to divorce as there are to marry, so the fact that divorces are on the rise in the United States is not surprising. Certainly, when one observes the vast numbers of marriages breaking up, it causes one to wonder if it is possible in this present day for couples to last throughout the seemingly all-encompassing pledge and commitment of an enduring marriage.

With approximately fifty percent of all marriages ending in divorce, it is not surprising why you are about to read this self-help book. It also seems relevant to indicate that over one million children each year are affected by divorce. Marriage dissolutions create hotly disputed issues and thorny problems, which cause lifestyle changes, financial divisions, property allocations, and countless other complexities.

The objective of this book is to assist you in considering your options in deciding various divorce issues and strategies. This book provides a broad outline of the factors that courts examine when determining divorce-related issues. In addition, you will learn the way a divorce proceeding progresses. The required information to allow you to file your own divorce action, should you choose to do so, is also presented.

Understanding the legal process in a divorce action and possessing a general knowledge of the laws in the domestic relations area can help reduce the rancor involved in your case. This basic understanding can ultimately enhance the willingness of both parties to make the process easier.

As you read this book, it is critical to keep in mind that no book can address every factual situation possible. It is wise to gather various sources of information to assist you in your understanding of this topic and to be certain that you are interpreting the law correctly based upon your particular situation. This book is designed and generally written for *uncontested divorces*. An uncontested divorce is one that will not involve complex issues of financial distribution, custody, support, and, most importantly, hostility on the part of your spouse. Even if your assets and backgrounds are complex, if there are no hotly contested issues creating an impasse between you and your spouse, you may still wish to handle the matter on your own.

Critical to the advancement of your divorce matter is understanding the fact that divorce significantly depletes the parties' overall accumulated wealth. The divorce causes the entire asset base viewed as a whole to be divided between two individuals. Certainly, the resulting outcome is that each individual has less than the whole. Functioning with reduced means becomes a new way of life for divorcing couples.

Retaining the legal services of a divorce or matrimonial attorney is expensive. In a divorce situation that becomes contested, it is quite routine for an individual to incur legal fees in the $15,000–$25,000 range. Despite all of the monies paid out, it is not unusual for an individual to observe little advancement or result in his or her case.

Although this book is designed to enable you to proceed through the divorce maze without the need to hire an attorney, it is recommended that you consider the complexities of this process. It is generally unlikely that a layperson could not proceed with ease through the intricacies of most divorce cases and thus we suggest using this book as a reference guide and a line of support in your particular situation.

Should you choose to retain the services of an attorney, be aware of what is taking place in your case. You will have the knowledge to engage in meaningful discussions with your attorney. You will not waste time in having your lawyer repeatedly explaining the basic aspects of the divorce process, since you will have gained a comprehensive understanding and working knowledge of the basics in your thorough review of this book.

You will find that in certain instances, specific requirements exist that are peculiar and unique to your locale. In such circumstances, it is best to prepare the general forms as supplied in this book and subsequently make needed changes or alterations when so instructed. Given the number of counties in New Jersey, it would be burdensome to the format of this book to include the assortment of idiosyncrasies particular to each and every county filing office. However, a list of New Jersey county filing offices is provided in Appendix B.

This book is a convenient guide to move you through the complexities of the legal system in the most understandable and simple manner possible. For the most part, confusing legal terminology has been removed. Be alert to the fact that the term spouse will refer to your husband or wife (as applicable), and the terms child and children are used interchangeably.

In New Jersey, divorce cases are generally filed with the *Clerk of the New Jersey Superior Court, Chancery Division, Family Part* for the county in which the parties live. Throughout this book, we will use the term "Superior Court Clerk" or "clerk" to identify this court official. Please keep in mind that different judges and courts in different counties may have their own unique procedures, forms, and ways of handling matters. The office of the Superior Court Clerk can often inform you if they have any special forms or particular requirements, or direct you to the Family Division Manager in your county, who can provide further information. You should be aware that in all cases personnel at the clerk's office are not permitted to provide legal advice.

The first two chapters of this book give you an overview of the law and the legal system. Chapter 3 helps you decide whether you want to hire an attorney. Chapters 4 and 5 help you evaluate your situation and provide you with an idea of what you may expect if you decide to proceed with divorce. The remaining chapters show you the forms that you need, the manner in which they must be completed, and the procedures to follow. A chapter is also included that discusses special circumstances that may affect the handling of your divorce.

In addition, there are several appendices. Appendix A contains *selected* New Jersey Statutes and Rules of Court dealing with divorce, property division, alimony, child support, child custody, and domestic violence. (Although these provisions are discussed in the book, it is sometimes helpful to read the law exactly as it is written.) Appendix B contains the addresses of the twenty-one county courthouses in New Jersey. Appendix C lists the names and telephone numbers of the family division manager in each county. Appendix D provides the hotlines for county customer service bureaus for assistance in child support matters. Appendix E contains New Jersey child support guidelines. Appendix F contains forms you may need to prepare and file in various types of divorce procedures.

You will not need to use all of the forms. This book tells you which forms you need, depending upon your situation, and guides you in filling in the necessary information. Be sure to read Chapter 7 "Legal Forms and General Procedures" before you use any of the forms in this book.

# Marriage

## chapter 1

This chapter addresses what marriage actually is. It explains the obligations and rights you have in the marriage, addresses the option to terminate the marriage, and examines if divorce is the actual direction in which you wish to proceed.

Commonly, *marriage* or the *bonds of matrimony* are considered a contractual relationship. It is a legal agreement in one aspect, and for the majority of married couples, it engenders some aspect of a religious pact. Only the legal aspects are addressed in this guide.

The vows uttered in the wedding ceremony and documents signed in advance of that ceremony (marriage license and a marriage certificate) create a binding pledge about the way the marriage will endure. Definitive rights and obligations exist for the husband and wife. Despite the focus that a wedding centers upon various ceremonial aspects of the marital union, the reality is that certain legal monetary and property rights are created as a direct result of the marriage. Thus, these monetary and property rights cannot be terminated without a legal proceeding.

The marital bond creates certain rights and obligations in finances and in property. It establishes particular requirements with regard to support and care of any children produced by the parties. Sadly, most couples fail to understand that these rights and obligations have been formed until divorce proceedings begin.

## THE DIVORCE PROCEEDING

Usually, breaking the marriage contract is undertaken by the divorce proceeding. In such a proceeding, a court makes findings of fact and conclusions of law that result in the breaking of the marital union. The couple's assets and debts are also divided according to either agreement or law. Decisions regarding support, custody, visitation with respect to any of the couple's children, alimony, and other issues are addressed.

**Grounds**     Divorce is granted under specific circumstances. Following are the *grounds* for divorce in New Jersey.

*Adultery.* Engaging in sexual relations with someone other than your spouse.

*Willful and continued desertion.* For the term of twelve or more months, a person has been absent from his or her spouse by choice and has not returned at any point.

*Extreme cruelty.* Physical or mental suffering inflicted on a person, which endangers the safety or health of the victim spouse. It makes it improper or unreasonable to expect the victim to continue to live with his or her spouse.

*Separation.* When a couple lives apart for a period of eighteen months with no reasonable prospect of reconciliation.

*Voluntarily induced addiction.* Repeatedly using any narcotic drug or being habitually drunk.

*Institutionalization for mental illness.* When a spouse is put into an in-patient program for psychiatric reasons, and stays for a period of twenty-four or more consecutive months after the beginning of the marriage and preceding the filing of the divorce complaint.

**_Imprisonment._** When a spouse is put in prison for eighteen or more consecutive months after a marriage.

**_Deviant sexual conduct._** An act or acts voluntarily performed by one of the spouses without the consent of the other spouse.

In reviewing these grounds, it is important to consider the differences between those that are legally based in _fault_ and _no-fault_. Those that are _fault_-based are:

- adultery;

- desertion;

- extreme cruelty;

- addiction;

- institutionalization;

- imprisonment; and,

- deviant sexual conduct.

The only _no-fault_ ground for divorce in New Jersey is separation. This ground is most commonly used, because it provides a basis for a straightforward _dissolution of a marriage_. For example, in New Jersey, using separation as grounds, the process can be completed in a period of eighteen months, provided that you and your spouse live _separate and apart_ during that period.

Obtaining a divorce on fault grounds is much more difficult, expensive, and time consuming. This process entails proof of very specific events such as adultery, barbarous treatment, fraud, incapacity of the mind, or abandonment. Because proof of these elements is required, most fault divorces should not be attempted without an attorney. (Fault divorces are beyond the scope of this book and are not extensively covered.)

**Separation**    Two questions often arise when a divorce is filed on the basis of separation.

> 1. What does it mean to live separate and apart?
>
> 2. When does the eighteen-month period begin to run?

Living *separate and apart* means that you and your spouse are living separate lives, with no intention of ever getting back together. To make it clear that you are living separate and apart, most divorce lawyers would advise you to move out of your home, or direct your spouse to leave the marital home. Clearly tell your spouse (in front of a friend or relative who can witness) that you never intend to live with him or her again.

The required eighteen-month period begins to run when you and your spouse separate with the intention to end your marriage. If your spouse does not object to the date of separation that you select, that date will usually be accepted by the court. However, if your spouse does not agree as to the date of your separation, you will need to prove that you separated on that date. If you cannot prove that date, the court will typically go by the date you filed a **VERIFIED COMPLAINT FOR DIVORCE**. (see form 4, page 187.) The following sample case shows the type of problems that can arise if it is not made clear the date you and your spouse began living separate and apart.

---

### Example:

John moves out and ten months later, Mary files for divorce, expecting that she will get her divorce decree in about eight months when the eighteen-month separation period is done. However, John files a response saying that he only moved out because he was exploring business or employment opportunities in another city and always intended to move back in with Mary.

Likely result: the court rules that there is no evidence that the parties intended to separate at the time John moved out; therefore, the separation period must be calculated from the date when Mary filed her **VERIFIED COMPLAINT FOR DIVORCE**. She will have to wait almost eighteen months before she can get a divorce decree.

---

In rare cases, a couple has been considered to live separate and apart while continuing to live in the same house. In such instances, the couple went to great trouble to separate their lives, such as sleeping in separate bedrooms and keeping separate food supplies. There are also many cases where a couple did this and a court determined that they were not living separate and apart.

In any event, such arrangements are not recommended, as they provide your spouse with an opportunity to deny the separation, which may greatly delay finalizing a divorce. In such instances, it is also more difficult to establish the date when the separation began.

## ANNULMENT

The basic difference between a divorce and an annulment is that a *divorce* says, "this marriage is broken," while an *annulment* says, "a marriage never existed." As annulments are more difficult and complicated to prove, they are not used very often. Annulments are only possible in a few circumstances, usually when one party deceived the other. If you decide that you want an annulment, you should consult an attorney. If you are seeking an annulment for religious reasons and need to go through a church procedure (rather than, or in addition to, a legal procedure), you should consult your clergyperson. Generally, a divorce is easier to obtain than an annulment.

However, in order to get an annulment, you will need to prove, through the use of documents and sworn testimony, that one of the following circumstances exists.

- ✪ One of the parties has *another wife or husband* living at the time of the other marriage.

- ✪ The marriage is incestuous, with one or both of the parties being within the degrees of *consanguinity* (family relationship) prohibited by law.

- ✪ One or both parties were physically and incurably *impotent*, with the nonimpotent spouse not knowing of such impotency at the time of the marriage.

✪ One party did not have the *mental capacity* to get married. This means the person was suffering from mental illness or disability (such as being severely retarded), or under the influence of intoxicants, drugs, or similar agents.

✪ There was a lack of mutual assent to the marriage. The marriage took place due to *duress* imposed upon one or both spouses, or there was *fraud* as to one or more of the essentials of marriage.

✪ One or both parties were *under the age of 18* at the time of the marriage, unless the marriage was confirmed by the underage party upon reaching age 18.

If your spouse wants to stop an annulment, there are several arguments he or she could make to further complicate the case. This area of the law is not as well defined as divorce, and annulments are much less common than divorces. The annulment procedure can be extremely complicated and should not be attempted without a lawyer.

## LEGAL SEPARATION

There is no formal *legal separation* under New Jersey law. This procedure is available in some states, and is used to divide the property and provide for child custody and support in cases in which the husband and wife live separately, but remain married. This is usually used to break the financial rights and obligations of a couple whose religion does not permit divorce. Some states refer to this procedure as *divorce from bed and board*. It is an old procedure that is gradually fading from use.

New Jersey does provide the ability to obtain child support and determine custody and visitation rights without getting a divorce, but it does not allow for the division of property. (This procedure for child support without divorce, often mistakenly called a "legal separation," is beyond the scope of this book.)

# HOW DIVORCE MAY AFFECT YOUR LIFE

Divorce is, first and foremost, a choice made by one, or sometimes both spouses. Before you choose to begin the divorce process, you must seriously consider how divorce will affect your life. This section assists you in reviewing these factors and offers to you a wide variety of options in the event that you wish to attempt to preserve your marital relationship. Even if you are completely sure that you want a divorce, you should still read this section in order to understand what may result.

In divorce, spouses break both their matrimonial bonds and their marriage contract. The stress created at this juncture centers upon enduring the divorce process, which can be very lengthy, and the spousal interaction during the process. Ironically, compared to the other aspects of divorce, the actual divorce proceeding does not last very long. However, the proceeding is plainly the most emotionally challenging and psychologically volatile phase of a divorce.

Three important aspects are addressed in the divorce procedure:

- ✪ breaking the bonds of matrimony for the couple, which gives each the legal right to remarry;

- ✪ separation and distribution of the couple's property and responsibility for obligations and debts (also termed *equitable distribution*); and,

- ✪ where applicable, the custody, support, and care of the couple's children.

Although it is procedurally and theoretically possible for a divorce action to be concluded within a matter of months, legal disputes and respective court entanglements within a divorce proceeding can cause the proceeding to continue for years. Many of these impediments are caused by the emotional aspects related to battles over children and money. Undoubtedly, a divorce will have a monumental effect upon the social and emotional lives of you and your spouse, which will persist long after you are *legally* divorced.

**Absence of Company**

Your marriage may have been an unhappy one but, nonetheless, you may still perceive some degree of purposelessness or isolation after a divorce. You may not miss your spouse specifically, however, you may rather feel the absence of another individual being near.

**Feelings of Sorrow**

Divorce is often termed *the death of a marriage*. As in any situation of loss of any person with whom you have been close, you will notice a sense of bereavement or mourning. This factor can draw you through all of the customary thoughts connected with heartache. Anger, frustration, guilt, depression, and denial are all feelings and emotions associated with the divorce process. It can be an enormously intricate and painful task to move on with your new life.

**Change in Friends**

It is not at all unusual for you to learn that old friends with whom you and your spouse interacted as a married couple may no longer call or visit. Friends typically are divided up like assets in a marriage break-up. Often, being single again means that you no longer suit the *married friends* clique.

**Being Single and Dating Again**

If you are hoping to escape from the lonely nights and days you may feel compelled to re-enter the world of dating. The singles scene is often quite off-putting and easier said than done. If you have custody of the children, the situation becomes even more daunting.

**Monetary Considerations and Concerns**

Countless married couples spend their lives just trying to keep afloat financially. After a divorce (when the proverbial pie is split), economic deprivation is likely. The spouses must readjust their lives to be once again autonomous and self-supporting. The *noncustodial parent* has the added consideration of paying child support to the *custodial parent*. This fact can further drain finances.

**Effect Upon Children**

The effect upon your children, and upon your ongoing relationship with them, can often be the most painful and permanent aspect of a divorce. Your relationship with your children may become over-wrought as they work through their own feelings of depression, culpability, guilt, disillusionment, and resentment. This strain may persist for months or years. You and your children may even require professional counseling. Child support issues and the partial custody, shared custody, or visitation issues inherent in divorce cases will compel communication with your ex-spouse and will have a further effect upon the perceptions of the children.

Children are often caught in the middle of their parents' uncoupling and, as a result, can feel powerless, rejected, humiliated, or unloved.

This is a time when family roles are redefined. Even though they are no longer a couple, parents must find ways to continue their roles as mother and father to their children. Some New Jersey municipalities and counties offer programs to assist divorcing spouses in minimizing negative impacts on children at a time when parents are naturally preoccupied with their own adjustments. Recognizing that their joint roles as parents will continue to exist, these programs help parents begin to restructure their relationship and make plans in the best interest of their children.

## ALTERNATIVES TO DIVORCING

You have taken several steps already in the assessment of your marital situation. You may have decided to purchase this self-help book—and by the time you have skimmed a few chapters and perhaps have even read this section, it may be clear to you that you wish to move forward with the divorce process. If, however, you wish to make a final attempt to preserve your marriage after you have read this far, you should consider the following options.

**Communicate with Your Spouse**

Choose an appropriate time (not during a high-stress period for your spouse) to discuss problems. Set certain basic rules for the discourse, such as:

- ✪ talk about the way in which you feel and do not cast blame upon one another;

- ✪ listen while the other speaks and do not interrupt;

- ✪ acknowledge the positive aspects of each other and of the marriage;

✪   discuss how you wish to see the marriage proceed and discuss the ways in which it may have changed negatively over the years; and,

✪   agree to undertake various communication-related activities, which will bring you together as a couple.

## Alter Your Philosophy

Divorce occurs in many circumstances based upon the spouses' adamant refusal to alter an attitude or routine. But once divorced, change becomes inevitable. So, it may be preferable to make changes during the marriage to preserve the marital balance, rather than to make vast changes to survive in a postdivorce life. If you believe that change may be of assistance, make an effort. Divorce will always be available if the state of affairs does not improve.

**NOTE:** *Your acceptance of physical or mental abuse by your spouse is not advisable and, in most instances, will result only in an intensification of the abuse.*

## Marital Counseling

Professional marital counseling is available to you and your spouse to assist in determining what course of action you truly wish to take. A counselor will make inquiries, which will cause you to think hard and seriously about critical marital issues. Discussion and communication with your spouse is critical as well. The difficult aspect of this process is that it is hard to remain impartial and tolerant. Calm analysis aids in determining exactly what difficulties exist in the marriage. Discussion of possible solutions can often be best received when in the presence of a counselor.

Professional marriage counselors are best found by referral. Friends may be able to direct you to someone who assisted in their situation. Priests, pastors, rabbis, and other clergy, doctors, and therapists may be able to refer you to a marital counselor. Of course, you may also find marital counselors in the telephone book under the heading "Marriage Counselors" or "Family Counselors." You may visit a marriage or family counselor independently, or you and your spouse may attend a counseling session together.

**Trial Separation**    You and your spouse may wish to try a period of time away from each another for a short time. Perhaps take time to visit a friend in another town, take a separate vacation, or even, in very serious cases, relocate into separate dwellings for a time. This trial separation will provide each of you an opportunity to assess the way in which you feel living alone, how much you miss the other spouse, the importance of your marital issues or difficulties, and other feelings.

# The Legal System

## chapter 2

An overview of the legal system used throughout America is provided for you in this chapter. This section also offers information to assist you in maneuvering your way through New Jersey's version of that system with less anxiety and pressure. There are certain functions of the legal system that you must understand. By learning these functions, you will experience much less tension and dissatisfaction as you continue through the process.

## FACT VERSUS FICTION

Three sets of fundamental rules shape and control our legal system.

1. *Rules of Law.* The fundamental substance of the law, such as a regulation instructing a judge how to award personal property to you.

2. *Rules of Procedure.* These rules govern the manner in which matters or questions related to your case are to be dealt with in court.

3.  *Rules of Evidence.* These rules establish the way in which your facts are to be proven or presented to the court.

The idea is that these rules allow each side to portray the case most favorable to his or her own side knowing that a judge (or in other cases, a jury) will somehow find the truth by sorting through all of the information presented. *Stability* in the law and in the rules is to be generally fixed. This stability notion is thought to provide predictability to our world and to our society. Unfortunately, our legal system often does not work this way.

Rules are put in place as attempts to make the legal system fair and just. Our system has grown and developed with such rules and in most cases, the rules make sense. Regrettably, our labors to find fairness and justice have resulted in a multifaceted and complex maze of rules. The rules are intended to be appropriate to all people and in all cases. From time to time, the rules give the impression that they provide an unfair result in certain situations. Nevertheless, the rules in the law are still adhered to. You may note that just as in a game of baseball, where an umpire can decide a result through making a bad call, so too, can a judge or a jury in a trial. You may note also that sometime, one side can achieve its result through dishonesty.

People are often shocked to find that judges do not follow the rules in all circumstances. Some judges are disposed to make a decision merely based upon what they think seems fair under the conditions.

Sadly, what may appear to be fair to one judge may depend upon his or her personal ideas and philosophy, and may be well outside of the law. For example, there is no general rule in divorce law that affords one parent priority in child custody. Nevertheless, many judges stand by the notion that it is in the child's best interest to keep that child with his or her mother. A judge who believes this may find a way, in the absence of any legal provision, to rule that the mother retain custody—even if the mother is unfit.

Keep in mind that whatever your divorce situation seems to suggest, the process will take longer than you expect. Patience is required to get through the legal system with the least amount of nervous tension. Even lawyers get frustrated at the lengthy processes to get a case completed. However, it is critical not to let your frustrations be detected. In all events, maintain your position and remain composed, well mannered, and tolerant.

Bear in mind that simply basing your case upon the way in which your friend's divorce case developed is a major mistake. No matter how similar your friend's case seems to be to yours—no two cases will have the exact same result. Judges and circumstances will create differences and there are usually other conditions your friend did not understand.

Be aware and always remember that there are two sides to every legal issue, so do not expect to have every detail move in your favor. Whatever the ultimate result, it is always less than the whole picture before the divorce. As previously referenced, viewing your marital status as a *whole pie*, divorce results in a slicing of that pie. Although any particular matter may not be decided in your favor, the goal is to keep as much of the pie intact as possible. A positive approach is essential.

## THE COURT SYSTEM IN NEW JERSEY

New Jersey possesses an efficient court system that processes thousands of cases, including divorce cases, each year. *Original jurisdiction*, meaning the ability to hear all the evidence, argument, and facts of a case, for most matters, is in the New Jersey Superior Court. The Superior Court has three divisions: *Law, Chancery,* and *Appellate*. The Law and Chancery Divisions sit in each of the twenty-one counties of the state, and operate in smaller subsections called *Parts*. The Appellate Division hears appeals from the Law and Chancery Divisions in all counties, but sits primarily in the state's larger county seats. Matrimonial cases are commenced and decided under the jurisdiction of the Chancery Division, Family Part.

The Chancery Division, Family Part also administers pretrial mediation or *Early Settlement Panels* (ESPs). Because of the large volume of divorce cases in New Jersey, nearly all persons who are parties in a divorce case are required to participate in these panels. They are designed to narrow issues of disagreement between spouses and, in many cases, arrive at an overall resolution of these issues, which can then be incorporated into a **Final Judgment of Divorce**. (see form 18, p.223.)

When a divorce case is concluded, either party can *appeal* the outcome and decisions of the Superior Court. The appeal is heard in the Appellate Division. Additional appeals from an Appellate Division decision in a case require the making of a *Petition For Certification* to the New Jersey Supreme Court, which must decide to hear a further appeal from the Appellate Division. Certification is rarely granted.

## THE PLAYERS

The law and the legal system have a host of individuals who operate within the system. It is imperative to know who the key players are and the way in which they will be involved with your case.

**Judge**    The power to decide whether you obtain a divorce, the manner in which your property will be divided, the way in which your custody matter will proceed, how custody of the children will be arranged, and how much the other will pay for child support often rests within the review of the judge. The judge is the last person you should cause to become unsettled or aggravated. For the most part, judges, like attorneys, carry significant burdens of responsibility and large caseloads, and they often prefer a situation in which your case can be concluded with ease and with deliberate speed. Thus, the more in which you and your spouse agree upon, and the more complete your documents and filings, the more you will please the judge. Generally, your only contact with the judge will be at certain divorce-, custody-, or support-related hearings.

**Judge's Secretary**    A key player and one not to be overlooked is the judge's secretary. The judge's secretary may set certain hearing dates for the judge and frequently can answer many of your questions about the procedure and what the judge may prefer or require in your particular case. Clearly, you do not wish to make an enemy of the secretary. This means that you should not repeatedly telephone or call the judge's secretary, and by all means, you should not pepper the secretary with a barrage of questions. A few questions are considered acceptable. You might commence your communication with the judge's secretary by indicating that you simply are seeking to ensure that you have your documents and filings in order for the judge. You will get much farther in your dealings with the court with polite inquiries as opposed to demanding requests and impositions.

**Clerk of the New Jersey Superior Court**

In New Jersey, divorce cases are filed with the Clerk of the New Jersey Superior Court. While a secretary usually works for only one judge, the clerk handles the files for all of the judges in the county where the court is located. The clerk's office is the central place where all of the court files are kept. The clerk files your court papers and keeps the official records of your divorce. While the clerk or employees of the clerk cannot give you legal advice (such as advising you what to say in your court papers), they can help explain the system and the procedures (such as telling you what type of papers must be filed). The clerk has the power to accept or reject your papers, so you do not want to anger the clerk. If the clerk tells you to change something in your papers, just change it. Do not argue or complain.

**Lawyers**

Lawyers serve to direct you though the maze of the legal system. A lawyer will guide one's own client, while employing strategies that may confuse, manipulate, or outmaneuver the legal opposition. When you commence your interaction with your spouse's attorney (if he or she has one), it is advisable to be courteous and dignified. Hostility will not serve your case, nor will it advance your goals. Generally, the opposing lawyer is carrying out his or her legal tasks to attain the most desirable outcome and best result for his or her client. As is the case in all professions and walks of life, some people are truly disagreeable individuals. In a situation in which that person is a legal representative, you may find that such lawyers simply cannot be swayed by reason. If your spouse retains this type of lawyer, it is a good idea for you to hire the services of an attorney as well. Read Chapter 3 with care to determine whether or not you wish to retain legal counsel.

**This Book**

This book serves as your map through the legal system. In many cases, the dangers along the way are relatively small. If you start getting lost, or the dangers seem to be getting worse, you can always hire a lawyer to jump to your aid. You may wish to contact the Lawyer

Referral Service for the county in which you reside. Your county's bar association can assist you in this regard. Check the Yellow Pages or look on the Internet for your local bar association or referral service.

The following sections give you a general overview of the law and procedures involved in obtaining a divorce. To most people, including many lawyers, the law appears very complicated and confusing. Fortunately, many areas of the law can be broken down into fairly simple and logical steps. Divorce is one of those areas.

## DIVORCE LAW

The law relating to divorce, as well as to any other area of law, comes from two sources:

1.  the New Jersey Statutes, which are the laws passed by the New Jersey Legislature and

2.  the past decisions of the New Jersey courts (called case law).

This book is designed so that you should not need to research the law. However, a portion of the New Jersey Statutes and New Jersey Rules of Court, relating to property division, alimony, child support, and domestic violence can be found in Appendix A of this book. For most situations, the law is clearly spelled out in the statutes, and the past court decisions are not necessary. However, if you wish to learn more about how to find these court decisions, see the section entitled "Legal Research" later in this chapter.

**Residency Requirements**  In order for you to file for divorce in New Jersey, either you or your spouse must be a resident of New Jersey for at least six months immediately before filing a complaint for divorce.

## DIVORCE PROCEDURE

As for procedures, a simple divorce may be viewed as a five-step process.

❑    File a **VERIFIED COMPLAINT FOR DIVORCE** with the clerk requesting a divorce.

❑    Have your spouse served with the **COMPLAINT** and a **SUMMONS** by the sheriff of the county in which the spouse resides (this may be the same county in which the **COMPLAINT** is filed).

❑    Enter into negotiations with your spouse, or your spouse's attorney, regarding the division of all marital property and assets. (In New Jersey, these negotiations are facilitated by the use of early settlement panels (ESPs).)

❑    Have your spouse agree to and sign a property settlement agreement dividing the assets and debts of the marriage.

❑    If statutory time guidelines are satisfied, ask the court to schedule the matter for a final hearing.

**Complaint**    The **VERIFIED COMPLAINT FOR DIVORCE** is a written request for the court to grant a judgment of divorce. A **VERIFIED COMPLAINT FOR DIVORCE** is provided in Appendix F of this book, and full instructions are provided in Chapter 8. The **COMPLAINT** must include a **CASE INFORMATION STATEMENT**, which sets forth the assets and debts of the marriage. Once the **COMPLAINT** is completed, it is filed with the clerk. A filing fee of $250 is required.

**Service of Process**    After you have prepared and filed the **COMPLAINT**, you need to officially notify your spouse. Even though your spouse may already know that you are filing for divorce, you still need to have him or her officially notified, or *served*, with the **COMPLAINT**. This is done by having the **COMPLAINT** and a **SUMMONS** delivered to your spouse by the sheriff of the county in which your spouse lives.

**Proposal**    Once all of your paperwork is filed, you need to contact your spouse or your spouse's attorney. This is often done by contacting the party in writing, with a request for a statement of assets, pension plan funds, 401(k) information, valuable marital property, etc. However, you may already have this information at your fingertips, in which case you may send a letter offering a *proposal* of property distribution. This process can be done verbally and less formally, and may even be completed before the **VERIFIED COMPLAINT FOR DIVORCE** is filed. This can often be done over the telephone. Child support and custody agreements can be finalized at meetings with court officials, such as an ESP.

**Settlement**   Finally, you have discussed all property matters and asset distribution and have reached a fair settlement to both parties satisfaction. You agree as to how your property should be divided, how custody of your children is to be arranged, and how the children will be supported. If it applies to your situation, there may also be an agreement as to whether alimony will be paid. If you cannot locate your spouse, or get signed consent for a settlement, the procedure will be different and other forms may be needed.

## LEGAL RESEARCH

If you need or want to find out more about the divorce law in New Jersey, this section gives you some guidance.

**Statutes**   The main source of information on New Jersey divorce law is that portion of the New Jersey Statutes Annotated (NJ Stat. Ann.) entitled "Divorce and the Nullity of Marriage," beginning at Section (Sec.) 2A:34-1 and continuing through Section 2A:34-52. Each statute is followed by summaries, called *annotations*, of actual cases that discuss and interpret that section of the statutes. Selected portions of these statutes are found in Appendix A.

You can usually find the full New Jersey Statutes Annotated at your local public library or on the Internet; however, check to be sure they have the most recent edition. You will also find it at your nearest law library, located in each New Jersey county courthouse or at a university campus where a law school is located.

In New Jersey, law schools are operated by Rutgers University (with campuses at Camden and Newark) and Seton Hall University (with a single campus in Newark). Most law schools in the New York City metropolitan area (including Brooklyn, Columbia, Cardozo, Fordham, Hofstra, New York University, New York Law School, Pace, and St. John's) and the Philadelphia metropolitan area (including the

University of Pennsylvania, Villanova, Temple, and Widener) will also possess a current version of the New Jersey Statutes Annotated in their libraries.

You can also find the statutes online at **www.njleg.state.nj.us**. Scroll down the page to "Laws and Constitution" and click "Statutes."

**Case Law**

In addition to the laws enacted by the legislature, law is also made by judicial decisions in various cases each year. To find this *case law*, you will also need to go to a law library. Do not be afraid to ask librarians for assistance. They cannot give you legal advice, but they can tell you where the books are located.

Case law may be found in the *New Jersey Digest*, which is a set of books that give short summaries of cases. The digest is arranged alphabetically by subject. Find the chapter on "Divorce," then look for the headings of the subject you want. The actual opinions of New Jersey courts are found in the *New Jersey Superior Court Reports* (containing decisions of the Law, Chancery, and Appellate Divisions) and the *New Jersey Reports* (containing only decisions of the New Jersey Supreme Court).

In limited instances, an opinion of the Appellate Division or Supreme Court may be published in the *Atlantic Reporter*. There are two series of the *Atlantic Reporter*, the older cases being found in the *Atlantic Reporter* (abbreviated "A."), and newer cases being found in the *Atlantic Reporter Second Series ("A.2d.")*. For example, if the digest gives you a reference to "*Gibbons v. DeSimone*, 149 A.2d. 721," this tells you that the case titled "Gibbons v. DeSimone" can be found by going to Volume 149 of the Atlantic Reporter Second Series, and turning to page 721.

**Rules of Court**

You should also pay attention to the New Jersey Rules of Court, which contains the rules and procedures applied in the various courts in New Jersey. The Rules of Court also contains some approved forms.

**Practice Manuals**

You may also find practice manuals, which are books, or sets of books, covering specific areas of the law. A divorce practice manual will explain the law, and usually provide sample forms. There are several excellent manuals of this type that you may wish to use in conjunction with this volume.

# Lawyers

## chapter 3

Many reasons and aspects will have an impact upon your decision to hire an attorney to represent you in a divorce case. Such reasons may include:

- how at ease you consider yourself to be in addressing your legal matter on your own;

- whether your case is more complex and problematic than most; and,

- the amount of resistance you encounter from your spouse.

It may be prudent to hire an attorney if you encounter a judge with a hostile attitude, or if your spouse retains a lawyer. Keep in mind that there is no court appointed counsel in divorce or custody cases, so if you require an attorney, you will have to hire one or seek aid from the local volunteer legal aid agency (which may only be available to you if you meet certain *reduced means* criteria).

It is recommended that you consider hiring an attorney when you no longer feel at ease in self-representation. This stage will vary significantly from person to person, thus, there is no easy way to be more exact.

The section that follows discusses some of the advantages and disadvantages of securing the services of an attorney. It will further provide you with various fundamentals that you may wish to consider in making this determination.

## HIRING A LAWYER

Making the decision as to whether or not you desire legal assistance in your divorce matter is affected by a number of considerations. Lawyers are as different in their fee structures as they may be in appearance, personality, and individuality. Generally, divorce attorneys' hourly service fees range in cost between $200 and $500. Such attorneys *bill for time,* which means that the client will receive a charge from the attorney for every communication undertaken on the client's behalf from telephone calls to drafting letters to court appearances.

Some attorneys utilize a *flat fee structure*, which may serve to save the client significant costs in the long run. An attorney who uses the flat fee method of legal service will charge per legal event. For example, should you wish to hire a counsel for a divorce, a flat fee for the filing and negotiation of the divorce can be obtained. Keep in mind that whatever you think a divorce will cost at the outset—it will cost more.

**Advantages to Having a Lawyer**

The following are some positive aspects to retaining the services of an attorney.

- ✪ Judges and other attorneys may value your case more sincerely. Many judges prefer both parties to have attorneys as this aids in a more effective move through the court system since both sides are knowledgeable about practice and procedure relevant to case issues. (A *Pro Se litigant*—an individual representing oneself—quite often squanders a great deal of time on issues that have absolutely no bearing upon the facts or the outcome of the case.)

- ✪ The lawyer may act as the first line of defense between you and your spouse, often leading to a more rapid course through the legal system by decreasing the possibility for pure emotion to override facts.

✪ The lawyer often feels more enthusiastic about completing a case when there is an attorney representing the other side. Most attorneys prefer to deal with other attorneys rather than a layperson.

✪ The lawyer is hired to worry about all of the details of your case, thus you can rest and be assured that your matter is being handled by a professional. By hiring legal counsel, you need only become generally aware of the information of this book, as it will be the responsibility of your attorney to file the correct documents in the accurate format and to transact matters with the clerk of court, the judge, the process server, your spouse, and your spouse's counsel.

✪ The lawyer provides professional representation to address your legal difficulties. In the event your case is complex, or abruptly becomes complicated, it is an advantage to have an attorney who is familiar with your situation to be on the scene. It can also be reassuring to have advice and answers to your questions provided by an attorney.

**Advantages to Representing Yourself**

Conversely, there are also advantages to self-representation. Some of those advantages include the following.

✪ The cost of hiring counsel can be used for your living expenses.

✪ Certain judges feel more compassionate toward a *Pro Se litigant* (person not represented by an attorney). Once in a while, this judicial compassion results in the unrepresented individual being able to gain some leeway with the court and procedural requirements.

✪ Your case may move more rapidly. Many, if not all attorneys, have a profound caseload, resulting in gaps of time in dealing with cases. Since you are the person most concerned about advancing your own case, you will be able to drive it through the system attentively and with determination.

As you will learn from the following section, deciding upon an attorney takes effort and it is tricky to know whether you are selecting an attorney with whom you will be pleased. You may investigate the option of hiring an attorney who will be agreeable to receiving an hourly fee to respond to your questions and to provide aid if you require it. This way you will reduce legal costs, however, you will still receive some professional aid. Further, this association will establish a relationship with a counsel who will be somewhat aware of your divorce case in the event the matter becomes complicated and the full-time service of an attorney is needed.

## SELECTING A LAWYER

Deciding upon a lawyer is a two-part procedure. You first need to determine with which attorney you will schedule a consultation. Second, you then must come to a decision if you wish to hire that attorney. The following are helpful hints to aid you in making that decision.

**Ask a Friend**

Perhaps the best way in which to find a lawyer is to ask someone you know who has used the services of an attorney to recommend one to you. This is especially helpful if the lawyer represented your friend in a divorce, custody, support, or other family law matter.

**Contact a Lawyer Referral Service**

In New Jersey, each county bar association operates a service that is designed to match a client with an attorney handling cases in the area of law the client needs. The referral service does not guarantee the quality of work, nor the level of experience or ability of the attorney. Finding a lawyer in this manner will at least connect you with one who is practicing in the area of family law and probably has some experience in divorce. You can find a referral service by looking in the Yellow Pages under "Attorney Referral Services."

**Telephone Directory**

Also check under the heading for "Attorneys" in the Yellow Pages. Many of the lawyers and law firms will place display ads indicating their areas of practice and educational backgrounds. Look for firms or lawyers that indicate they practice in areas such as *divorce, family law*, or *domestic relations*. Large, flourishing ads are not necessarily indicative of expertise. Keep in mind that some lawyers, and often the best lawyers, do not need to advertise.

**Ask Another Lawyer**

If you have used the services of an attorney in the past for some other matter (for example, a real estate closing, a traffic ticket, or a will) you may want to call and ask if he or she could refer you to an attorney whose ability in the area of family law is respected.

**Make the Call**

From your search, you should select three to five lawyers worthy of further consideration. Your first step will be to call each attorney's office, explain that you are interested in seeking a divorce, and ask the following questions.

✪ Does the attorney (or law firm) handle this type of matter?

✪ What is the attorney's fee range and what is the cost of an initial consultation? (Do not expect to get a definite answer on a divorce fee, but the attorney may be able to give you a range or an hourly rate. You will probably need to meet with the lawyer for anything more detailed.)

✪ How soon can you schedule an appointment? (Most offices require you to make an appointment. Once you get in contact with the attorney at the appointment, ask the following questions.)

- How much will it cost?

- How will the fee be paid?

- How long has the attorney been in practice, generally; and in New Jersey, specifically?

- What percentage of the attorney's cases involve divorce cases or other family law matters? (Do not expect an exact answer, but you should get a rough estimate that is at least 20%.)

- How long will it take? (The attorney should be able to give you an average range and discuss things that may make a difference.)

If you get acceptable answers to these questions, ask yourself the following questions about the lawyer.

- ✪ Do you feel comfortable talking to the lawyer?

- ✪ Is the lawyer friendly toward you?

- ✪ Does the lawyer seem confident in him- or herself?

- ✪ Does the lawyer seem to be straightforward with you, and able to explain issues so you understand?

If you get satisfactory answers to all of these questions, you probably have a lawyer with whom you will be happy to work. Most clients are happiest with an attorney with whom they feel comfortable.

## WORKING WITH A LAWYER

In general, you will work best with your attorney if you keep an open, honest, and friendly attitude. If you want to know something or if you do not understand something, ask your attorney. If you do not understand the answer, tell your attorney and ask him or her to explain it again. You should not be embarrassed to ask questions. Many people who say they had a bad experience with a lawyer either did not ask enough questions or had a lawyer who would not take the time to explain things to them. If your lawyer is not taking the time to explain what he or she is doing, it may be time to look for a new lawyer.

**Relay All Information**

Remember that anything you tell your attorney is confidential. An attorney can lose his or her license to practice if he or she reveals information without your permission. So do not hold back. Tell your lawyer everything, even if it does not seem important to you. There are many things that seem unimportant to a nonattorney, but can change the outcome of a case. Also, do not hold something back because you are afraid it will hurt your case. It will definitely hurt your case if your lawyer does not know information until he or she hears it in court from your spouse's attorney. But if your lawyer knows in advance, he or she can at least plan to eliminate or reduce damage to your case.

**Listen**
It will do you no good to argue because the law or the system does not work the way you think it should. For example, if your lawyer tells you that the judge cannot hear your case for two weeks, do not demand that he or she set a hearing tomorrow. By refusing to accept reality, you are only setting yourself up for disappointment.

**Be Patient**
It is essential to be patient both with the system, which is often slow, and with your attorney. Do not expect your lawyer to return your phone call within an hour. Your lawyer may not be able to return it the same day. Most lawyers are very busy. It is rare that an attorney can maintain a full caseload and still make each client feel as if he or she is the only client.

**Check with the Secretary**
Your lawyer's secretary can be a valuable source of information. Be friendly and get to know the secretary. Often he or she will be able to answer your questions, and you will not get a bill for the time you talk to the secretary.

**Your Spouse**
It is your lawyer's job to communicate with your spouse or with your spouse's lawyer. Let your lawyer do his or her job. Many lawyers have had clients lose or damage their cases when the clients decided to say or do something on his or her own.

**Squeaking Wheel**
Many lawyers operate on the old principle of *the squeaky wheel gets the grease*. Work on a case tends to be put off until a deadline is near, an emergency develops, or the client calls. There is a reason for this. Many lawyers take more cases than can be effectively handled in order to earn the income they desire. Your task is to become a *squeaky wheel* that does not squeak too much. Whenever you talk to your lawyer, ask the following questions.

- ✪ What is the next step?

- ✪ When do you expect it to be done?

- ✪ When should I talk to you next?

Call your lawyer if you do not hear back in a timely fashion. Do not remind your lawyer of the missed call—just ask how things are going.

If you can no longer work with your lawyer, it is time to either go at it alone or get a new attorney. You will need to send your lawyer a letter stating that you no longer desire his or her services and are discharging him or her from your case. Also state that you will be coming by his or her office the following day to pick up your file. The attorney does not have to give you his or her own notes or other work he or she has in progress. He or she *must* give you the essential contents of your file (such as copies of papers already filed or prepared and billed for, and any documents that you provided). If the lawyer refuses to give you your file for any reason, contact the New Jersey Bar Association about filing a complaint, or grievance, against the lawyer.

**NOTE:** *You will need to settle any remaining fees charged for work that has already been done by the lawyer.*

# Preliminary Considerations

The following things should be done or considered before you begin the divorce process.

## RESIDENCY

In order to be eligible to file for divorce in New Jersey, either you or your spouse must be a resident of New Jersey for a period of at least one year immediately before filing. It is important to distinguish between the terms *resident* and *domiciliary*. You are a resident of a state if you live in that state at least part of the time. You are a domiciliary of the state you consider to be the primary and permanent state where you live. A person may be a resident of more than one state, but may only be a domiciliary of one state.

---

### Example 1:

You live seven months of the year in Florida and five months in New Jersey. You consider Florida to be the primary place you live and use your Florida address for your voter registration, income tax returns, car registration, and driver's license, and to receive most of your important mail. You are a domiciliary of Florida and a resident of both Florida and New Jersey. You may file for divorce in New Jersey, provided you have been a resident for at least the past year.

### Example 2:

Your main home is Princeton, New Jersey, but you also own a condominium in Erie, Pennsylvania, because that is where you vacation. You typically spend Monday through Friday in New Jersey and stay in Erie, Pennsylvania, on weekends. You consider New Jersey to be the primary state in which you live and use your New Jersey address for your voter registration, income tax filing, automobile registration, driver's license, and mail. You are a domiciliary of New Jersey, and a resident of both New Jersey and Pennsylvania. You may file for divorce in New Jersey, provided you have been a resident for at least the past year.

---

It is not necessary that you or your spouse have been physically in New Jersey for the entire one-year period before filing for divorce, but only that the period of your residency began at least one year ago. For example, during the one-year period, you may leave New Jersey for business, visiting relatives, and vacation, or to return to the state where you are domiciled, as long as you do not abandon your residence in New Jersey.

Generally, residence will only become an issue if your spouse makes it one. There is no conclusive test that can be applied to decide whether a person is, or is not, a resident. In a dispute over residency, the court will look at all the circumstances and determine whether you or your spouse meets the residency requirement. However, if you are clearly a resident of another state, there is little need to stretch the definition of residency in order to file for divorce in New Jersey. You can probably get a divorce more quickly and easily in another state.

## GROUNDS FOR DIVORCE

As stated in Chapter 1, there are eight legal grounds for divorce available in New Jersey. However, six of the seven fault grounds (adultery, desertion, deviant sexual conduct, addiction, institutionalization, and imprisonment) involve complicated proof problems and highly specialized fact scenarios. Accordingly, only the extreme cruelty (*fault*) and separation (*no-fault*) grounds are addressed in depth. The others may require the assistance of an attorney.

**Extreme Cruelty**

If you and your spouse agree that you want a divorce, and there is a general level of mutual discord in the marriage based upon abusive or cruel behavior of any kind (verbal or physical) by one or both spouses, you can obtain a divorce under New Jersey Statutes Annotated, Section 2A:34-2 (c). This may be done provided that you do not file a complaint for divorce until after three months from the date of the last act of cruelty, which will be stated in the complaint.

The term *extreme cruelty* has a very broad meaning in New Jersey law. There is no fixed and definite factual formula for establishing extreme cruelty; each situation is evaluated separately to determine the acts complained of and their effect upon the spouse(s). The standard for establishing this ground is very subjective, requiring primarily that one or both spouses show that he or she, in fact, finds it improper or unreasonable to cohabit with the other spouse. For example, actions willfully taken by one spouse to destroy the peace of mind and happiness of the other have been conclusively established to be extreme cruelty. Other actions that have been considered as extreme cruelty include, but have not been limited to, threats, false accusations, coercion, denial of sexual relations, and homosexual conduct.

**Separation**

If you and your spouse have separated, agreed that you want a divorce, and will cooperate in filing the necessary papers, you can obtain a divorce under New Jersey Statutes Annotated, Section 2A:34-2 (d). This may be done provided that you and your spouse have lived s*eparate and apart* for a period of eighteen months, and there is no reasonable prospect of reconciliation.

If you desire to file for divorce and cannot meet the requirements under either of these grounds, you have two choices.

1. File using one or more of the remaining grounds, if applicable. As the proof standards for the remaining grounds are much more stringent, you should seriously consider retaining an attorney.

2. Move to another state and become a resident there, so that you can file for divorce in that state. Some states may have a shorter residency period than New Jersey.

---

### – Caution –

Many problems can arise if you try to establish residency in another state. If you think you may want to do this, you should consult an attorney in New Jersey and an attorney in the state where you intend to file for divorce.

---

## RELATING WITH YOUR SPOUSE

You need to evaluate your situation with respect to your spouse. Have both of you already agreed to get a divorce? If not, what kind of reaction do you expect from your spouse? Your expected reaction can determine how you proceed. If he or she reacts in a rational manner, you can probably use the ground of *separation* or the broader ground of *extreme cruelty* to obtain a divorce. However, if you expect an extremely emotional (and possibly violent) reaction as a result of filing for divorce, you will need to take steps to protect yourself, your children, and your property. You will have to start out expecting to employ all necessary court procedures.

Unless you and your spouse have already mutually decided to get a divorce, you do not want your spouse to know you are thinking about filing for divorce. This is a defense tactic, although it may not seem that way at first. If your spouse knows or suspects that you are planning a divorce, he or she may take certain steps to prevent you from getting a fair result. These steps include withdrawing money from bank accounts, hiding information about income, and hiding assets. So do not let on about your intentions until you have collected all of the information you will need and are about to file with the court, or until you are prepared to protect yourself from violence, if necessary.

**– Caution –**

Tactics such as withdrawing money from bank accounts and hiding assets raise potential legal action. If you try any of those tactics, you risk being placed in a very negative light before the court. This can result in anything from having disputed matters resolved in your spouse's favor to being ordered to produce the assets (or being jailed for contempt of court).

Theoretically, the *system* would prefer that you keep evidence of the assets (such as photographs, sales receipts, or bank statements) to present to the judge if your spouse hides them. Then your spouse will risk being jailed. However, once your spouse has taken assets and hidden them, or sold them and spent the money, even a contempt order may not get the money or assets back.

If you determine that you need to get the assets in order to keep your spouse from hiding or disposing of them, be sure you keep them in a safe place. Make a thorough list of them to be utilized at the appropriate time. Do not dispose of the assets. If your spouse claims later that you took them, you can explain to the judge why you were afraid that your spouse would dispose of them, and that you merely got them out of his or her reach.

## GATHERING FINANCIAL INFORMATION

It is extremely important that you collect all of the financial information you can, including originals or copies of the following:

- ✪ your most recent income tax return (and your spouse's if you filed separately);

- ✪ the most recent W-2 tax forms for yourself and your spouse;

- ✪ any other income reporting papers (such as interest, stock dividends, etc.);

- ✪ your spouse's most recent pay stub, hopefully showing year-to-date earnings (otherwise try to get copies of all pay stubs since the beginning of the year);

- ✪ deeds to all real estate;

- ✪ titles to cars, boats, or other vehicles;

- ✪ your will and your spouse's will (including any trust documents);

- ✪ life insurance policies;

- ✪ stocks, bonds, or other investment papers;

- ✪ pension or retirement fund papers and statements;

- ✪ health insurance cards and papers;

- ✪ bank account or credit union statements;

- ✪ your spouse's Social Security number and driver's license number;

- ✪ names, addresses, and phone numbers of your spouse's employer, close friends, and family members;

- ✪ credit card statements, mortgage documents, and other credit and debt papers;

- ✪ a list of vehicles, furniture, appliances, tools, etc., owned by you and your spouse;

- ✪ copies of bills or receipts for recurring, regular expenses, such as electric, gas or other utilities, car insurance, etc.;

- ✪ copies of bills, receipts, insurance forms, or medical records for any unusual medical expenses (including for recurring or continuous medical conditions) for yourself, your spouse, or your children; and,

✪   any other papers showing what you and your spouse earn, own, or owe.

Make copies of as many of these papers as possible, and keep them in a safe, private place (where your spouse will not find them). Try to make copies of new papers as they come in, especially as you get close to filing court papers.

## NEGOTIATION

It is important to remember that many key aspects to receiving exactly what you desire in a divorce center upon effective negotiation. Your marital property settlement can be crafted (and later entered as an order of court) in any fashion you choose, providing that your spouse agrees to the settlement proposal. Keep in mind that the better your skill at presenting the proposal to your spouse, the better your chances he or she will accept it with little or no change. The more favorable you make your spouse's offer appear, the more likely he or she will not entirely object to your terms. Negotiation is both a skill and an art. If you feel as though you should not attempt to undertake this process, you should consult an attorney.

# Property, Debts, and Alimony

## chapter 5

This chapter explains how property and debts are divided, when alimony is awarded, and if so, how the amount and duration of alimony are determined. These subjects are grouped together because they are interrelated and must be considered in any divorce, regardless of whether you and your spouse have children. If you and your spouse are trying to come to an agreement on these matters, this chapter will help you decide what proposal to offer or accept. By applying the information in this chapter to your situation, you will get an idea of what to expect if a judge must decide these matters.

## PROPERTY

This section is designed to acquaint you with the manner in which property is divided in a divorce. It will also assist you in completing the **PROPERTY DIVISION WORKSHEET** (see form 2, p.183.) This worksheet enables you to list and describe your property.

Your property, assets, and debts will fall into one of two categories—marital or nonmarital property. Trying to determine how to divide assets and debts can be difficult. Under New Jersey's *equitable dis-*

*tribution law*, marital property belongs to both you and your spouse, while nonmarital property belongs to you or your spouse individually.

In making this distinction, the following rules apply.

1.  If the asset (or debt) was acquired *after* the date you were married, it is presumed to be a marital asset or debt. It is up to you or your spouse to prove otherwise.

2.  A nonmarital asset (or debt) is one that was acquired *before* the date of your marriage.

    -   It is also a nonmarital asset if you acquired it through a gift or inheritance (as long as it was not a gift from your spouse). Income from nonmarital property is also seen as nonmarital property (for example, rent you receive from an investment property you had before you got married).

    -   If you exchange one of these assets or debts after your marriage, it is still nonmarital. (For example, you had a $6,000 car before you were married. After the marriage, you traded it for a different $6,000 car. The replacement car remains nonmarital property.)

    -   Items acquired after you and your spouse separated are nonmarital property.

    -   You and your spouse may sign a written agreement that certain assets and debts are to be considered nonmarital (or marital if you so agree).

3.  Marital assets and debts are those acquired during your marriage, even if they were acquired by you or your spouse individually.

    -   This includes the increase in value of a nonmarital asset during the marriage, or if marital funds are used to pay for or improve the property.

- All rights accrued during the marriage, such as pension, retirement, profit-sharing, insurance, and similar plans, are marital assets.

- It is also possible for one spouse to make a gift of nonmarital property to the other spouse, therefore making it marital property.

4. Real estate that is in both names is considered marital property, and it is the responsibility of the spouse claiming otherwise to prove it.

5. Finally, determining the status of an asset or debt as marital or nonmarital (as well as the value of any asset) is made as of the date of a settlement agreement or the date the complaint for divorce was filed, whichever is first.

**Detailed Listings of Property**

The **PROPERTY DIVISION WORKSHEET** (see form 2, p.183) calls for a detailed listing of your property and is divided into four columns as follows.

*Item of property.* In this column, you should give a brief description of property and identify if the item is marital or nonmarital. After listing the item, place an "N" for nonmarital property or an "M" for marital property.

*Estimated value.* Enter an estimated value of the property in the next column. This should be based on the value of the item at the time it was purchased or received, or your own best estimate, unless you have a more specific valuation of the item.

*Husband or wife.* You should insert whether the property will be kept by you or your spouse.

*Notes.* Enter special information or additional facts to better describe the property item.

Use these columns to list and identify your property. Describe property on the worksheet as follows.

***Cash.*** For each account of any kind, list the name of the bank, savings & loan, credit union, etc., and the account number. This should include certificates of deposit (CDs). The balance of each account should be listed. Make copies of the most recent bank statements for each account.

***Stocks and bonds.*** All stocks, bonds, or other paper investments should be listed. Write down the number of shares and the name of the company that issued them. Also, copy any notation such as *common* or *preferred* stock or shares. This information can be obtained from the stock certificate itself or from a statement from the stock broker. Make a copy of the certificate or the statement.

***Real estate.*** List each piece of property you and your spouse own. The description might include a street address for the property, a subdivision name and block/lot number, or other identifying characteristics of the property. There may also be a municipal or county tax identification number.

Real estate (or any other property) may be in both of your names (joint), in your spouse's name alone, or in your name alone. The only way to know for sure, is to look at the deed to the property. (If you cannot find a copy of the deed, try to find mortgage papers or payment coupons, homeowners insurance papers, or a property tax assessment notice.) The owners of property are usually referred to on the deed as the grantees, and after their names it will list how they hold title.

---

### Example:
GRANTEE: John and Mary Smith, as joint tenants with right of survivorship.

---

In assigning a value to the property, consider the market value, which is the amount for which you will probably sell the property. You could consider the amount for which similar houses in your neighborhood have sold. A local realtor can provide you with this information. You may also consider how much you paid for the property. Do not use the tax assessment value, as this is usually considerably lower than the market value.

**Vehicles.** This category includes cars, trucks, motor homes, recreational vehicles (RVs), motorcycles, boats, trailers, airplanes, and any other means of transportation for which New Jersey requires a title and registration. Your description should include the following information (which can usually be found on the title or on the vehicle itself).

- ✪ *Make.* You should also provide the year the vehicle was made.

- ✪ *Model.* All vehicles have a model series name; for example, Chrysler makes vehicles such as the *Sebring* and the *300M*, while Ford makes vehicles called the *Mustang*, *Taurus*, and *F150 Truck*.

- ✪ *Vehicle Identification Number* (VIN). This is found on the vehicle, the title, and the registration. Make a copy of the title or registration. For a value, go to your public library and ask for the NADA blue book for cars, trucks, or whatever vehicle you have. This book gives the average values for used vehicles. Your librarian can help you find what you need. If you have Internet access, there are hundreds of websites that deal with the issue of used car value. Another source to use is the classified advertising section of a newspaper, which helps you find selling prices for vehicles. You might also try calling a dealer to see if it can give you a rough idea of the value. Be sure you take into consideration the condition of the vehicle and the mileage.

**Furniture.** List furniture as specifically as possible. Include the type (such as sofa, coffee table, etc.), the color, and if you know it, the manufacturer, line name, or style. Furniture usually does not have a serial number, although if you find one, write it on the list.

**Appliances and hardware.** This category includes such items as refrigerators, lawn mowers, and power tools. These items will probably have a make, model, and serial number on them. You may have to look on the back, bottom, or another hidden place for the serial number, but try to find it.

*Jewelry and valuables.* If you own an expensive piece of jewelry or other collectible, identify the name of the insurer and policy number, include it in your list, along with an estimated value. Be sure to include silverware, original art, gold, coin collections, antiques, etc. Be as detailed and specific as possible. Do not list *costume jewelry*. You can plan on keeping your own personal watches, rings, etc.

*Life insurance with cash surrender value.* Any life insurance policy that you may cash in or borrow against, should be listed. If you cannot find a cash surrender value on the policy, call the insurance company and ask for the information.

*Other big ticket items.* This is simply a general reference to anything of significant value that does not fit into one of the categories already discussed. Examples might be a portable spa, an above-ground swimming pool, golf clubs, pool tables, camping, hunting or fishing equipment, farm animals, exotic pets, or machinery.

*Pensions.* Dividing pensions and retirement benefits is complex. Whenever these types of benefits are involved and you cannot agree on how to divide them, you should consult an attorney or accountant to determine the value of the benefits and how they should be divided.

**Property *Not* to List**

Do not list your clothing and other personal effects. Pots, pans, dishes, and cooking utensils should not be listed unless they have some unusually high value.

**Dividing the Property**

Once you have completed your list, go through it and try to determine who should receive each item. Ideally, you and your spouse will be able to divide the listed items fairly. However, if this is not possible, you will need to create a reasonable settlement proposal to submit to your spouse or your spouse's attorney. Consider each item and make a check mark to designate whether that item should go to the husband or wife. You may make the following assumptions:

✪    your nonmarital property will go to you;

✪    your spouse's nonmarital property will go to your spouse;

✪    you should get the items that only you use; and,

✪    your spouse should get the items only used by your spouse.

The remaining items should be divided, evening out the total value of all the marital property and taking into consideration who would really want that item.

When you make your initial settlement proposal, you and your spouse may argue over some or all of the items on your list. Arguments over the value of property may also need to be resolved. In some instances, this can be resolved by retention of an appraiser to set a value on the marital property.

## DEBTS

This section relates to the **DEBT DIVISION WORKSHEET** upon which you will list your debts. (see form 3, p.185.) Although there are cases in which, for example, the wife gets the car but the husband is ordered to make the payments, generally whoever gets the property also gets the debt owed on that property. This is a fair and legally sustainable arrangement in many cases. On the **DEBT DIVISION WORKSHEET**, list each debt owed by you or your spouse. As with nonmarital property, there are also nonmarital debts. These are debts that you incurred before you were married and remain your responsibility after your divorce.

---

### – Caution –

If you and your spouse are jointly responsible for a debt, you are not relieved of your obligation to pay simply because your spouse agrees to pay (or is ordered to pay) the debt in the divorce proceeding. If your spouse does not pay, the creditor can still pursue you (and sue you) for payment.

---

The **DEBT DIVISION WORKSHEET** is divided into four columns, designated as follows.

*Creditor.* Enter the name of the bank, credit union, credit card company, or other entity to whom you and your spouse owe money.

*Amount of debt.* Enter the amount or balance owed.

*Husband or wife.* Insert whether the debt will be paid by you or your spouse.

*Notes.* Enter additional descriptive information pertaining to the debt, such as its monthly installment or payment status.

# ALIMONY

Alimony may be granted to either the husband or the wife. In reality, there are few cases in which a wife will be ordered to pay alimony to her husband.

New Jersey courts recognize four types of alimony.

1.  *Permanent.* This can continue for a long period of time, possibly until the death of the party receiving the alimony. This is typically awarded when one of the parties is unable to work due to age or a physical or mental illness.

2.  *Rehabilitative.* This type of alimony is awarded specifically to enable one of the spouses to get the education or training necessary to find a job. This is usually awarded when one of the parties has not been working during the marriage.

3.  *Limited duration.* This is temporary in nature, granted for a finite period in recognition of a dependent spouse's contributions to a relatively brief marriage.

4.  *Reimbursement.* This is awarded on a retroactive basis to compensate a spouse who made financial sacrifices providing the other spouse the opportunity to obtain advanced education (such as an M.D., M.B.A., doctorate, or law degree) or an enhancement to their professional license, through which both spouses expected to raise their standard of living.

New Jersey's alimony statute, N.J.S.A. 2A:34-23, requires a court to consider, but not be limited to, the following factors when making a determination on a request for alimony. These factors are used to determine whether alimony should be awarded, and if so, how much to award and for how long:

- ✪ actual need and ability of the spouses to pay;

- ✪ duration of the marriage;

- ✪ age, physical, and emotional health of the spouses;

- ✪ standard of living established in the marriage and the likelihood that each spouse can maintain a reasonable, comparable standard of living;

- ✪ earning capacities, educational levels, vocational skills, and employability of the spouses;

- ✪ length of absence from the job market of the spouse seeking alimony;

- ✪ parental responsibilities for the children;

- ✪ time and expense necessary to acquire sufficient education or training to enable the spouse seeking alimony to find appropriate employment;

- ✪ availability of training and employment, and the opportunity for future acquisitions of capital assets and income;

- ✪ history of the financial or nonfinancial contributions to the marriage by each spouse, including contributions to the care and education of the children and interruption of personal careers or educational opportunities;

- ✪ equitable distribution of property ordered and any pay outs on equitable distribution, directly or indirectly, out of current income, to the extent that this consideration is reasonable, just, and fair;

✪  income available to either spouse through investment of any assets held by that spouse;

✪  tax treatment and consequences to both spouses of any alimony award, including the designation of a portion of the payment as nontaxable; and,

✪  any other factors that the court may deem relevant.

As an alternative to requesting alimony, you may want to try to negotiate to receive a greater percentage of the property or a lump-sum payment. This may be less of a hassle in the long run, but it could change the tax consequences of your divorce. Consult your accountant regarding either of these alternatives.

# Child Custody, Visitation, and Support

This chapter initially addresses the handling and resolution of child custody, visitation, and support issues. Through application of the information contained in this chapter to your circumstances, you will obtain an idea of what to expect if a court must rule on these issues. In addition, if you and your spouse are attempting to reach an agreement on these matters, this chapter will assist you in determining whether a custody, visitation, or support proposal is sensible and fair. Child support is determined by a set of established guidelines, which are contained in New Jersey Rule of Court (*Rule*) 5:6A and Appendix IX-F to that Rule. (see Appendix E.)

## CHILD CUSTODY OVERVIEW

The decision to live apart is very difficult. However, it is most painful when children are involved in the family separation. Children have no part in either parent's determination to live separately. When parents do separate, there is an enormous effect upon their young lives. Children feel torn, questioning the proper way in which to show affection to both parents when they are no longer together as a family. Despite the end of a couple's relationship, a mother and father have an undeniable responsibility and duty to continue to care for their children and make decisions that directly affect them. The parents' decisions will ultimately manifest itself through their children's behavior, stability, and confidence. Though the couple's relationship may terminate, both the mother and father will legally continue to be parents.

## CUSTODY BY PARENTAL AGREEMENT

It is always preferable that both parents reach an agreement regarding their shared custody arrangements. If they are successful in reaching such an agreement, they may have that agreement formalized in a court order. The court must approve the agreement, and this can often be done without significant difficulty, provided the agreement is in the *best interests* of the children. This legal term is used by the courts to determine what actions most positively affect the welfare of the child.

In addition, after a filing for divorce, these arrangements are often fostered by the New Jersey Superior Court, Law Division, Family Part in the various counties. The court will encourage, if not direct, both spouses to attend parenting seminars designed to assist the spouses in reaching common ground on issues of custody. This frequently results in a custody agreement between the spouses, which will be readily approved by the court.

Even though the divorcing parents may have verbally agreed to certain custody arrangements (which may function without reduction to writing), it is highly recommended that a formal custody order be obtained. Such an order is an invaluable backup document, or a guide, whenever disagreements occur as to custody arrangements.

## MEDIATION

If parents are unable to reach an agreement on custody, the court is required by law to refer the dispute to *mediation* (the process of hiring, or having appointed by the court, an individual to hear the facts of your divorce matter and to aid both parties in finding a mutually agreeable settlement).

Mediation may include conferences between the spouses or a formal mediation process. If mediation is unsuccessful, the court may order an investigation by the Family Part into the character and fitness of the parents, the economic condition of the family, and the financial ability of a spouse to pay alimony or support. The investigation may also include psychological, psychiatric, or mental health evaluations of one or both spouses. The result of these investigations will be a *Child Custody and Parenting Time Investigation Report*, which must be prepared and filed with the court within forty-five days of the court's order. The report is intended to provide the court with information concerning the factors it must consider, under New Jersey Statutes Annotated, Section 9:2-4. (see Appendix A, p. 127), in custody decisions affecting minor children. These factors include:

- the parents' ability to agree, communicate, and cooperate in matters relating to their child or children;

- any history of unjustified accusations against the other parent in attempts to restrict his or her time spent with the child;

- the interaction and relationship of the child with his or her parents and siblings;

- the history of domestic violence, if any;

- the safety of the child and the safety of either parent from physical abuse by the other parent;

- the preference of the child when of sufficient age and capacity to reason and form an intelligent decision;

- the needs of the child;

- the stability of the home environment offered;

- the quality and continuity of the child's education;

- the fitness of the parents;

- the geographical proximity of the parents' homes;

- the extent and quality of the time spent with the child prior to or subsequent to the separation;

- the parents' employment responsibilities; and,

- the age and number of the children.

Pursuant to Rule 5:8-5, in conjunction with these reports, conflicting parties must submit a custody and parenting time or visitation plan with the court within seventy-five days after the parties have filed their last *responsive pleading*. This plan must include:

- addresses of the parties;

- employment of the parties;

- the type of custody requested with the reasons for selecting the type of custody:

  - joint legal custody with one parent having primary residential care;

  - joint physical custody;

  - sole custody to one parent, parenting time (visitation) to the other; or,

  - other custodial arrangement;

- a specific schedule as to parenting time including, but not limited to, weeknight, weekends, vacations, legal holidays, religious holidays, school vacations, birthdays, and special occasions (family outings, extracurricular activities, and religious services);

- access to medical and school records;

- the impact of a possible change of residence by a parent;

✪   participation in making decisions regarding the children; and,

✪   any other pertinent information.

## CUSTODY BATTLES WITHIN A DIVORCE

In a divorce, generally, if you are the wife, the odds start out in favor of you getting custody. However, do not depend solely upon the odds. Begin by reviewing the guidelines set forth in the prior section. Invariably, the court will utilize many of these in making a custody award. For each item listed, write down an explanation of how that item applies to you.

Child custody is very difficult to negotiate in a divorce. Tragically, it is an issue more often manipulated or used as a threat by one of the parties in order to get something else, such as a greater share of the property or a reduced child support obligation. If the essential issue in your divorce is one of these other matters, do not be alarmed by a threat of a custody battle. In such cases, the other party probably does not truly wish to possess custody and will not engage in a protracted struggle for it. If the critical issue is custody, you will rarely be able to negotiate for it, and ultimately the court will have to intervene and make a determination.

**Moral Fitness**     In some instances, a custody determination will depend upon the *moral fitness* of one or both parents. If you become involved in this sort of a custody battle, it is recommended that you seek legal counsel. Allegations of moral unfitness (such as illegal drug use, child abuse, or immoral sexual conduct) can require lengthy hearings involving the testimony of numerous witnesses and presentation of evidence. In some cases, the services of a private investigator will be needed. For such a hearing, you will need an attorney who knows the fine points of family law, knows the right questions to ask of witnesses, and is skilled in the rules of evidence.

But if the only question is whether you or your spouse has been the main caretaker of your children, it may not be necessary for you to get an attorney. You can always ask willing friends, neighbors, and relatives to attend hearings to testify on your behalf as witnesses.

However, should you have a need to *subpoena* (the legal document that requires the opponent to provide something or someone requested by you to the court) unwilling witnesses to testify, you need to hire an attorney.

**Best Interests**    New Jersey (and many other states) seeks to ensure that each minor child has frequent and continuing contact with both parents after the parents have separated or dissolved their marriage. The primary goal of New Jersey law is to ensure that child custody disputes be resolved in a manner protecting the *best interests* of the child, not of the parent. To this end, state policy encourages parents to share the rights and responsibilities of child rearing. (NJ Stat. Ann., Sec. 9:2-4.) (see Appendix A, p.127.)

In spite of this policy, many judges still believe that, all things being equal, a young child is better off with his or her mother. Therefore, a judge may go to great lengths to find that all things are not equal and justify a decision to award custody to the mother. At the same time, though, New Jersey courts are very reluctant to eliminate the participation of a willing and responsible spouse from parenting activities. Because of this, more cases than ever before show fathers being awarded significant custodial rights.

**Shared Custody**    Ideally, the court will order that the legal custody for a minor child be shared to a significant degree by both parents, unless the court finds that shared parental custody would be detrimental to the child. This is commonly known as *shared* or *joint* (partial) custody. However, because few parents can put aside their anger at each other to agree on what is best for their child, shared custody may lead to more fighting.

If you and your spouse cannot agree upon how these matters will be handled, you will be leaving this important decision up to the court. With the decision based to a significant degree on the criteria discussed earlier in this chapter, think carefully before you leave this decision to the court. The court cannot possibly know your children as well as you and your spouse, so it makes sense for both of you to work out the custody arrangements.

**Court Factors**    It is difficult to predict the outcome of a custody battle. There are too many factors and individual circumstances to make such a guess. The only exception is when one parent can prove the unfitness of the other. The most common charges against a spouse are drug abuse, physical abuse, or sexual abuse. However, unless there has been an arrest and conviction, it is difficult to prove. In general, do not charge your spouse with being unfit unless you can prove it. Judges are not impressed with unfounded allegations, and such charges often do more harm than good.

**Child's Preferences**

If your children are older (not infants), it may be a good idea to seriously consider their preferences of whom they would like to live. Your fairness and respect for their wishes may benefit you in the long run. (If they are primarily residing with the other parent, just be sure that you keep in close contact with them and visit them often.)

Knowing their preferences may assist you in voicing your position. In limited instances, noninfant children may be questioned by a judge (in the judge's chambers, not in open court) in the course of the court's fact-finding leading to a custody determination.

## CHILD SUPPORT

In New Jersey, as in most states, the question of child support is mostly a matter of mathematical calculation. Getting a fair child support amount depends on the accuracy of the income information presented to the court. If you feel fairly sure that the information your spouse presents is accurate or that you have obtained accurate information about his or her income, there is not much to debate. The court will take the income information provided, apply the Child Support Guidelines (*Guidelines*) provided in Rule 5:6A, Appendix IX-F (discussed on p.56–68) and order that amount to be paid.

The guidelines can be modified or disregarded only when the parties prove to the court that an exception should be made. In most instances, there will not be much room to argue about the amount of child support, so there usually is not a need to get an attorney. However, if you believe that your spouse has not provided accurate income information, this may be the time to consult an attorney who will know how to obtain more accurate income information.

**Guidelines**    If child support is involved in your case, you should first work out what you think the court will order based upon the guidelines discussed on the succeeding pages. Do this before attempting to reach an agreement with your spouse on the amount of support. If you will be receiving child support, you may want to ask for more than the guidelines require and negotiate down to what the guidelines suggest. If you will be paying child support, you may want to try for slightly less than the guidelines call for, but keep in mind that the court will rely upon the guidelines if you and your spouse are agreeing to less. This does not mean the court will reject your agreement, but you may need to offer an explanation as to why you are not following the guidelines.

You can tell your spouse there is little room for negotiation on child support, as the court will probably require it be set according to the statute. If your spouse will not agree on something close to the guidelines, it is better to let the court decide. Once again, the controlling factor in any question of support is not the best interest of the spouses, but of the child.

The guidelines calculate child support using the following steps.

***Step 1.*** Define the parental role of each spouse. In an instance of *sole parenting*, the children live in the custody of a *custodial* parent, who provides for their day-to-day needs. The other, or *noncustodial* parent, generally exercises visitation privileges equivalent to two overnight visits (*overnights*) by the children per week. In an instance of *shared parenting*, a *parent of primary residence* is: (a) the parent with whom the children live for more than 50% of overnights each year, or (b) the parent who provides the children with a residence while they attend school. A *parent of alternate residence* is the parent with whom the children reside when they are not with the parent of primary residence.

***Step 2.*** Select a **CHILD SUPPORT GUIDELINES WORKSHEET**. The form of these Worksheets has been approved by the New Jersey Supreme Court, and copies of these forms can be found in Appendix IX-C and Appendix IX-D of the New Jersey Rules of Court, which can be found in Appendix E of this book. The proper worksheet must be completed and made part of the permanent case file for each child support order, which is based upon the guidelines.

There are worksheets for sole parenting and shared parenting. The worksheets are complex, and use of a calculator is recommended to check the accuracy of your entries. Complete the top of the worksheet, which identifies the case name, parties, county of venue, and docket number.

***Step 3A.*** If you are completing a **Sole Parenting Worksheet** (p.152), you must make line-item entries for the custodial and the noncustodial parent and a *combined* entry, which is the total of both entries.

⟡   On Line 1, determine and enter the weekly gross taxable income. Gross income includes:

- wages, salary, fees, tips, and commissions;

- net income from business, minus ordinary and necessary operating expenses;

- gains from dealings in property;

- interest and dividends;

- rent, less ordinary, and necessary expenses;

- bonuses and royalties;

- alimony and separate maintenance payments received from current or past relationships;

- annuities or an interest in a trust;

- life insurance and endowment contracts;

- distributions from government and private retirement plans (including Social Security, Veterans Administration, Railroad Retirement Board, deferred compensation, Keoghs, and IRAs);

- personal injury awards or other civil lawsuits;

- interest in a decedent's estate or trust;

- disability grants or payments (including Social Security disability);

- profit sharing plans;

- workers' compensation;

- unemployment compensation benefits;

- overtime, part-time, and severance pay;

- net gambling winnings;

- sale of investments (net capital gain) or earnings from investments;

- income tax credits or rebates;

- unreported cash payments;

- the value of in-kind benefits (something being used in place of cash); and,

- imputed income.

⟡ On Line 1a, enter the mandatory nontaxable retirement contributions. On Line 1b, enter the amount of alimony paid. On Line 1c, enter the amount of alimony received. On either line, include current and past relationships.

⟡ Then, add Lines 1, 1a, 1b, and 1c together and place this figure on Line 2, which is the adjusted gross taxable income of both spouses.

⟡ Fill in the amount of federal, state, and local income tax withheld each week from your income and insert this figure on Line 2a. Then, enter on Line 2b the amount paid under child support orders from past relationships.

If the spouses have paid mandatory union dues, these amounts should be placed on Line 2c. Line 2d asks you to insert, as a deduction, the weekly support obligation for other legal dependents of the spouses. Ideally, this figure should be taken directly from a worksheet prepared for the support of these other legal dependents.

◈ Next, subtract the total of Lines 2a, 2b, 2c, and 2d from Line 2. The resulting figure is the net taxable income for the spouses. Enter this figure on Line 3.

◈ Next, on Line 4, enter the nontaxable income of the spouses. Income not subject to *federal tax* includes:

- accident and health insurance proceeds;

- black-lung benefits;

- child support payments;

- federal Employees Compensation Act payments;

- interest on a state or local obligation;

- scholarships and fellowships grants;

- veterans' benefits;

- workers' compensation;

- welfare and other public assistance benefits;

- life insurance proceeds paid due to the death of the insured;

- Social Security benefits;

  **NOTE:** *Exceptions may apply for a spouse having an income greater than $25,000 if single, or $32,000 if married, and filing a joint return.*

- casualty insurance and other reimbursements; and,

- earnings from tax-free government bonds or securities.

Income not subject to *state tax* includes:

- federal Social Security benefits;

- railroad retirement benefits;

- proceeds of life insurance contracts payable by reason of death;

- employee death benefits;

- value of property acquired by gift, bequest, devise, or inheritance (except income from any such property, or if the gift, bequest, devise, or inheritance is income);

- amounts received under workers' compensation, including income from suits, agreements, accident, or health insurance resulting from personal injuries or sickness;

- compensation paid by the United States for services in the Armed Forces performed by an individual not domiciled in New Jersey;

- grants or scholarships received from educational institutions;

- payments of up to $10,000 for a married couple filing jointly, $5,000 for a married couple filing separately, and $7,500 for a single taxpayer from an annuity, endowment, or life insurance contract, or payments of any such amount received as a pension, disability, or retirement benefits for persons at least 62 years old or disabled under Social Security;

- New Jersey Lottery winnings;

- permanent and total disability under a public or private plan and certain accident/health insurance benefits, including veterans' benefits;

- unemployment insurance and Temporary Disability benefits;

- interest on obligations issued by the state or any county, municipality, school, or other governmental body of New Jersey and obligations statutorily free from tax under state or federal law;

- amounts contributed by an employer on behalf of an employee to a trust that meets the requirements of I.R.C. section 401(k) in the year when contributed;

- earnings from tax-free government bonds or securities; and,

- state or federal income tax refunds.

    **NOTE:** *This list is not all-encompassing. There may be other types of income that are considered nontaxable. Confer with your accountant or tax professional if you have any questions.*

◈ Once you have entered the figure for nontaxable income, add Lines 3 and 4 together and enter the total on Line 5, which will be your net income.

◈ Then, on Line 6, determine and insert each parent's percentage share of the net income figure, which is the net income of each parent divided by the total net income of both parents.

◈ You must then look up and enter, on Line 7, the basic child support amount attributable to each parent from the schedules prepared in Appendix IX-F to Rule 5:6-A. This number will be keyed to the spouses' share of the net weekly income that they contribute and will vary dependent upon the number of children of the marriage.

❖ Next, enter on Line 8 (based again upon the percentage contribution of the spouses to net income stated on Line 6) the dollar amount attributable to each spouse for work-related child care expenses. To facilitate your calculation of these figures, Appendix IX-E to Rule 5:6-A provides a sub-worksheet for net child care costs.

❖ On Line 9, insert that share of the spouse's health insurance premium applicable to the children of the marriage.

❖ On Line 10, place each spouse's share of the unreimbursed health care expenses over $250 per child, per year.

❖ If the court has ordered or approved parental payment of certain extraordinary expenses for the children, the parental contribution for these expenses should be entered on Line 11, again based upon the Line 6 percentage share.

❖ On Line 12, any government benefits provided to the children should be entered as a deduction for each spouse, also based upon the Line 6 percentage.

❖ Line 13 summarizes the total amount of child support for which both spouses will be responsible, by the addition of Lines 7, 8, 9, 10, and 11, with Line 12 then subtracted from this figure.

❖ At Line 14, each spouse's share of this amount is determined by multiplying the Line 6 percentage by the number on Line 13.

❖ Thereafter, a series of deductions from the proportional support obligation are to be entered on Line 15 (net work-related child care paid), Line 16 (amounts paid for children's health insurance premium), Line 17 (nonreimbursed health care expenses paid in excess of $250 per child per year), Line 18 (court-approved extraordinary expenses paid), and Line 19 (adjustment parenting time expenses).

NOTE: *The figure to be entered on Line 19 is the result of an equation in which the amount on Line 7 (basic child support) is multiplied by the percentage of parenting time spent by each spouse with the children, which is then multiplied by a factor of .037.*

◆ Having calculated these deductions, you should then subtract the amounts on Lines 15, 16, 17, 18, and 19 from Line 14. Enter the resulting number on Line 20. This is the net child support obligation of the parties.

◆ This net obligation may be adjusted by deductions for dependents from other relationships, and if one or both spouses request this, these adjustments should be reflected and entered on Lines 21 and 22.

> **NOTE:** *It is very important to consider the financial impact of child support obligations from previous marriages, if these obligations exist. Indeed, the calculations involved in preparing the worksheet may well warrant consultation with an attorney to review all of your worksheet entries to ensure their accuracy. The Line 21 child support obligation reflecting this "other dependent deduction" should then be added to the Line 22 obligation not reflecting this deduction, with the sum being divided by 2. This number should be placed in Line 23 as the "adjusted child support order."*

◆ Some final adjustments remain. For the noncustodial parent, the number entered on Lines 20 or 23 (if adjusted) should be subtracted from Line 5 (net income), with the result placed on Line 24, while for the custodial payment, the amount on Line 5 should be inserted on Line 24.

◆ If the noncustodial parent's Line 24 entry is greater than 105% of the poverty guideline, you may skip Line 25 and insert the figure from Lines 20 or 23 on line 26, which will become the final Child Support Order.

If the noncustodial parent's Line 24 entry is less than 105% of the United States poverty guideline for one person ($188 per week at the time this book went to press) and the custodial parent's Line 24 entry is greater than this poverty guideline, Line 25 must be completed, where a figure equivalent to 105% of the poverty guideline ($197.40) must be subtracted from the noncustodial parent's net income.

◈ The Line 25 figure must also be inserted on Line 26 as the final Child Support Order.

**Step 3B.** If you are completing a **SHARED PARENTING WORKSHEET**, you must make line-item entries for the parent of primary residence and the parent of alternate residence (see Step 1 on page 56), as well as a *combined* entry (the total of both entries).

◈ On Line 1, determine and enter the weekly gross taxable income (See Step 3A for a description of what gross income includes.) On Line 1a, enter the mandatory nontaxable retirement contributions. On line 1b, enter the amount of alimony paid, and on Line 1c, enter the amount of alimony received, including current and past relationships on both lines.

◈ Then, take the Line 1 figure, subtract from it the figures on Lines 1a and Line 1b, then add the figure inserted on Line 1c. The result is the adjusted gross taxable income, which should be placed on Line 2.

◈ Calculate the amount of federal, state, and local income tax withheld and insert this figure on Line 2a. Then, enter on Line 2b the amount paid under child support orders from past relationships.

◈ If the parents have paid mandatory union dues, these amounts should be placed on Line 2c. On Line 2d, the weekly support obligations for other legal dependents and their spouses must be inserted.

◈ Next, subtract the total of Lines 2a, 2b, 2c, and 2d from Line 2. The resulting figure is the net taxable income of the parents. Enter this figure on Line 3.

◈ Next, on Line 4, enter the nontaxable income of the spouses (See Step 3A for a description of nontaxable income). Again, this list is not all encompassing and there may be other types of income that are considered nontaxable. If you have any questions about this, it is highly recommended that you confer with your accountant or tax professional.

◈ Once you have entered the figure for nontaxable income, add Lines 3 and 4 together and enter the total on Line 5, which will be your net income.

◈ Then, on Line 6, calculate and insert each parent's percentage share of the net income figure.

◈ On Line 7, enter the number of overnights with each parent.

◈ On Line 8, calculate and insert each parent's percentage share of the total number of overnights.

◈ You must then look up and enter on Line 9 the basic child support amount attributable to each parent from the schedules prepared in Appendix IX-F to Rule 5:6-A.

◈ The fixed parenting expenses of the parent of alternate residence should then be calculated by multiplying the percentage of overnight visits of the parent of alternate residence (Line 8) by the basic child support amount on Line 9, then multiplying this figure by a factor of .038, then multiplying the resulting figure by 2, with the product being placed on Line 10.

◈ Government benefits provided to the children should be entered on Line 11.

◈ Thereafter, the shared parenting basic child support amount is determined by adding the figures on Lines 9 and 10 and subtracting the amount on Line 11.

◈ Then, the parent of alternate residence's share of the shared parenting basic support amount is calculated by multiplying that parent's total on Line 6 by his or her total on Line 12, with the product being entered on Line 13.

◈ The shared parenting variable expenses for the parent of alternate residence are then figured by multiplying the parent's total on Line 8 by that on Line 9, with that product being multiplied by a factor of .037. The result of these calculations is then placed on Line 14.

◈ An adjusted shared parenting basic child support amount, determined by subtraction of the figures on Lines 10 and 14 from Line 13, is then entered on Line 15.

◈ Thereafter, the net work-related child care expenses paid are to be entered on Line 16, and additional entries should be made for the amounts paid for the children's health insurance premium (Line 17), unreimbursed health care expenses paid in excess of $250 per child per year (Line 18), and court-approved extraordinary expenses paid (Line 19).

◈ The sum of the expenses entered on Lines 16–19 should be inserted on Line 20.

◈ Calculation is then made for the share of total supplemental expenses for which the parent of alternate residence is responsible. This figure is obtained by multiplying Line 6 by Line 20 for the parent of alternate residence and placing the product on Line 21.

◈ The net work-related child care expenses, health insurance premiums, unreimbursed health care expenses, and court-approved extraordinary expenses paid by the parent of alternate residence are then entered on Lines 22, 23, 24, and 25, respectively.

◈ Then, the parent of alternate residence's total payments and supplemental expenses (the sum of Lines 22–25) and net supplemental expenses (the sum of Lines 21–26) are placed on Lines 26 and 27, respectively.

◈ On Line 28, the figures on Lines 15 (adjusted basic child support) and 27 are added to create the *net child support obligation* for the parent of alternate residence.

◈ If neither parent seeks a deduction from his or her obligation due to the existence of an obligation to other dependents from previous relationships, Lines 29–31 should not be completed; if such an adjustment is desired, these lines should be completed to reflect the child support obligation of the parent of alternate residence with this other-dependent deduction (Line 29) and without the deduction (Line 30).

◈ The Line 29 obligation should be added to the Line 30 obligation, with that sum being divided by 2 and placed on Line 31. This is the adjusted child support obligation for the parent of alternate residence.

◈ Again, some final adjustments must be made. For the parent of alternate residence, the number entered on Line 28 or 31 should be subtracted from Line 5 (net income), with the result placed on Line 32.

◈ The income of the parent of primary residence should also be entered in its designated area. If this amount is greater than 105% of the poverty guideline for one person (see Step 3A, p.57), Line 33 need not be completed and the amount from Line 28 or 31 may be placed on Line 34, which is the amount that will be the basis for the final Child Support Order.

However, if the number on Line 32 is less than 105% of the poverty guideline, and the income of the parent of primary residence is greater than 105% of the poverty guideline, calculate the support by subtracting 105% of the poverty guideline from the net income of the parent of alternate residence (Line 5). Place this calculation on Lines 33 and 34.

◈ In certain circumstances, if the child support obligor is the parent of alternate residence, Line 35 must be completed. On this line, the net income of the parent of primary residence (Line 5) is added to the net income of other members of the parent's household. This sum is then added to the Child Support Order figure on Line 34 for the parent of alternate residence.

The following test is then applied—if the number on Line 35 is less than the household income threshold for the combined net income of both the parent of primary residence and the total number of persons in that parent's household, it is inappropriate to use a **SHARED CUSTODY WORKSHEET.** A **SOLE CUSTODY WORKSHEET** must be used.

***Step 4.*** On either type of worksheet, there is a section called "Comments, Rebuttals and Justification for Deviations." If you are seeking a support figure that does not follow the guidelines, this should be completed. You should set forth any special circumstances that would justify a further adjustment. Under Rule 5:6A, in deciding whether to deviate from the amount of support determined by the guidelines, the court will consider:

- unusual needs and unusual fixed obligations of the parents;

- other legal dependents of either parent;

- multiple family obligations;

- employment status of the parents;

- assets of the parties;

- unpredictable and recurring expenses for the children;

- government benefits paid to or for the children; and,

- other relevant and appropriate factors, including the best interests of the child.

## CHILD SUPPORT ENFORCEMENT AND COLLECTION

Once the Child Support Order is finalized, the court will direct, through the order, that all payments made under the order be made through the *probation division* in the county where the parent having the support obligation resides. In the majority of cases, this is done through income withholding. This is preferable because a spouse's compliance with child support guidelines is continually monitored by the probation division, enabling enforcement activity to be more directly imposed against a nonpaying spouse—through arrest, if necessary. New Jersey Court Rule 5:7-4 provides:

✪ that if support is not paid through immediate income withholding, the child support provisions of an order or judgment are subject to income withholding when past-due child support (*arrearage*) has accrued in an amount equal to or in excess of the amount of support payable for fourteen days;

✪ that any payment or installment of an order for child support or those portions of an order that are allocated for child support shall be fully enforceable and entitled to full faith and credit (recognizable by other courts) and shall be a judgment (having the effect of a lien) by operation of law on or after the date it is due;

✪ that no payment or installment of an order for child support or those portions of an order that are allocated for child support shall be retroactively modified by the court except for the period during which the party seeking relief has pending an application for modification;

✪ that the occupational, recreational, and professional licenses, including a license to practice law, held or applied for by the nonpaying spouse may be denied, suspended, or revoked if:

  • a child support arrearage accumulates that is equal to or exceeds the amount of child support payable by the nonpaying spouse for a period of six months;

  • the nonpaying spouse fails to provide health care coverage for the child as ordered by the court within six months;

- a warrant for the nonpaying spouse's arrest has been issued by the court for failure to pay child support as ordered, for failure to appear at a hearing to establish paternity or child support, or for failure to appear at a child support hearing to enforce a child support order;

✪ that the driver's license held or applied for by the nonpaying spouse may be denied, suspended, or revoked if:

- a child support arrearage accumulates that is equal to or exceeds the amount of child support payable for six months or

- the nonpaying spouse fails to provide health care coverage for the child, as ordered by the court within six months; and,

✪ that the driver's license held or applied for by the nonpaying spouse shall be denied, suspended, or revoked if the court issues a warrant for the spouse's arrest for failure to pay child support as ordered, failure to appear at hearing to establish paternity or child support, or for failure to appear at a child support hearing to enforce a child support order, while said warrant remains outstanding.

Though the spouses can agree to pay each other directly, this can lead to problems in the long term, as there is less threat of punishment to a nonpaying spouse. Thus, spouse-to-spouse payment is not recommended.

# Legal Forms and General Procedures

## chapter 7

You may tear the forms out of this book to file with the court. However, it is better to photocopy the forms and keep the originals blank should you make mistakes or need additional copies.

Most of the forms in this book are based upon forms commonly used by New Jersey attorneys in cases before the New Jersey Superior Court. Therefore, courts or attorneys are unlikely to object to them. While the forms in this book are legally correct, you may, however, encounter a judge who is very particular about how he or she wants the forms drafted. If you encounter any problem with the forms in this book being accepted by a judge, you can try one or more of the following:

- ✪ ask the judge what is wrong with the forms, then correct them to suit the judge;

- ✪ a small number of judges provide attorneys appearing before them with written guidelines as to the desired format for pleadings in matters before them. Ask the judge if he or she provides such instructions, and if so, ask to be provided with a copy. Use those guidelines along with the instructions in this book in preparing your pleadings; or,

✪    consult an attorney.

Although the instructions in this book tell you to "type in" certain information, it is not absolutely necessary to use a typewriter. If typing is not possible, you can print the information required in the forms, as long as it can easily be read. Black ink should be used.

A list of the forms used in this book can be found at the beginning of Appendix F. Most of the forms in the appendix have similar headings (also known as *captions*) which identify the court, the parties, and the docket number. The top portion of these forms should be completed as follows.

◈    Fill in the name of the county where you will file your papers.

◈    Fill in the docket number, which should be provided by the clerk when the initial **COMPLAINT** for divorce is filed. In some instances, the clerk will mail the **COMPLAINT** and attachments back to you with the docket number entered on the **COMPLAINT**. Thereafter, you must fill in the same number on any papers you file.

◈    Fill in your full name on the line marked "Plaintiff" and your spouse's full name on the line marked "Defendant." Do not use nicknames or shortened versions of names. Use the names as they appear on your marriage license, if possible.

When completed, the top portion of your forms should look like the following example.

```
YOUR NAME (OR LAW FIRM'S NAME)
YOUR ADDRESS (OR LAW FIRM'S ADDRESS)
PHONE NUMBER (OR LAW FIRM'S PHONE NUMBER)
If not represented by attorney: YOUR NAME, Pro Se
If represented by attorney: ATTORNEY'S NAME
_____

                                         :NEW JERSEY SUPERIOR
                                          COURT
JULIET CAPULET,                          :CHANCERY DIVISION

                                         :FAMILY PART
          Plaintiff,                     :WARREN COUNTY
                                         :
vs.                                      :Docket No.
                                         :
                                         :
                                         :
ROMEO MONTAGUE,                          :CIVIL ACTION
                                         :
          Defendant,                     :
_____
```

At the end of many of the forms there will be a place for you to sign your name. In some instances, your signature may have to be notarized, in which case a provision is included on the form for completion by a notary public. Please note that in New Jersey, attorneys are considered to be a notary public.

## FILING WITH THE CLERK OF THE SUPERIOR COURT

Once you decide which forms you need, and prepare them, you may commence your case by filing a **VERIFIED COMPLAINT FOR DIVORCE** with the clerk. (see form 4, p.187.) First, make at least five copies of your complaint and attachments, if any (the original and one copy for the clerk, one for yourself, one for your spouse, and one extra if needed).

Filing is fairly simple. The following information will help the process go smoothly. Call the office of the Clerk of the Superior Court in the county where you will be filing your complaint. You can find the phone number under the county government section of your phone directory. Ask the following questions as well as any other questions that come to mind, such as the location of the clerk's office and office hours.

- How much is the filing fee for a **VERIFIED COMPLAINT FOR DIVORCE**?

- Does the court have any special forms that need to be filed with the **COMPLAINT**?

- How many copies of the **COMPLAINT** should be filed with the clerk?

Next, take your **COMPLAINT** and any other forms you determine you need to the clerk's office to file. (Instructions for completing these forms are provided in other parts of this book.) The clerk handles many different types of cases, so be sure to look for signs telling you which office or window to go to. You should be looking for signs that say such things as "Family Part," "Filing," etc.

Once you have found the right place, simply hand the papers to the clerk and say, "I'd like to file this." The clerk will briefly examine the complaint, then either accept it for filing (and collect the filing fee, or direct you to where to pay it), or tell you that something is not correct. If you are told something is wrong, ask the clerk to explain to you what is wrong and how to correct the problem. Although the clerk is not permitted to give legal advice, the types of problems he or she can spot are usually very minor things that he or she can tell you how to correct. It is often possible to figure out how to correct it from their explanation.

## SERVICE OF THE COMPLAINT UPON YOUR SPOUSE

The laws of New Jersey require that a person be notified of a legal proceeding that involves him or her. This includes any proceeding involving divorce, custody, visitation, or support. This gives your spouse a chance to respond to your **COMPLAINT**.

**Personal Service**

The usual way to notify your spouse that you filed for divorce is called *personal service*. A sheriff's officer of the county in which your spouse lives will do this. You must complete a **Summons** (form 9, p.197), which is then attached to the **Complaint** after it is filed. You must then provide the **Summons** and **Complaint** to the sheriff's office, together with your spouse's last known address. There is a fee for this service, and will vary by the destination for service in a particular county.

If your spouse lives out of state, even though you may file your **Complaint** in the county in which you live, your spouse must be served in that state. In those instances, you will have to pay the out-of-state sheriff or constable the fees that are set locally. This will be more expensive.

Finally, you may wish to utilize an approved process server, which will serve the **Summons** and **Complaint** for a set charge. This is a more recent development in New Jersey process service, and you should make sure that your *process server* is approved by the New Jersey Superior Court. The sheriff or process server will provide you with an *Affidavit of Service*, which verifies proper service under the Rules of Court.

## OTHER NOTICE

Once your spouse has been served with the **Complaint**, you may simply mail him or her copies of any papers you file later. You must sign a statement called a *Certification of Service* verifying that you mailed copies to your spouse. Some of the forms in this book will include a *Certification of Service* section for you to complete. If any form you file does not contain one, you will need to complete the **Certificate of Service**. (see form 12, p.209.)

## TRACK DESIGNATION

After your **Verified Complaint for Divorce** is filed, your case will be assigned to one of four judicial management tracks as follows.

1. *Priority Track.* Involving contested custody or parenting time issues. (see Chapter 6.)

2. *Complex Track.* Requiring substantial court and litigant resources in preparation for trial and at trial because of the number of parties involved, the number of claims and defenses raised, the legal complexity of the issues presented, the factual difficulty of the subject matter, and other factors or a combination thereof.

3. *Expedited Track.* Involving a case that can be tried with minimal pretrial proceedings.

4. *Standard Track.* Any case not assigned to one of the other tracks.

**NOTE:** *It is strongly recommended that you retain counsel for any case falling into Tracks 1 and 2. Keep in mind that cases in Tracks 3 and 4 may have unique complexities and could also warrant retention of an attorney.*

## CASE INFORMATION STATEMENTS

Both spouses in a divorce proceeding must file a **MATRIMONIAL CASE INFORMATION STATEMENT** (CIS) and serve it on the other spouse within twenty days after the responding spouse has answered the **COMPLAINT**. (see form 1, p.173.) The CIS is each party's statement of contested issues, assets, and debts accumulated in the marriage, property owned by the spouses, spousal income, and other important information. Care must be taken in the preparation of the CIS, which also must be updated and amended on a continuing basis up to twenty days prior to the final hearing date on the divorce. (see Rule 5:5-2 in Appendix A, p.138.)

## EARLY SETTLEMENT PANEL

All counties have an *Early Settlement Panel* (ESP) in conjunction with the Presiding Family Part Judge in each county and that county's bar association. The majority of cases are referred to ESP by the presiding judge after review of the pleadings and CISs submitted by the spouses. When a case is referred to the ESP, the spouses and their counsel must participate. The purpose of the ESP is to set forth the positions of each party as to material issues such as property division, child support, and custody. If one or both spouses do not participate in the ESP, the nonparticipating spouse(s) will be penalized, either through an award of legal fees to the other spouse, or a dismissal of pleadings filed by the nonparticipating spouse.

## MOTIONS

In conjunction with your divorce filing, there may be related issues that must be settled promptly, such as child support and spousal support. Though in New Jersey, as in other states, the long-term resolution of these issues is usually addressed during and at the conclusion of the divorce proceeding. You, or your children, if they are living with you, may need short-term assistance now. To do this, you must file a *motion* with the court seeking support from the other spouse on a temporary, or *Pendente Lite* basis. A sample that may fit your situation is provided as form 13, p.211.

In New Jersey, motions are generally heard on Fridays, and motions must be filed at least sixteen days prior to the hearing date. Your spouse will have the right to oppose your motion. Be careful in filing the motion to have your facts straight, because you will have to make your request under oath, by use of an *Affidavit or Certification*. A **SAMPLE CERTIFICATION IN SUPPORT OF MOTION** that may fit your needs is included as form 14, p.213.

**NOTE:** *Motions can also be used to resolve other temporary issues, such as adjustment of custody and visitation schedules and control of spousal behavior (such as unauthorized relocation of children of the marriage by the parent of alternate residence (see Chapter 6)). However, motions should not be used frivolously. Only use motions when you have a legitimate dispute with your spouse over an issue that is material to the divorce. Otherwise, the court may give you a fine, or at least a warning.*

## COURTROOM DECORUM

There are certain standards of decorum that are used in a court. They are not difficult, and most of them make sense. These are essentially rules of good conduct and manners, and are designed to keep the proceedings orderly. Some of these are written down and some are unwritten customs that have developed over many years.  Following these suggestions will make the judge respect you for your maturity and professional manner, and may also increase the likelihood that you will receive the things you request.

**Display Respect and Reverence for the Court**

New Jersey judges are expected to treat all *litigants* with courtesy, respect, and dignity. You must hold yourself to a similar standard of decency and respect. Showing respect to the court basically means that you must not do anything to make the judge angry with you, such as being argumentative. Be polite and call the judge "Your Honor" when you speak to him or her, such as "Yes, Your Honor," or "Your Honor, I brought proof of my income." Although some lawyers address judges as "Judge," this is not proper. You should wear appropriate and conservative clothing (a coat and tie for men and a dress or suit for women). Do not wear T-shirts, blue jeans, shorts, or revealing clothing.

**Listen to the Judge**

Any time the judge is talking, you need to be listening carefully. Even if the judge interrupts you, stop talking immediately and listen. Judges can become upset if you do not allow them to interrupt.

**Do Not Talk Over One Another**

Each person is allotted his or her own time to speak in court. The judge can only listen to one person at a time, so do not interrupt your spouse when it is his or her turn. As difficult as it may be, stop talking if your spouse interrupts you. Let the judge tell your spouse to keep quiet.

**Speak Only to the Court**

Many divorcing spouses come into court and begin arguing with each other. They turn away from the judge, face each other, and begin arguing as if they were in a room alone. Invariably, this can have several negative results—the judge cannot understand what either spouse is saying; they both look foolish for losing control; and, the judge becomes angry with both of them. Whenever you speak in a courtroom, you are speaking to the court on the public record. Therefore, only look at, and speak to, the judge. Try to pretend that your spouse is not there. Remember, you are there to convince the judge that you should have the children, visits, support, etc., that you seek. You do not need to convince your spouse.

**Speak when Instructed to Do So**

The usual procedure is for you to present your case first. When you have completed saying all you came to say, your spouse will have a chance to say whatever he or she came to say. Let your spouse have his or her say. When he or she is finished, you will be provided another chance to respond to what has been said.

**Focus on the Facts of the Case**

Many people tend to get off the track and start telling the judge all the problems with their marriage. This wastes time and aggravates the judge. Do not do this. Organize your presentation in a brief and succinct manner. When asked questions by the judge, answer them simply and to the point.

**Retain Your Composure**

Judges like matters to go smoothly in their courtrooms. They do not tolerate shouting, name calling, crying, or other displays of emotion. Generally, judges do not like family law cases because they get too emotionally charged. So give your judge a pleasant surprise by keeping calm and focusing on the issues.

**Display Respect for Your Spouse**

Even if you do not respect your spouse, act as though you do. All you have to do is refer to your spouse as "Mr. Smith" or "Ms. Smith" (using his or her correct name, of course).

## chapter 8

# Uncontested Divorce

Many divorce cases can proceed through the court system with ease. The cases that are unchallenged, or do not involve your spouse's objections over a variety of issues, can be considered *uncontested*.

## NEGOTIATION

An uncontested divorce is usually one that has become uncontested through a lot of negotiations back and forth among the spouses. Though the techniques involved in negotiation are beyond the scope of this book, use these few basic rules as guidelines.

**Ask for More than You Want**

By asking for more than you want, you have some room to compromise by giving up a few things. You may end up with close to what you really want. With property division, this means you will review your **PROPERTY DIVISION WORKSHEET** and compile a list, comprised of those items which you really want, would like to have, and do not care much about. Also consider the items that your spouse would place in these categories. Your list should be divided as follows:

- ✪ everything you really want;

- ✪ everything you would like to have; and,

- ✪ items you do not care about.

Be sure to also consider your debts, as well as what may be owed on each item and who is (or should be) responsible for the debt. For example, after considering your postdivorce income and expected expenses, it may be to your advantage to take a paid-off older car rather than a newer car with a large payment.

Your list will eventually consist of things you can probably get with little difficulty (you really want and your spouse does not care), those items that you will fight over (you both really want), and those items that need to be divided, but can probably be easily divided equally (you both do not really care).

Regarding child support or alimony, ask for more than you really want (or less than you are willing to pay, if you will be paying). Hopefully, your spouse will make a counteroffer that is close to what you would prefer. Use the child support calculations in Chapter 6 to get an idea of what the court would probably order, then ask for a bit more (or a bit less if you will be paying support). But remember that the court will probably order an amount close to what the child support guidelines call for, so there will not be too much room for negotiation.

**Let Your Spouse Start the Bidding**

The first person to mention a dollar figure loses. Whether it is a child support figure or the value of a piece of property, it is important to get your spouse to make an offer first. If your spouse starts with a figure that you had in mind, it will be much easier to get to your figure. If your spouse begins with a figure far from yours, you know how far in the other direction to begin your bid.

**Give Your Spouse Time to Think and Worry**

Your spouse is probably just as afraid about the possibility of losing to the support counselor's or custody conciliator's decision, and would like to settle. Do not be afraid to state your *final offer*, then walk away. Give your spouse a day or two to think it over. Maybe he or she will call back and make a better offer. If not, you can always *recon-*

*sider* and make a different offer in a few days, but do not be too willing to do this or your spouse may think you will give in even more.

**Know Your Bottom Line**

Before you begin negotiating, try to set a point that you will not go beyond. If you have decided that there are four items of property that you absolutely must have, and your spouse is only willing to agree to let you have three, it is time to end the bargaining session and go home.

**Remember What You Have Learned**

By the time you have read this far, you should be aware of two things:

✪ your property will be divided in a roughly equal portion and

✪ the court will probably come close to the child support guidelines in what it orders as a child support payment.

This awareness should give you an approximate idea of the way in which matters will turn out, which should help you to set your bottom line on such matters.

## UNCONTESTED DIVORCE PROCEDURE

There are two ways that a case can be considered *uncontested*. One is if you and your spouse agree to everything from the beginning. The other is if you and your spouse negotiate or argue, but eventually reach an agreement.

Most lawyers have had the following experience. A new client comes in and says she wants to file for divorce. She has discussed it with her husband and it will be a simple, uncontested divorce. However, once the papers are filed, the husband and wife begin arguing over a few items of property. The lawyer then spends a lot of time negotiating with the husband. After much arguing, an agreement is finally reached. The case will proceed in the court as *uncontested*, but only after a lot of *contesting* out of court.

For purposes of this book, an *uncontested case* is where you will do your arguing and deciding *before* you go to court, and the court will only be approving your decision. In all probability, you will be seeking a divorce on the grounds of *extreme cruelty* as discussed in Chapter 5.

You can also seek an uncontested divorce on the grounds of *separation*, but if you and your spouse have only just separated, the process will probably take longer due to the eighteen-month separation requirement.

A *contested case* is where you and your spouse will do your arguing *in* court, and leave the decision to the court. You may not know if you are going to have a contested case until you try the uncontested route and fail. In addition, you should at least consult with an attorney if you become embroiled in a contested case.

Unfortunately, unlike some states, New Jersey does not have a formal *uncontested* or *on the papers* divorce procedure. Nevertheless, obtaining an uncontested divorce is relatively straightforward under the standard divorce procedure established in the New Jersey Statutes and New Jersey Court Rules. However, before you can file for a divorce on an uncontested basis, the following threshold requirements must be met.

- ✪ You or your spouse must have resided in New Jersey for at least the past year (unless your claim is for alimony). (NJ Stat. Ann., Sec. 2A:34-10.)

- ✪ You and your spouse do not have any *minor* or *dependent* children. (A *minor child* is under the age of 18. A *dependent child* may be over the age of 18 and still be dependent upon a parent for support due to mental or physical illness, disease, or disability. In some cases, the child's attendance at college can also extend the period of dependency.)

- ✪ You and your spouse agree on who will have custody and child support terms, so that there will be no need for a hearing on these matters.

- ✪ You and your spouse have agreed as to how your property and debts will be divided.

If you meet these four requirements, and you are *not* seeking a divorce on the grounds of separation, your divorce can be completed in a relatively short time, depending on the court's number of cases.

Even if you do not meet each of these requirements, you should still read this chapter because it will help you to better understand the other procedures. If the only requirement you do not meet is that you cannot agree on the division of your property, you may want to reconsider your position on the property. Read this chapter, then compare this simple procedure to the procedure in Chapter 9. Once you see how much easier it is when you have an agreement, you may want to try harder to resolve your differences.

To begin your divorce case the following forms will be filed with the Clerk of the Superior Court (see Chapter 7 for filing instructions):

- ✪ **CIVIL CASE INFORMATION STATEMENT** (This describes the type of case before the court.) (form 8);

- ✪ **VERIFIED COMPLAINT FOR DIVORCE** (form 4 or form 5);

- ✪ **CERTIFICATION OF INSURANCE COVERAGE** (form 6);

- ✪ **MATRIMONIAL CASE INFORMATION STATEMENT** (form 1);

- ✪ Cover Letter (see sample form 7); and,

- ✪ Filing Fee. ($250)

Complete and file all necessary forms and *serve* them upon your spouse. Your spouse should file an **APPEARANCE** (form 10, p.199) and his or her own **MATRIMONIAL CASE INFORMATION STATEMENT** (form 1, p.173.) In some cases your spouse may elect not to file an **APPEARANCE** or **CASE INFORMATION STATEMENT**, and you will receive what is called a *Default Judgment* thirty-five days after your spouse is served. Though this may seem the most direct route to an uncontested divorce, it may in fact lengthen the time for the case to conclude. The court will more closely scrutinize a divorce in which only one spouse's pleadings and information are submitted to the court.

You and your spouse will discuss and resolve all property distribution (and child custody and support if applicable) after all forms are filed. As discussed in Chapter 2, the Early Settlement Panel may also be helpful in resolving these issues. Your agreement should be reduced to writing.

After reaching agreement, whether mutually or through the Early Settlement Panel, your case can be set down for a *final hearing* before a Superior Court, Chancery Division, Family Part judge. The faster you are able to reach such agreement, the more quickly your divorce can be concluded. If the court approves the agreement that you have reached, a **FINAL JUDGMENT OF DIVORCE** can be entered. (see form 18, p.223.) You may also be asked to file other appropriate forms with the court in order to complete the case.

## VERIFIED COMPLAINT FOR DIVORCE

The **VERIFIED COMPLAINT FOR DIVORCE** is the primary *pleading* used to open your case and ask for a divorce. Form 4 is used if the grounds for divorce is separation, and form 5 is used if the grounds for divorce is extreme cruelty. Both forms are completed in much the same way, with form 5 requiring more facts regarding the cruelty. The instructions that follow are specifically for form 4, but can easily be followed to complete form 5. Complete the **VERIFIED COMPLAINT FOR DIVORCE** as follows.

◈ Complete the top portion of the form according to the instructions in Chapter 7.

◈ Type in your name, address, and county of residence on the first two lines in the first unnumbered paragraph.

◈ In Paragraph 1, type in the name of your spouse and the date of your marriage. Identify whether your wedding ceremony was "civil" or "religious."

◈ In Paragraph 2, state that you were a bona fide resident of New Jersey when your cause of action (for divorce) arose.

◈ In Paragraph 3, type in the name and address of your spouse, including the county where he or she resides, even if in another state.

◈ Beginning in Paragraph 4, begin the description of the facts that caused you to file for divorce. You may need more than one paragraph. However, since the divorce is consensual in nature and you are most likely seeking divorce on grounds of separation or extreme cruelty, frame the facts in a manner that makes clear that it is improper or unreasonable to expect you and your spouse to continue to live together with any level of harmony.

◈ When you have completed the foregoing description of the facts, in the succeeding paragraph, give the number of children you and your spouse have (including any adopted children), and their names and birthdays. Of course, if there are no children of the marriage, this is unnecessary.

◈ In the next paragraph, state whether there have been any previous proceedings between you and your spouse respecting the marriage or its dissolution or respecting your maintenance (as the Plaintiff) in any way. If there have been such proceedings (such as for domestic violence), these should be *briefly* described.

◈ Add the *Ad Dammum* clause, which begins: "WHEREFORE, Plaintiff demands Judgment:" and after which you recite the relief you seek, including dissolution of your marriage, child custody, support, alimony, etc.

◈ You may sign and date the **COMPLAINT**, and type in your name, address, and telephone number beneath the signature line.

◈ Add the Rule 4:5-1 Certification. This requires that you state that (1) you are the plaintiff and (2) that you certify that "to the best of [your] knowledge, information, and belief, [you] are not aware of any other action or arbitration proceeding pending or contemplated concerning the subject matter of this Complaint in any court, nor are you aware of any other persons who should be joined in this matter."

◈ You must then add the "Certification of Non-Collusion," where you, as the plaintiff in the proceeding for divorce, must state under oath that "the allegations of the Complaint for Divorce are true to the best of your knowledge, information, and belief; and that the complaint is made in good faith, and without collusion, for the causes set forth in it." You must sign and date this verification.

# PROPERTY SETTLEMENT AGREEMENT

Whether you and your spouse agreed upon everything from the start, went through extensive negotiations to reach an agreement, or reached agreement through the use of an Early Settlement Panel and/or counsel, you need to put your agreement into writing. Even if you do not agree with everything, you should put what you do agree with into a written settlement agreement. (Remember, child custody and support agreements will be handled through the court; see Chapter 4 for more information.)

It is common practice for attorneys to create a custom **PROPERTY SETTLEMENT AGREEMENT** (PSA) for each case. There is not a pre-approved, or standard PSA form. However, form 11 in Appendix F can be used as a guide and modified to your specific situation.

Use this form as a guide to create your own form. Do not simply copy the form and reuse it. You will need to specifically and succinctly list, and clearly spell out, how your property and debts will be divided.

Complete the **PROPERTY SETTLEMENT AGREEMENT** as follows.

◈ Make certain your names appear just as they appear on your original **VERIFIED COMPLAINT FOR DIVORCE**.

◈ Just below the document title (Property Settlement Agreement), fill in the name and address information indicated for you and your spouse.

◈ At the bottom of the "Background" section, after the sentence beginning with "NOW, THEREFORE," fill in the month, day, and year the PSA is signed by both parties.

◈ After the word "Background," fill in the date on which you and your spouse were married and the date you filed for divorce where indicated.

◈ Article 2 ("Child") contains standard language pertaining to custody and visitation of your child or children. If you and your spouse can reach agreement on these issues, you can adapt this section to match your circumstances.

◈ Article 3 ("Child Support") again contains fairly standardized language on the issue of child support. Be mindful of the appropriate amounts of child support applicable to your situation. This is discussed in Chapter 6.

◈ Article 4 ("Equitable Distribution of Property") sets forth the division of the real and personal property, assets, and debts of the parties.

◈ At Article 4.1 (a) set forth your intentions as to the division and/or sale of your real estate (or real property). List all of your real estate. If you do not own any real estate, after the words "Real Estate," type in "No real estate is owned by the parties, either individually or jointly." There are several options for dealing with the division of your real estate.

   • First, one of you may buy out the other and keep the property. If this is your desire, type in: "Husband and Wife own real estate located at [*give address of property*]. Husband/Wife shall retain the property. Husband/Wife shall remit the amount of $ [*insert amount agreed upon*] to cover buy out of the other party's interest."

   • Second, both of you could sell the property and divide the proceeds. To do this, type in: "Husband and Wife own real estate located at [*give address of property*]. The parties agree that this property shall be sold and the proceeds divided (after payment of commissions, closing costs, and other sales expenses) as follows: [*insert percentage or dollar amount*] to Husband, and [*insert percentage or dollar amount*] to Wife."

   • Third, one of the parties may simply be allocated the property (such as when there is more than one piece of real estate or one party will get more of the personal property). To do this, type in: "Husband/Wife shall retain real estate located at [give address of property]." If one of you will keep the property and be responsible for an existing mortgage, be sure to list the mortgage as that person's responsibility. As with other joint debts, be aware that you will both still be responsible for a joint mortgage debt even if one of you keeps the property and agrees to pay the mortgage.

## Example:

Martin and Marsha get divorced and agree that Marsha will keep the house and pay the mortgage. Marsha fails to make payments and the mortgage company forecloses. When the mortgage company sells the house, it gets $10,000 less than the mortgage balance. The mortgage company then sues Martin for the $10,000. (If your spouse is going to keep property that is mortgaged, he or she must get a new mortgage so that only your spouse is responsible to pay.)

◈ In Article 4.1 (b) list the personal property that the Husband and Wife will divide. You can also separately list the property divided and attach this separate list to the PSA, incorporating the list by reference. Describe each item clearly.

   **NOTE:** *These paragraphs provide that each of you will keep your own clothing and personal effects. It is not necessary to list all of these items. However, if there are any such items that are particularly valuable (such as a mink coat or valuable jewelry), it is a good idea to list them just to make it clear who is to get the item.*

◈ In Article 4.1 (c), list all pension, retirement, IRAs, or profit sharing plans and the spouse who will receive each.

◈ In Article 4.1 (d), list all bank, credit union, or other financial institution accounts and the recipient spouse.

◈ In Article 4.1 (e), list your motor vehicles and indicate if the vehicles are to be retained and by which spouse.

◈ In Article 4.1 (f), list the life insurance policies currently in effect on each spouse's life, the beneficiaries, and the agreed treatment of the policies.

◈ In Article 4.1 (g) ("Liabilities and Obligations"), list all debts for which the husband and wife will be responsible. Give the name of the person or company to whom the debt is owed and the account number. Remember that if the debt was incurred by you and your spouse jointly, you are both still liable for repayment. In other words, even if your spouse agrees to pay the debt, if he or she fails to pay, then the creditor can still come after you. You could then drag your spouse back to court for violating the settlement agreement, but your credit rating would still be damaged.

---

## Example:

Joe and Mary have a joint credit card. In their PSA, they agree that Joe can keep the card and will be responsible to pay it. If Joe runs up charges over the next year then declares bankruptcy, the credit card company can still sue Mary, and the delinquency will go on Mary's credit report. She can drag Joe back to court, but if he is in such bad financial shape that he had to file for bankruptcy, there is very little the court can do to force him to repay her. Worse, there is nothing the court can do to repair her credit rating. What Mary should have done was to be sure the credit card was cancelled, and let Joe get his own credit card after the divorce.

---

◈  Article 5 sets forth any arrangements you and your spouse have regarding alimony and expenses of the divorce case. This paragraph provides: "Each of the parties hereto releases the other from subsequent claims for alimony, alimony pendente lite, or spousal support, except as follows." If neither of you are to pay alimony, simply type in the word "None" below that sentence. If you do have an agreement for alimony, you will need to fill in the details.

---

## Example:

"Husband shall pay alimony to Wife in the amount of $200 per month, beginning on March 1, 2006, and continuing on the first day of each month thereafter, until February 1, 2010. No alimony shall be paid after February 1, 2010."

---

→ Article 6 addresses the issue of modification and breach of the PSA.

→ Article 7 is concerned with the continuing legal effect of the PSA, as well as the possible tax implications for the spouses based upon child/dependent deductions.

## WIFE'S RETAKING OF PRIOR NAME

If you are the wife, and you desire to resume your maiden name, or another name you had before you were married, you are entitled to do so under New Jersey law. (NJ Stat. Ann., Sec. 2A:34-21.) This can generally be accomplished by including a demand in the *Ad Dammum* clause of your **COMPLAINT** that you wish to resume your name prior to your marriage. When your final hearing takes place, the judge handling the hearing will ask you certain questions to ensure that you are not resuming your premarital name for purposes of deception or avoidance of creditors.

## FINAL HEARING

Provided that no issues remain in dispute between the spouses, the case will often be scheduled for a final hearing. In the event that issues of property or debt division, alimony, child support, or other issues remain in dispute, the plaintiff must file a **NOTICE OF EQUITABLE DISTRIBUTION, ALIMONY, CHILD SUPPORT, AND OTHER RELIEF** within twenty days of the hearing date. (see form 16, p.217.) Entry into a **PROPERTY SETTLEMENT AGREEMENT** obviates this requirement.

At the final hearing, a Family Part Judge will ask questions and hear sworn testimony from both spouses as to the grounds for divorce and agreements between the spouses that have been reduced to writing. If the judge finds everything in order, a **JUDGMENT OF DIVORCE** will ordinarily be entered.

# FINAL JUDGMENT OF DIVORCE

You will also need to provide the court with a **FINAL JUDGMENT OF DIVORCE**. (see form 18, p.223.) To complete the final judgment form, all you need to fill in is the caption information according to the instructions in Chapter 7. In the vast majority of cases, the PSA will be attached to the **FINAL JUDGMENT OF DIVORCE** and its terms will be incorporated by reference into the **FINAL JUDGMENT OF DIVORCE**. Therefore, language verifying the attachment and incorporation of the PSA should be included in your form of **FINAL JUDGMENT OF DIVORCE**. The judge will fill in the rest of the form and sign it. The **FINAL JUDGMENT OF DIVORCE** will generally be provided to you at the conclusion of your final hearing.

# Contested Divorce

## chapter 9

When you have been unable to reach sufficient common ground with your spouse to permit an uncontested divorce, you must prepare to handle your divorce on a *contested* basis. Though the more complex procedure involved in a contested form of divorce is beyond the scope of this book, the following information is important to consider if you are confronted by the necessity of a contested case.

A contested divorce is much more difficult, challenging, and lengthy than the uncontested divorce explained in the previous chapter. There is no model contested divorce. In some instances, the contested issues between the spouses are relatively harmless. You and your spouse may agree that you want a divorce—you may even agree on the grounds for your divorce. Nevertheless, disagreement on one or more issues unrelated to these fundamental *threshold* considerations will make your divorce contested. In those instances, the assistance of the Early Settlement Panel process, practical advice from an attorney, or formal or informal mediation (also known as *Alternative Dispute Resolution*, see Chapter 10) can be invaluable in working out spousal differences, enabling a divorce to be concluded in a practical and efficient manner.

At the other extreme, you and your spouse may be experiencing bitter conflict based upon those *threshold* considerations. *Fault* grounds for divorce (see Chapter 2) may be in dispute, and one spouse may allege acts that are denied by the other. One spouse may have abandoned the other, adultery may be evident, or drug addiction, mental illness, or deviant sexual activity may have created a gap of anger and disappointment between the spouses. Issues of child support and custody only aggravate the conflict in these instances. In addition, the existence of domestic abuse or child neglect may prevent any civil contact between the spouses. In the majority of contested or fault ground cases, you must seriously consider retaining an attorney.

## FILING AND PROCEDURES

To begin a contested divorce case, you will file the same forms discussed in Chapter 8 and will observe a similar procedure. Refer to Chapter 8 for instructions on completing these forms. The differences in completing these forms will briefly be discussed.

The following forms will be completed and filed with the Clerk of the Superior Court.

- **VERIFIED COMPLAINT FOR DIVORCE**, alleging *fault* grounds (Adultery, Extreme Cruelty, Voluntarily Induced Addiction, Institutionalization for Mental Illness, Imprisonment, Deviant Sexual Conduct) as necessary (form 4, p.187 or form 5, p.189);

- **CIVIL CASE INFORMATION STATEMENT** (form 8, p.195);

- **MATRIMONIAL CASE INFORMATION STATEMENT** (again, only if completed; otherwise, you may file it within twenty days after your spouse files an *Answer* to your complaint (form 1, p.173); and,

- Cover Letter. (See form 7 for sample.)

You complete and file the necessary pleadings and forms with the clerk and *serve* them upon your spouse. Your spouse will file an *Answer* to your **COMPLAINT** and their own **MATRIMONIAL CASE INFORMATION STATEMENT** (see form 1, p.173), contesting the grounds that you have claimed for divorce, or other issues raised in your **COMPLAINT**. Through mandatory participation in an Early Settlement Panel, you will have the opportunity to discuss and resolve issues of property distribution, child custody, and support. You and your spouse attend one or more hearings, and present evidence and sworn testimony in order to get the disputes resolved.

**NOTE:** *When used as a fault or contested ground for divorce, extreme cruelty should be interpreted much more literally as a series of continued acts of mental or physical cruelty. These are acts such as physical abuse, verbal humiliation, willful acts of disrespect for the marriage, intentional disregard for the husband/wife relationship, etc. Used in this fashion, it goes beyond the mere allegation made in an uncontested divorce that the continuance of the marriage is unreasonable and/or the marriage is irretrievably broken. (see Chapter 8.)*

## PROSECUTING THE CASE

This book cannot transform you into a trial lawyer. It is *very risky* to attempt to handle a contested case yourself. There are three significant differences between a contested and an uncontested case.

1.  In an uncontested case, the court will usually go along with whatever you and your spouse have worked out. But in a contested case, all of your allegations will come up against a challenge and you will need to prove that you are entitled to what you are asking. This means you will likely have one or more court proceedings before a judge, where you will need to present papers and *testimony* as evidence.

    You may need to have witnesses testify for you; indeed, for most of the fault grounds, independent or corroborative testimony is an absolute necessity. Absent such testimony, even with the existence of highly credible or probative written or documentary evidence, your case will boil down to your word against that of your spouse.

2.  You may have to do some extra work to get the evidence you need, such as sending out *subpoenas*, serving *interrogatories*, taking one or more *depositions* of witnesses, or even hiring a private investigator. Also, you will need to pay extra attention to assure that your spouse is properly notified of any court hearings, and that he or she is sent copies of any papers you file with the clerk.

3.  Your case will have more *procedural treatment*. There will be a greater number of hearings, pretrial motions (see Chapter 10) by you and your spouse, a pretrial conference, and trial calls, along with those existing steps discussed in previous chapters to encourage settlement or a more expedited resolution of your case. As a result, you will have to be more prepared for your case on a continuing basis.

**Hiring an Attorney**

Though you should seriously consider hiring an attorney in a contested case, you should not assume that you need an attorney just because your spouse has hired one. Sometimes it will be easier to deal with the attorney than with your spouse. The attorney is not as emotionally involved and may see your settlement proposal as reasonable. Discuss issues with your spouse's attorney first to see if matters can be worked out. You can always hire your own lawyer if your spouse's lawyer is not reasonable.

---

### – Caution –

Be very cautious about signing any papers until you are certain you understand exactly what they mean. You may want to have an attorney review any papers prepared by your spouse's lawyer before you sign them.

---

## YOUR SPOUSE'S RESPONSE

After receiving copies of the divorce papers, your spouse may contact an attorney. The attorney will then notify you that he or she is representing your spouse. Typically, your spouse will have a period of thirty-five days in which to file an *Answer* to your complaint. The

*Answer* will be filed with the Clerk of the Superior Court, and a copy will be served upon you by mail—directly by your spouse or through his or her attorney. In the *Answer*, your spouse may *admit* certain allegations, *deny* certain allegations, or answer by stating he or she *neither admits nor denies* the allegation.

If your spouse also wants a divorce and agrees with the grounds upon which your are requesting it, but is arguing about one or more of the other *nonthreshold* issues (property division, child custody, child support, or alimony), you may still proceed with the divorce as discussed in Chapter 8. However, if your spouse does not want the divorce under any circumstances due to disagreement with your claims as to the reasons why your marriage should not be continued (for example, he or she may disagree with a claim of spousal or child abuse, adultery, drug addiction, etc.), you must consider two options.

1.    You may persist in prosecuting your initial claim for a divorce upon the fault ground that you originally filed under. You may wish to do this on principle alone. However, you must be ready to accept the struggle—and expense, if you use an attorney—incident to a contested divorce. It is also possible that your persistence will overcome your spouse's resistance due to the suffering and expense he or she is also suffering. Ideally, this could result in a negotiated resolution of your case in advance of trial.

2.    If you and your spouse have been separated for eighteen months or more, you may amend your **COMPLAINT** to allege that you and your spouse have lived separate and apart for at least eighteen months and that there is no reasonable prospect of reconciliation. You may then proceed with the divorce to its conclusion, but this is not a perfect solution. If you have custody or property issues in dispute, those disputes could remain open during the remaining life of your case. It will be highly difficult, however, for a contesting spouse to defeat or disprove a claim of separation. In addition, while your case is pending, you can use the court's continuing jurisdiction to resolve issues of custody and property, preventing your spouse from being unresponsive to your claims on these issues.

**NOTE:** *When you decide to seek a divorce, work to reach consensus with your spouse on as many issues as possible. Though you and your spouse may desire to hurt each other in the divorce process, **try to step back from your situation and pragmatically consider if this is really the right thing to do**. A bitterly contested divorce is a painful, humiliating, psychologically damaging, and expensive process for all participants—especially for children.*

# Special Circumstances

## chapter 10

Many divorce cases have unique and special circumstances. These are events and situations that do not necessarily occur in every, or even in most, cases. Following is a discussion of a few of the possible situations that may arise in your case.

## WHEN YOU CANNOT AFFORD COURT COSTS

If you cannot afford to pay court costs, such as filing fees and sheriff service fees, you will need to make an application to the Superior Court, Chancery Division, Family Part for a waiver of these fees. (Court Rule 1:13-2.) You should go to the clerk's office, located at your county courthouse, and advise the clerk that you wish to file for divorce, but are unable to afford the filing fee and other court costs. The clerk will provide you with the necessary information in order that you may file an application to have the court costs either waived or reduced.

If you are involved in a divorce or custody case and are experiencing financial hardship, your county may have a legal aid service, legal services project, or other program whereby private attorneys will be appointed to handle your custody case at no charge to you. These are volunteer lawyers who offer their time and service to handle such cases.

## ALTERNATIVE DISPUTE RESOLUTION

New Jersey is one of the leading states in America with respect to its use of mediation or *Alternative Dispute Resolution* (ADR) programs to resolve potential litigation, including divorces. Many New Jersey matrimonial attorneys utilize ADR as a cost-effective means of resolving differences between spouses, saving some of the expense and time involved in contested divorce litigation. The bar association in your local county can often refer you to those attorneys skilled in ADR.

## DOMESTIC VIOLENCE

A significant level of hostility and frustration accompanies the dissolution of any marriage and affects the spouses and children deeply. Usually, despite these hard feelings, the parties can manage to be civil as the marriage is being terminated. However, sometimes civility is impossible for one or both of the parties, resulting in abusive or violent behavior toward the other spouse or the children. Though more often than not the male spouse seems to exhibit such behavior, there are an increasing number of instances in which female spouses are abusive.

Either way, when such behavior occurs, it must be stopped. Unfortunately, many battered spouses do not know there are legal means to thwart abuse, and they do not have to accept abuse as part of the price for getting out of a marriage. Thankfully, New Jersey's legislature has acted strongly to ensure that no battered spouse need feel powerless against his or her abuser.

New Jersey's *Prevention of Domestic Violence Act* forces the arrest and prosecution of an abusive spouse by a police officer if the officer finds *probable cause* to believe that an act of domestic violence has occurred. (NJ Stat. Ann., Sec. 2C:25-21.) Another law sets forth a very broad definition of the acts comprising *domestic violence*. (NJ Stat. Ann., Sec. 2C:25-19(a).) These acts include the following:

- ✪ homicide;

- ✪ assault;

- ✪ terroristic threats;

- ✪ kidnapping;

- ✪ criminal restraint;

- ✪ false imprisonment;

- ✪ sexual assault;

- ✪ criminal sexual conduct;

- ✪ lewdness;

- ✪ criminal mischief;

- ✪ burglary;

- ✪ criminal trespass;

- ✪ harassment; and,

- ✪ stalking.

As a result of the arrest for domestic violence, a battered spouse may also obtain a *Temporary Restraining Order* (TRO) against the abusive spouse. The police officers who perform the arrest can tell you how to get a TRO, which is issued by a judge of the superior court. A judge is always on duty in each of the twenty-one counties to sign and issue TROs. New Jersey law also enables a New Jersey court to issue a TRO when an assault has taken place in another state (for example, the neighboring states of Delaware, Maryland, New York, and Pennsylvania) and the victim has escaped to New Jersey.

Because of the highly charged atmosphere that accompanies domestic violence, the police officer must provide you with an explanation of the conditions a judge can order in a TRO. (NJ Stat. Ann., Sec. 2C:25-23.) These include:

- ✪ that your spouse is temporarily forbidden from entering the residence in which you live;

- ✪ that your spouse is temporarily forbidden from having contact with you and/or your relatives;

- ✪ that your spouse is temporarily forbidden from bothering you at work;

- ✪ that your spouse has to pay temporary child support or support for you;

- ✪ that you are to be given temporary custody of your children; and,

- ✪ that your spouse pay you back any money you have to spend for medical treatment or repairs because of the violence.

The arresting officer must also file a complete domestic violence offense report, which is provided to the court in the municipality and county bureau of investigation where the offense takes place, as well as the New Jersey State Police. (NJ Stat. Ann., Sec. 2C:25-24.)

The TRO remains in effect until a hearing can be held in the Superior Court, Law Division, Family Part, ordinarily on an expedited basis. At that hearing, a judge will more fully consider the claims and defenses of both spouses and either dissolve the TRO or issue a final restraining order (which remains in effect until dissolved by the court). In some cases, the TRO will be dissolved but the court will approve *civil restraints* under which restraints are imposed by agreement and consent of the spouses.

---

## – Caution –

Domestic violence is a life-threatening reality. If you are being attacked by your spouse, or fear that such an attack may take place, seek a TRO. In addition, many communities have shelters to provide counseling, information, and temporary safety to domestic violence victims, where necessary. Look up the telephone number for the shelter in your area and keep it handy.

---

## PROTECTING YOUR CHILDREN

If you are apprehensive that your spouse may attempt to kidnap your children, you should make certain that the day-care center, baby-sitter, relative, or whomever you leave the children with at any time, is aware that you are in the process of a divorce and that the children are only to be released to you personally (not to your spouse or to any other relative or friend).

To prevent your spouse from taking the children out of the United States, you can apply for a passport for each child. Once a passport is issued, the government will not issue another. So get their passport and lock it up in a safe-deposit box. (This may not prevent them from being taken to Canada or Mexico, where passports are not currently required, but will prevent them from being taken overseas.)

If your spouse is determined, crafty, and resourceful, there is no cast-iron way to prevent the concerns discussed in this chapter from occurring. All you can do is place as many obstacles in his or her way as possible, and prepare for him or her to suffer legal consequences (e.g., a fine or jail time) for acting inappropriately.

## SPOUSE'S REMOVAL OF PROPERTY

If you genuinely fear that your spouse will attempt to remove money from your joint bank account(s) or hide important papers showing what property you own, you may want to take this same action before your spouse can act. However, you can find yourself in a great deal of trouble with the court should you try to take or hide joint assets. You should make a complete list of any property you do take and include these items in your lists of property. You may need to convince a court that you only took these items temporarily to preserve them until a hearing was set.

Also, do not spend any cash you take from a bank account, or sell or give away any items of property you take. Any cash should be placed in a separate bank account (without your spouse's name on it) and kept separate from any other cash you have. Any papers, such as deeds, car titles, stock or bond certificates, etc., should be placed in a safe-deposit box without your spouse's name on it. The idea is not to take these things for yourself, but to get them in a safe place so your spouse cannot hide them and deny they ever existed.

## TEMPORARY SUPPORT AND CUSTODY

If your spouse has left you with the children, the mortgage, and monthly support bills, and is not helping you financially during the pendency of your divorce, you may want to make a motion to the court to order the payment of *temporary (pendente lite) support* for you and the children during the divorce procedure. (NJ Stat. Ann., Sec. 2A:34-24.) The law empowers the Superior Court, Chancery Division, Family Part to order suitable support and maintenance to be paid and provided by a spouse for the other spouse and their children.

The statute further provides that if a spouse fails to comply with a pendente lite support order, the court may impose a lien against the property of that spouse that is located in New Jersey. Of course, if you are the only spouse bringing in income and paying the bills, it is highly unlikely that you will obtain any temporary support.

**Temporary (Pendente Lite) Support**

To make a motion for pendente lite support, you will need to file a **NOTICE OF MOTION**, a **CERTIFICATION IN SUPPORT OF MOTION** (which must be signed before a Notary Public), a **FORM OF ORDER** granting the motion, and a **CERTIFICATION OF SERVICE**. Sample forms of these documents are contained in Appendix F (see forms 13, 14, 15, and 12, respectively). You may also wish to call the Family Division Manager in the county where your divorce is filed if you have any questions on how to file a motion (or respond to a motion if one has been filed against you by your spouse). Please note, however, that the Family Division Manager cannot give legal advice.

Under Court Rule 5:7-2 (a), you must also submit a completed **MATRIMONIAL CASE INFORMATION STATEMENT**. (see form 1, p.173.)

**NOTE:** *If you have already submitted a CIS in your pending case, and there is a change in economic circumstances for you and your spouse, be sure to update the CIS when you file your motion, or no later than eight days before the motion hearing date.*

If child support is in issue, both spouses must submit a **FINANCIAL STATEMENT FOR SUMMARY SUPPORT ACTIONS**. (see form 17, p.219.) The **AFFIDAVIT/CERTIFICATION** sets forth the facts of your spouse's nonsupport and contains your request for reasonable temporary support based upon the income and expenses listed in your CIS. (see sample form 14, p.213.) The **AFFIDAVIT/CERTIFICATION** may not exceed fifteen pages in length.

Your motion must be filed with the Clerk of the Superior Court, and a filing fee must be paid at the time of filing. You must also serve your spouse with all the materials (pleadings and attachments) that you have filed, and you must certify to the court (through your **CERTIFICATION OF SERVICE** (form 12, p.209)) that you served your spouse with the papers no less than twenty-nine days prior to the motion hearing date. The motion will generally be heard by the Superior Court judge to whom your divorce has been assigned, on the next available motion date at least twenty-nine days from the time you file. The clerk or Family Division Manager in the county where you file can provide you with this date, which must be filled in on your **NOTICE OF MOTION**. (see sample form 13, p.211.) In very limited circumstances, on request to the court, the motion may be heard on an expedited basis.

**Temporary Child Custody**

To seek a **TEMPORARY ORDER AWARDING CHILD CUSTODY**, you must also make a motion to the court. Again, you will need to file a **NOTICE OF MOTION**, a **CERTIFICATION**, and a form of **ORDER GRANTING TEMPORARY CUSTODY** and setting forth a proposed custody schedule, which must also take into account the visitation rights of the other spouse.

In filing your motion, keep in mind the custody factors discussed at length in Chapter 6, as they will weigh heavily in the court's determination. Do not make a motion for temporary custody without reviewing these factors and realistically assessing if a request is warranted. At the same time, if you are aware of facts that indicate that your spouse is unfit to be a custodial parent (examples would be prior episodes of child abuse or a substance addiction), emphasize these facts in your **CERTIFICATION**. If you know others who can give sworn and credible testimony as to your spouse's lack of parental fitness, you may wish to ask them to submit their own **CERTIFICATION** in support of your motion.

## TAXES

The United States Internal Revenue Code is complicated and ever-changing. For this reason, it is impossible to give detailed legal advice with respect to taxes in a book such as this. Any such information could easily be out of date by the time of publication. Therefore, it is strongly recommended that you consult your accountant, lawyer, or tax professional about the tax consequences of a divorce. A few general concerns are discussed in this chapter to give you an idea of some of the tax questions that can arise.

**Exchange or Transfer of Property**

You and your spouse may be exchanging title to property as a result of your divorce. Generally, there should not be any tax to pay as the result of such a transfer. However, either spouse receiving a share of property will be responsible to pay any tax that may become due upon sale of that share.

The Internal Revenue Service (IRS) has issued numerous rulings about how property is treated in a divorce. You need to be very careful if you are transferring tax shelters, or making other complicated financial arrangements.

**Alimony**

Alimony can cause the worst tax problems of any aspect of divorce. The IRS is always making new rulings on whether a property settlement agreement is really a division of property, or a veiled form of alimony. The basic rule is that *alimony* is treated as income to the person receiving it, and as a deduction for the person paying it. Therefore, in order to manipulate IRS regulations, some couples attempt to show a transfer of property or cash as an element of their **PROPERTY SETTLEMENT AGREEMENT** instead of as alimony, or some other variation on this theme.

As the IRS becomes aware of these tax games, it issues rulings on how it will view a certain arrangement. If you are simply talking about regular, periodic payments of cash from one spouse to another, the IRS will probably not question that such an arrangement is alimony. However, if you try to incorporate that arrangement in a property settlement, you may run into problems. You should consult a tax professional if you are considering any unusual or creative property settlement or alimony arrangements.

**Child Support**     There are simple tax rules regarding child support.

- ✪ The parent having custody gets to claim the children on his or her tax return (unless both parents file an IRS Form 8332 agreeing to a different arrangement each year (see form 19, p.225.)).

- ✪ Child support is not considered income to the parent receiving it.

- ✪ The parent paying child support cannot deduct it.

**IRS Form 8332**     If you are sharing physical custody, the parent with whom the child lives for the most time during the year is entitled to claim the child. To reverse this, IRS Form 8332 must be filed each year. If you do not have custody, but you and your spouse agreed that you can claim the child(ren), request that your spouse sign an open-ended IRS form which can be filed each year, so that you do not have to worry about it each year. A phone call to the IRS can help you get answers to questions on this point.

## PENSION PLANS

Pension or retirement plans of spouses are *marital assets*. They may be very valuable assets. If you and your spouse are young, and have not been working very long, you may not have pension plans worth worrying about. Also, if you have both worked, and have similar pension plans, it may be best to simply include a provision in your settlement agreement that each party shall keep his or her own pension plan.

However, if the spouses have been married a long time, and one spouse worked while the other stayed home to raise the children, the working spouse's pension plan may be worth a lot of money. It may be necessary to see you through retirement. If you and your spouse cannot agree on how to divide a pension plan, you should see an attorney. The valuation of pension plans, and how they are to be divided, is a complicated matter that you should not attempt without an attorney's guidance.

## SOCIAL SECURITY ISSUES AND BENEFIT ELIGIBILITY

Although many women choose a lifetime career outside the home, some women work for a few years, leave the labor force to raise their children, and then return to work. Other women choose not to work outside their home at all. They are usually covered by benefits and Social Security through their husband's work and can receive benefits when he retires, becomes disabled, or dies. Whether you work or have never worked, you should know what Social Security coverage means to you. You should also know about coverage for anyone you hire as a household worker or childcare provider.

Many women are not aware that they can receive benefits on their ex-husband's Social Security record if he is receiving Social Security benefits (or is deceased), their marriage lasted more than ten years, they are presently unmarried, and they are sixty-two or older. The same is true for ex-husbands receiving benefits from ex-wives. If a woman's ex-husband is deceased, she can receive benefits on his Social Security record even though they were not married for ten years or more. The amount of benefits the ex-wife will receive as a divorced spouse does not affect the ex-husband's amount, so if there was an amicable divorce, they can both receive benefits without affecting each other financially. You should contact Social Security and ask about your eligibility for benefits if you think you qualify.

Local Social Security Field Offices are listed on the next page.

**Atlantic County**
1350 Doughty Road
Egg Harbor Township, NJ 08234
800-772-1213
Fax: 609-484-0167

**Bergen County**
201 Rock Road
Suite 206
Glen Rock, NJ 07452-1740
800-772-1213
Fax: 201-612-8219

22 Sussex Street
Hackensack, NJ 07601
800-772-1213
Fax: 201-487-2254

**Burlington County**
Evergreen Plaza
1710 NJ Route 38
Mount Holly, NJ 08060
800-772-1213
Fax: 609-261-9431

**Camden County**
5 Executive Campus
Suite 100
Cherry Hill, NJ 08002
800-772-1213
Fax: 856-757-5001

**Cape May County**
1046 Route 47
Suite 8
Rio Grande, NJ 08242
800-772-1213
Fax: 609-886-2383

**Cumberland County**
149 West Broad Street
Bridgeton, NJ 08302
856-455-6044
Fax: 856-451-1197

**Essex County**
Halsted Commons
15-33 Halsted Street
East Orange, NJ 07018
800-772-1213
Fax: 973-674-7819

274 Springfield Avenue
Newark, NJ 07103
800-772-1213
Fax: 973-645-4787

396 Bloomfield Avenue
Montclair, NJ 07042
800-772-1213
Fax: 973-744-0497

970 Broad Street
Room 1035
Newark, NJ 07102
800-772-1213
Fax: 973-645-2505

**Gloucester County**
51 Charles III Drive
Glassboro, NJ 08028-9926
800-772-1213
Fax: 856-256-9795

**Hudson County**
79 Hudson Street
6th Floor
Hoboken, NJ 07030
800-772-1213
Fax: 201-656-4344

3000 Kennedy Boulevard
Jersey City, NJ 07306
800-772-1213
Fax: 201-451-3207

**Mercer County**
635 South Clinton Avenue
2nd Floor
Trenton, NJ 08608
800-772-1213
Fax: 609-989-0471

**Middlesex County**
190 Middlesex Turnpike
3rd Floor
Iselin, NJ 08830-2842
732-750-7950
Fax: 732-636-5207

52 Charles Street
New Brunswick, NJ 08901
800-772-1213
Fax: 732-214-0109

**Monmouth County**
3310 Route 66
Neptune, NJ 07753
800-772-1213
Fax: 732-774-9054

**Morris County**
2200 State Route 10
2nd Floor
Parsippany, NJ 07054-4507
800-772-1213

**Ocean County**
Yorktowne Plaza
2620 Yorktowne Boulevard
Brick, NJ 08723
800-772-1213
Fax: 732-477-0291

190 Saint Catherine Boulevard
Toms River, NJ 08755
800-772-1213
Fax: 732-244-1167

**Passaic County**
935 Allwood Road
Clifton, NJ 07012-1997
800-772-1213
Fax: 973-614-1535

21 Clark Street
2nd Floor
Paterson, NJ 07505

*Mailing address:*
200 Federal Plaza
Paterson, NJ 07505-1956
800-772-1213
Fax: 973-357-4132

**Somerset County**
29 Davenport Street
Somerville, NJ 08876
800-772-1213
Fax: 908-526-5360

**Sussex County**
Sussex County Mall
15 NJ Route 206 North
Newton, NJ 07860
800-772-1213
Fax: 973-383-5220

**Union County**
547 Morris Avenue
Elizabeth, NJ 07208
800-772-1213
Fax: 908-351-2970

## CONCLUSION

Divorce will always be a traumatic and exceedingly difficult process in one's life. Understanding the system and legal entanglements associated with a divorce can make the process less painful. The information provided in the preceding pages is intended as a guide and directive that will aid you in obtaining your goals and objectives. We hope that this book serves you well in maneuvering through the maze of legal issues and facilitates the result that you desire in your divorce.

# Glossary

## A

**abandon.** To intentionally and permanently give up, surrender, leave, desert, or relinquish all interest and ownership in property, a home or other premises, a right of way, or even a spouse, a family, or children.

**acceptance of service.** Agreement by a defendant (or his or her attorney) in a legal action to accept a complaint or other divorce papers without having a sheriff or process server show up at the door.

**accrue.** Growing or adding to, such as interest on a debt or investment that continues to accumulate.

**acknowledgment.** The section at the end of a document where a notary public verifies that the signer of the document states he or she actually signed it.

**action.** A lawsuit in which one party (or parties) sues another.

**adoption.** The taking of a child into one's family, creating a parent and child relationship, and giving him or her all the rights and privileges of one's own child, including the right to inherit as if the child were the adopter's natural child.

**adultery.** Consensual sexual relations when one of the participants is legally married to someone else. (In some states it is still a crime, and in many states it is grounds for divorce for the spouse of the married adulterer.)

**affidavit.** Any written document in which the signer swears under oath before a notary public or someone authorized to take oaths that the statements in the document are true.

**agreement.** Another name for a contract including all the legal elements—offer, acceptance, and consideration (payment or performance)—based on specific terms.

**alimony.** Support paid by one ex-spouse to the other as ordered by a court in a divorce case.

**allege.** To claim a fact is true.

**amend.** To alter or change by adding, subtracting, or substituting.

**antenuptial (prenuptial) agreement.** A written contract between two people who are about to marry, setting out the terms of possession of assets, treatment of future earnings, control of the property of each, and potential division if the marriage is later dissolved.

**appeal.** To ask a higher court to reverse the decision of a trial court after final judgment or other legal ruling.

**appraiser.** A professional who assesses the value of property.

**appreciation.** The increase in value through the natural course of events as distinguished from improvements or additions.

**arrears.** Unpaid money, when due, usually the sum of a series of unpaid amounts, such as rent, installments on an account or promissory note, or monthly child support.

**asset.** Any item or property with monetary value, including those with only sentimental value (particularly in the estates of the deceased).

# B

**bifurcate.** The order or ruling of a judge that one issue in a case can be tried to a conclusion, or a judgment given on one phase of the case, without trying all aspects of the matter. A typical example is when the judge will grant a divorce judgment without hearing evidence or making a ruling on such issues as division of marital property, child custody, or alimony.

**breach of contract.** Failing to perform any term of a contract, written or oral, without a legitimate legal excuse.

# C

**capital gains.** The difference between the sale price and the original cost (plus improvements) of property.

**case law.** Reported decisions of appeals courts and other courts that make new interpretations of the law.

**child custody.** Physical and/or legal control and responsibility of a minor under age 18 determined by the court.

**child support.** Funds ordered by the court to be paid by one parent to the custodial parent of a minor child after divorce or separation.

**civil procedure.** The complex body of rules and regulations set out in the New Jersey Rules of Court and Federal Rules of Civil Procedure that establish the format under which civil lawsuits are filed, pursued, and tried.

**claim.** To make a demand for money, property, or enforcement of a right provided by law.

**common-law marriage.** An agreement between a man and woman to live together as husband and wife without any legal formalities, followed and/or preceded by cohabitation on a regular basis (usually for seven years).

**complaint.** The first document filed with the court by a person or entity claiming legal rights against another.

**compromise.** An agreement between opposing parties to settle a dispute or reach a settlement in which each gives some ground, rather than continue the dispute or go to trial.

**consent decree.** An order of a judge based upon an agreement (almost always put in writing) between the parties to a lawsuit instead of continuing the case through trial or hearing.

**contempt of court.** There are essentially two types of contempt: a) being rude or disrespectful to the judge or other attorneys, or causing a disturbance in the courtroom, particularly after being warned by the judge; or, b) willful failure to obey an order of the court. (The latter can include failure to pay child support or alimony.)

**continuance.** Postponement of a date of a trial, hearing or other court appearance to a later fixed date by order of the court or upon a legal agreement by the attorneys.

**counselor.** A licensed attorney or lawyer.

**court.** 1. The judge, as in "The court rules in favor of the plaintiff," or 2. any official tribunal presided over by a judge or judges in which legal issues and claims are heard and determined.

**court calendar.** List of matters to be heard or set for trial or hearing by a court.

**court costs.** Fees for expenses that the courts pass on to attorneys, who then pass them on to their clients or to the losing party. (Court costs usually include: filing fees, charges for serving summons and subpoenas, court reporter charges for depositions, court transcripts, and copying papers and exhibits.)

**court docket.** *See docket.*

**credibility.** Whether testimony is worthy of belief, based on competence of the witness and likelihood that it is true.

**cross-examination.** Opportunity for the attorney (or an unrepresented party) to ask questions in court of a witness who has testified in a trial on behalf of the opposing party.

**custodial parent.** Parent who has primary responsibility for the care and control of the child.

**custody.** In domestic relations, a court's determination of which parent should have physical and/or legal control and responsibility for a minor child.

# D

**decree.** Synonymous with judgment except in some specific areas of the law.

**default judgment.** If a defendant in a lawsuit fails to respond to a complaint in the time set by law (thirty-five days), then the plaintiff can request that the default be entered into the court record by the clerk.

**defendant.** Party (individual) sued in a civil lawsuit or the party charged with a crime in a criminal prosecution.

**direct examination.** First questioning of a witness during a trial or deposition (out-of-court testimony), as distinguished from cross-examination by opposing attorneys and redirect examination when the witness is again questioned by the original attorney.

**dissolution.** A modern term for divorce.

**divorce.** Termination of a marriage by legal action.

**docket.** Cases on a court calendar.

**domestic relations.**  Term for the legal field involving divorce, dissolution, annulment, child custody, child support, and alimony.

**domestic violence.**  Continuing crime and problem of the physical beating of a wife, a girlfriend, and/or children, usually by the woman's male partner (although it can also be female violence against a male.)

**domicile.**  Place where a person has his or her permanent principal home.

# E

**Early Settlement Panels (ESPs).**  Because of the large volume of divorce cases in New Jersey, nearly all persons who are parties in a divorce case are required to participate in these panels. They are designed to narrow issues of disagreement between spouses and, in many cases, arrive at an overall resolution of these issues.

**equitable.**  Based on fairness and not upon legal technicalities.

**equitable distribution.**  Identification of assets accumulated during a marriage and their distribution in accordance with the legal or equitable interests of the spouses.

**exhibit.**  Document or object (including a photograph) introduced as evidence during a trial.

**expert testimony.**  Opinions stated during trial or testimony under oath before trial by a specialist qualified as an expert on a subject relevant to a lawsuit or a criminal case.

**expert witness.**  Person who is a specialist in a subject, often technical, who may present his or her expert opinion without having been a witness to any occurrence relating to the lawsuit.

# F

**fact.** Actual thing or happening that must be proved at trial by presentation of evidence.

# H

**hearing.** Any proceeding before a judge or other magistrate without a jury in which evidence is presented to determine some issue of fact.

**hearsay.** Secondhand evidence in which the witness is not telling what he or she knows personally, but what others have said to him or her.

**hearsay rule.** Testimony or documents that quote people not in court are not admissible as evidence.

# I

**income.** Money, goods, or other economic benefit received.

# J

**joint.** Referring to property, rights, or obligations that are united, undivided, and shared by two or more persons or entities.

**joint custody.** In divorce actions, a decision by the court (often upon agreement of the parents) that the parents will share custody of a child.

**jurisdiction.** Authority given by law to a court to try cases and rule on legal matters within a particular geographic area and/or over certain types of legal cases.

# L

**legal separation.** Court-decreed right to live apart, with the rights and obligations of divorced persons, but without divorce. (The parties are still married and cannot remarry.)

**legal services.** Work performed by a lawyer for a client.

# M

**marriage.** Joining of a male and female in matrimony by a person qualified by law to perform the ceremony (a minister, priest, judge, justice of the peace, or some similar official), after having obtained a valid marriage license.

**matter of record.** Anything, including testimony, evidence, rulings, and sometimes arguments, which has been recorded by the court reporter or court clerk.

**mediation.** The process of hiring, or having appointed by the court, an individual to hear the facts of your divorce matter and to aid both parties in finding a mutually agreeable settlement outcome.

**minor.** Anyone under age 18.

# N

**negotiation.** The give-and-take discussion or conference in an attempt to reach an agreement or settle a dispute.

**no-fault divorce.** Divorces in which neither spouse is required to prove fault or marital misconduct on the part of the other.

**noncustodial parent.** A parent who does not have primary responsibility over the child; often awarded visitation and ordered to pay child support to the custodial parent.

**notary public.** A person authorized by the state who resides to administer oaths, take acknowledgments, and certify documents.

# O

**objection.** Lawyer's protest to the legal propriety of a question that has been asked of a witness by the opposing attorney, with the purpose of making the trial judge decide if the question can be asked.

**offer.** Specific proposal to enter into an agreement with another.

**order to show cause.** Judge's written mandate that a party appear in court on a certain date and give reasons why a particular order should not be made.

# P

**parent.** Lawful or natural father or mother of a person. (The word does not mean grandparent or ancestor, but can include an adoptive parent as a replacement for a natural parent.)

**parental neglect.** Crime consisting of acts or omissions of a parent (including a stepparent, adoptive parent, or someone who, in practical terms, serves in a parent's role) that endangers the health and life of a child or fails to take steps necessary to the proper raising of a child.

**pendente lite.** Latin term for "awaiting the litigation (lawsuit)."

**plaintiff.** Party who initiates a lawsuit by filing a complaint with the clerk of the court.

**pleading.**   1. Every legal document filed in a lawsuit, petition, motion and/or hearing, including complaint, petition, answer, demurrer, motion, declaration, and memorandum of points and authorities. 2. The act of preparing and presenting legal documents and arguments.

**Pro Se litigant.**  Person not represented by an attorney.

**process server.**  Person who hand-delivers filed court documentation to a party involved in a legal matter or lawsuit.

# R

**real property.**  Land, structures, firmly attached and integrated equipment (such as light fixtures or a well pump), and anything growing on the land.

**relevant.**  Having some reasonable connection with, and in regard to evidence in trial; having some value or tendency to prove a matter of fact significant to the case.

**residence.**  Place where one makes his or her home.

# S

**separate and apart.**   The living of separate lives with no intention of ever getting back together.

**separate property.**  Property controlled by the spouse owning it.

**separation.**  Married persons living apart, either informally by one leaving the home or agreeing to separate while sharing a residence without sexual relations, or formally by obtaining a legal separation or negotiating a separation agreement setting out the terms of separate living.

**separation agreement.**  Agreement between two married people who agree to live apart for an unspecified period of time.

**special master.**  Person appointed by the court to carry out an order of the court, such as selling property or mediating child custody cases.

**spousal support.**  Payment for support of an ex-spouse (or a spouse while a divorce is pending) ordered by the court.

**statute.**  Federal or state written law enacted by Congress or a state legislature, respectively.

**subpoena.**  The legal document that requires the opponent to provide something or someone requested by you to the court.

# T

**tenancy by the entirety.**  Joint ownership of title by husband and wife, in which both have the right to the entire property. Upon the death of one, the other has title.

**title.**  Ownership of real property or personal property, which stands against the right of anyone else to claim the property.

# W

**witness.**  Person who testifies under oath in a trial (or a deposition, which may be used in a trial if the witness is not available) with first-hand or expert evidence useful in a lawsuit.

# New Jersey Statutes and Court Rules

## I.  New Jersey Statutes *cited in this book*

**N.J.S.A.** 9:2-4. **Legislative findings and declarations; parents' right to custody equal; custody order; factors; guardian ad litem; agreement as to custody**

The Legislature finds and declares that it is in the public policy of this State to assure minor children of frequent and continuing contact with both parents after the parents have separated or dissolved their marriage and that it is in the public interest to encourage parents to share the rights and responsibilities of child rearing in order to effect this policy.

In any proceeding involving the custody of a minor child, the rights of both parents shall be equal and the court shall enter an order which may include:

a. Joint custody of a minor child to both parents, which is comprised of legal custody or physical custody which shall include:

(1) provisions for residential arrangements so that a child shall reside either solely with one parent or alternatively with each parent in accordance with the needs of the parents and the child; and,

(2) provisions for consultation between the parents in making major decisions regarding the child's health, education and general welfare;

b. Sole custody to one parent with appropriate visitation for the non-custodial parent; or,

c. Any other custody arrangement as the court may determine to be in the best interests of the child.

In making an award of custody, the court shall consider but not be limited to the following factors: the parents' ability to agree, communicate, and cooperate in matters relating to the child; the parents' willingness to accept custody and any history of unwillingness to allow visitation not based on substantiated abuse; the interaction and relationship of the child with his or her parents and siblings; the history of domestic violence, if any; the safety of the child and the safety of either parent from physical abuse by the other parent; the preference of the child when of sufficient age and capacity to reason so as to form an intelligent decision; the needs of the child; the stability of the home environment offered; the quality and continuity of the child's education; the fitness of the parents; the geographical proximity of the parents' homes; the extent and quality of the time spent with the child prior to or subsequent to the separation; the parents' employment responsibilities; and, the age and number of the children. A parent shall not be deemed unfit unless the parents' conduct has a substantial adverse effect on the child.

The court, for good cause and upon its own motion, may appoint a guardian ad litem or an attorney or both to represent the minor child's interests. The court shall have the authority to award a counsel fee to the guardian ad litem and the attorney and to assess that cost between the parties to the litigation.

d. The court shall order any custody arrangement which is agreed to by both parents unless it is contrary to the best interests of the child.

e. In any case in which the parents cannot agree to a custody arrangement, the court may require each parent to submit a custody plan which the court shall consider in awarding custody.

f. The court shall specifically place on the record the factors which justify any custody arrangement not agreed to by both parents.

### N.J.S.A. 2A:34-2. Causes for divorce from bond of matrimony

Divorce from the bond of matrimony may be adjudged for the following causes heretofore or hereafter arising:

a. Adultery;

b. Willful and continued desertion for the term of 12 or more months, which may be established by satisfactory proof that the parties have ceased to cohabit as man and wife;

c. Extreme cruelty, which is defined as including any physical or mental cru-elty which endangers the safety or health of the plaintiff or makes it improper or unreasonable to expect the plaintiff to continue to cohabit with the defendant; provided that no complaint for divorce shall be filed until after 3 months from the date of the last act of cruelty complained of in the complaint, but this provision shall not be held to apply to any counterclaim;

d. Separation, provided that the husband and wife have lived separate and apart in different habitations for a period of at least 18 or more consecutive months and there is no reasonable prospect of reconciliation; provided, further that after the 18-month period there is no reasonable prospect of reconciliation;

e. Voluntarily induced addiction or habituation to any narcotic drug as defined in the New Jersey Controlled Dangerous Substances Act, P.L. 1970, c.226 or habitual drunkenness for a period of 12 or more consecutive months subsequent to marriage and next preceding the filing of the complaint;

f. Institutionalization for mental illness for a period of 24 or more consecutive months subsequent to marriage and next preceding the filing of the complaint;

g. Imprisonment of the defendant for 18 or more consecutive months after marriage, provided that where the action is not commenced until after the defendant's release, the parties have not resumed cohabitation following such imprisonment; and,

h. Deviant sexual conduct voluntarily performed by the defendant without the consent of the plaintiff.

### N.J.S.A. 2A:34-10. Jurisdiction in divorce proceedings; service of process; residence requirements

Jurisdiction in actions for divorce, either absolute or from bed and board, may be acquired when process is served upon the defendant as prescribed by the rules of the Supreme Court, and

(1) When, at the time the cause of action arose, either party was a bona

fide resident of this State, and has continued so to be down to the time of the commencement of the action; except that no action for absolute divorce shall be commenced for any cause other than adultery, unless one of the parties has been for the one (1) year next preceding the commencement of the action a bona fide resident of this State; or

(2) When, since the cause of action arose, either party has become, and for at least one (1) year next preceding the commencement of the action has continued to be, a bona fide resident of this State.

## N.J.S.A. 2A:34-21. Resumption of name or assumption of any surname

The court, upon or after granting a divorce from the bonds of matrimony to either spouse, may allow either spouse to resume any name used by the spouse before the marriage, or to assume any surname.

## N.J.S.A. 2A:34-23. Permanent or rehabilitative alimony, maintenance, and child support; security; failure to obey order; sequestration of property; receiver; modification of orders; retainer and counsel fees; factors in determination of amount of payments; equitable distribution of property

Pending any matrimonial action brought in this State or elsewhere, or after judgment of divorce or maintenance, whether obtained in this State or elsewhere, the court may make such order as to the alimony or maintenance of the parties, and also as to the care, custody, education, and maintenance of the children, or any of them, as the circumstances of the parties and nature of the case shall render fit, reasonable, and just, and require reasonable security for the due observance of such orders, including, but not limited to, the creation of trusts or other security devices, to assure payment of reasonably foreseeable medical and educational expenses. Upon neglect or refusal to give such reasonable security, as shall be required, or upon default in complying with any such order, the court may award and issue process for the immediate sequestration of the personal estate, and the rents and profits of the real estate of the party so charged, and appoint a received thereof, and cause such personal estate and the rents and profits of such real estate, or so much thereof as shall be necessary, to be applied toward such alimony and maintenance as the said court shall from time to time seem reasonable and just; or the performance of the said orders may be enforced by other ways according to the practice of the court. Orders so made may be revised and altered by the court from time to time as circumstances may require.

The court may order one party to pay a retainer on behalf of the other for expert and legal services when the respective financial circumstances of the parties make the award reasonable and just. In considering an application, the court shall review the financial capacity of each party to conduct the litigation and the criteria for award of counsel fees that are then pertinent as set forth by court rule. Whenever any other application is made to a court which includes an application for *pendente lite* or final award of counsel fees, the court shall determine the appropriate award for counsel fees, if any, at the same time that a decision is rendered on the other issue then before the court and shall consider the factors set forth in the court rule on counsel fees, the financial circumstances of the parties, and the good or bad faith of either party.

a. In determining the amount to be paid by a parent for support of the child and the period during which the duty of support is owed, the court in those cases not governed by court rule shall consider, but not be limited to, the following factors:

(1) Needs of the child;

(2) Standard of living and economic circumstances of each parent;

(3) All sources of income and assets of each parent;

(4) Earning ability of each parent, including educational background, training, employment skills, work experience,

custodial responsibility for children including the cost of providing child care and the length of time and cost of each parent to obtain training or experience for appropriate employment;

(5) Need and capacity of the child for education, including higher education;

(6) Age and health of the child and each parent;

(7) Income, assets, and learning ability of the child;

(8) Responsibility of the parents for the court-ordered support of others;

(9) Reasonable debts and liabilities of each child and parent; and,

(10) Any other factors the court may deem relevant.

b. In all actions brought for divorce, divorce from bed and board, or nullity the court may award one or more of the following types of alimony: permanent alimony; rehabilitative alimony; limited duration alimony; or, reimbursement alimony to either party. In so doing the court shall consider, but not be limited to, the following factors:

(1) The actual need and ability of the parties to pay;

(2) The duration of the marriage;

(3) The age, physical, and emotional health of the parties;

(4) The standard of living established in the marriage and the likelihood that each party can maintain a reasonably comparable standard of living;

(5) The earning capacities, educational levels, vocational skills, and employability of the parties;

(6) The length of absence from the job market of the party seeking maintenance;

(7) The parental responsibilities for the children;

(8) The time and expense necessary to acquire sufficient education or training to enable the party seeking maintenance to find appropriate employment, the availability of the training and employment, and the opportunity for future acquisitions of capital assets and income;

(9) The history of the financial or nonfinancial contributions to the marriage by each party including contributions to the care and education of the children and interruption of personal careers or educational opportunities;

(10) The equitable distribution of property ordered and any payouts on equitable distribution, directly or indirectly, out of current income, to the extent that this consideration is reasonable, just, and fair;

(11) The income available to either party through investment of any assets held by that party;

(12) The tax treatment and consequences to both parties of any alimony reward, including the designation of all or a portion of the payment as a non-taxable payment; and,

(13) Any other factors which the court may deem relevant.

When a share of a retirement benefit is treated as an asset for purposes of equitable distribution, the court shall not consider income generated thereafter by that share for purposes of determining alimony.

c. In any case in which there is a request for an award of permanent alimony, the court shall consider and make specific findings on the evidence about the above factors. If the court determines that an award of permanent alimony is not warranted, the court shall make specific findings on the evidence setting out the reasons therefore. The court shall then consider whether alimony is appropriate for any or all of the following:

(1) limited duration;

(2) rehabilitative; and,

(3) reimbursement.

In so doing, the court shall consider and make specific findings on the evidence about factors set forth above. The court shall not award limited duration alimony as a substitute for permanent alimony in those cases where permanent alimony would otherwise be awarded.

An award of alimony for a limited duration may be modified based either upon changed circumstances, or upon the nonoccurrence of circumstances that the court found would occur at the time of the award. The court may modify the amount of such an award, but shall not modify the length of the term except in unusual circumstances.

In determining the length of the term, the court shall consider the length of time it would reasonably take for the recipient to improve his or her earning capacity to a level where limited duration alimony is no longer appropriate.

d. Rehabilitative alimony shall be awarded based upon a plan in which the payee shows the scope of rehabilitation, the steps to be taken, and the time frame, including a period of employment during which rehabilitation will occur. An award of rehabilitative alimony may be modified based either upon changed circumstances, or upon the nonoccurrence of circumstances that the court found would occur at the time of the rehabilitative award.

This section is not intended to preclude a court from modifying permanent alimony awards based upon the law.

e. Reimbursement alimony may be awarded under circumstances in which one party supported the other through an advanced education, anticipating participation in the fruits of the earning capacity generated by that education.

f. Nothing in this section shall be construed to limit the court's authority to award permanent alimony, limited duration alimony, rehabilitative alimony, or reimbursement alimony, separately or in any combination, as warranted by the circumstances of the parties and the nature of the case.

g. In all actions for divorce other than those where judgment is granted solely on the ground of separation the court may consider also the proofs made in establishing such ground in determining an amount of alimony or maintenance that is fit, reasonable, and just. In all actions for divorce or divorce from bed and board where judgment is granted on the ground of institutionalization for mental illness the court may consider the possible burden upon the taxpayers of the State as well as the ability of the party to pay in determining an amount of maintenance to be awarded.

h. In all actions where a judgment of divorce or divorce from bed and board is entered the court may make such award or awards to the parties, in addition to alimony and maintenance, to effectuate an equitable distribution of the property, both real and personal, which was legally and beneficially acquired by them or either of them during the marriage. However, all such property, real, personal, or otherwise, legally or beneficially acquired during the marriage by either party by way of gift, devise, or intestate succession shall not be subject to equitable distribution, except that interspousal gifts shall be subject to equitable distribution.

**N.J.S.A. 2A:34-24. Abandonment or separation from obligee; order for support and maintenance; lien for overdue support; priority; order for security, bond or guarantee of support**

If an obligor shall abandon an obligee or separate from the obligee and refuse to or neglect to maintain and provide for the obligee, the court may order suitable support and maintenance to be paid and provided by the obligor for the obligee and their children. If the obligor fails to comply with the order of the court, entered in New Jersey or another jurisdiction, the court may impose a lien against the real and personal property of the obligor who lives in or owns property in New Jersey to secure payment of the overdue support and for such time as the nature of the case and circumstances of the parties render suitable and proper; such lien shall have priority from the time of proper filing or recording.

If the circumstances warrant, for such overdue support or maintenance, upon reasonable notice, the court may compel the obligor to give reasonable security, post a bond or other guarantee for such overdue support and for present and future support and maintenance and may, from time to time, make further orders touching the same, as shall be just and equitable, and enforce such judgment and orders in the manner provided in N.J.S.A. 2A:34-23.

## N.J.S.A. 2C:25-19. Definitions

As used in this act:

a. "Domestic Violence" means the occurrence of one or more of the following acts inflicted upon a person protected under this act by an adult or an emancipated minor:

    (1) Homicide, N.J.S.A. 2C:11-1 et seq.

    (2) Assault, N.J.S.A. 2C:12-1

    (3) Terroristic threats, N.J.S.A. 2C:12-3

    (4) Kidnapping, N.J.S.A. 2C:13-1

    (5) Criminal restraint, N.J.S.A. 2C:13-2

    (6) False imprisonment, N.J.S.A. 2C:13-3

    (7) Sexual assault, N.J.S.A. 2C:14-2

    (8) Criminal sexual contact, N.J.S.A. 2C:14-3

    (9) Lewdness, N.J.S.A. 2C:14-4

    (10) Criminal mischief, N.J.S.A. 2C:17-3

    (11) Burglary, N.J.S.A. 2C:18-2

    (12) Criminal trespass, N.J.S.A. 2C:18-3

    (13) Harassment, N.J.S.A. 2C:33-4

    (14) Stalking, N.J.S.A. 2C:12-10

When one or more of these acts is inflicted by an unemancipated minor upon a person protected under this act, the occurrence shall not constitute "domestic violence," but may be the basis for the filing of a petition or complaint pursuant to the provisions of section 11 of P.L. 1982, c. 77 (N.J.S.A. 2A:4A-30).

b. "Law enforcement agency" means a department, division, bureau, commission, board, or other authority of the State or of any political subdivision thereof which employs law enforcement officers.

c. "Law enforcement officer" means a person whose public duties include the power to act as an officer for the detection, apprehension, arrest, and conviction of officers against the laws of this State.

d. "Victim of domestic violence" means a person protected under this act and shall include any person who is 18 years of age or older or who is an emancipated minor and who has been subjected to domestic violence by a spouse, former spouse, or any other person who is a present or former household member. "Victim of domestic violence" also includes any person, regardless of age, who has been subjected to domestic violence by a person with whom the victim has a child in common, or with whom the victim anticipates having a child in common, if one of the parties is pregnant. "Victim of domestic violence" also includes any person who has been subjected to domestic violence by a person with whom the victim had a dating relationship.

e. "Emancipated minor" means a person who is under 18 years of age but who has been married, has entered military service, has a child or is pregnant or has been previously declared by a court or an administrative agency to be emancipated.

## N.J.S.A. 2C:25-21. Arrest; criminal complaint; seizure of weapons

a. When a person claims to be a victim of domestic violence, and where a law enforcement officer responding to the incident finds probable cause to believe that domestic violence has occurred, the law enforcement officer shall arrest the person who is alleged to be the person who subjected the victim to domestic violence and shall sign a criminal complaint if:

(1) The victim exhibits signs of injury caused by an act of domestic violence;

(2) A warrant is in effect;

(3) There is probable cause to believe the person has violated N.J.S.A. 2C:29-9, and there is probable cause to believe that the person has been served with the order alleged to have been violated. If the victim does not have a copy of a purported order, the officer may verify the existence of an order with the appropriate law enforcement agency; or,

(4) There is probable cause to believe that a weapon as defined in N.J.S.A. 2C:39-1 has ben involved in the commission of an act of domestic violence.

b. A law enforcement officer may arrest a person or may sign a criminal complaint against that person, or may do both, where there is probable cause to believe that an act of domestic violence has been committed, but where none of the conditions in subsection a. of this section applies.

c. (1) As used in this section, the word "exhibits" is to be liberally construed to mean any indication that a victim has suffered bodily injury, which shall include physical pain or any impairment of physical condition. Where the victim exhibits no visible sign of injury, but states that an injury has occurred, the officer should consider other relevant factors in determining whether there is probable cause to make an arrest.

(2) In determining which party in a domestic violence incident is the victim where both parties exhibit signs of injury, the officer should consider the comparative extent of the injuries, the history of domestic violence between the parties, if any, and any other relevant factors.

(3) No victim shall be denied relief or arrested or charged under this act with an offense because the victim used reasonable force in self defense against domestic violence by an attacker.

d. (1) In addition to a law enforcement officer's authority to seize any weapon that is contraband, evidence or an instrumentality of crime, a law enforcement officer who has probable cause to believe that an act of domestic violence has been committed shall:

(a) question persons present to determine whether there are weapons on the premises and

(b) upon observing or learning that a weapon is present on the premises, seize any weapon that the officer reasonably believes would expose the victim to a risk of serious bodily injury. If a law enforcement officer seizes any firearm purchaser identification card or permit to purchase a handgun issued to the person accused of the act of domestic violence.

(2) A law enforcement officer shall deliver all weapons seized pursuant to this section to the county prosecutor and shall append an inventory of all seized weapons to the domestic violence report.

(3) Weapons seized in accordance with the above shall be returned to the owner except upon order of the Superior Court. The prosecutor who has possession of the seized weapons may, upon notice to the owner, petition a judge of the Family Part of the Superior Court, Chancery Division, within 45 days of seizure, to obtain title to the seized weapons, or to revoke any and all permits, licenses and other authorizations for the use, possession, or ownership of such weapons pursuant to the law governing such use, possession, or ownership, or may object to the return of

the weapons on such grounds as are provided for the initial rejection or later revocation of the authorizations, or on the grounds that the owner is unfit or that the owner poses a threat to the public in general or a person or persons in particular.

A hearing shall be held and a record made thereof within 45 days of the notice provided above. No formal pleading and no filing fee shall be required as a preliminary to such hearing. The hearing shall be summary in nature. Appeals from the results of the hearing shall be to the Superior Court, Appellate Division, in accordance with the law.

If the prosecutor does not institute an action within 45 days of seizure, the seized weapons shall be returned to the owner.

After the hearing the court shall order the return of the firearms, weapons and any authorization papers relating to the seized weapons to the owner if the complaint has been dismissed at the request of the complainant and the prosecutor determines that there is insufficient probable cause to indict; or if the defendant is found not guilty of the charges; or if the court determines that the domestic violence situation no longer exists.

Nothing in this act shall impair the right of the State to retain evidence pending a criminal prosecution. Nor shall any provision of this act be construed to limit the authority of the State or a law enforcement officer to seize, retain, or forfeit property pursuant to chapter 64 of Title 2C of the New Jersey Statutes.

If, after the hearing, the court determines that the weapons are not to be returned to the owner, the court may:

(a) With respect to weapons other than firearms, order the prosecutor to dispose of the weapons if the owner does not arrange for the transfer or sale of the weapons within 60 days; or

(b) Order the revocation of the owner's firearms purchaser identification card or any permit, license or authorization, in which case the court shall order the owner to surrender any firearm seized and all other firearms possessed to the prosecutor and shall order the prosecutor to dispose of the firearms if the owner does not arrange for the sale of the firearms to a registered dealer of the firearms within 60 days; or

(c) Order such other relief as it may deem appropriate. When the court orders the weapons forfeited to the State or the prosecutor is required to dispose of the weapons, the prosecutor shall dispose of the property as provided in N.J.S.A. 2C:64-6.

(4) A civil suit may be brought to enjoin a wrongful failure to return a seized firearm where the prosecutor refuses to return the weapon after receiving a written request to do so and notice of the owner's intent to bring a civil action pursuant to this section. Failure of the prosecutor to comply with the provisions of this act shall entitle the prevailing party in the civil suit to reasonable costs, including attorney's fees, provided that the court finds that the prosecutor failed to act in good faith in retaining the seized weapon.

(5) No law enforcement officer or agency shall be held liable in any civil action brought by any person for failing to learn of, locate, or seize a weapon pursuant to this act, or for returning a seized weapon to its owner.

### N.J.S.A. 2C:25-23. Notice provided to victims; contents

A law enforcement officer shall disseminate and explain to the victim the following notice, which shall be written in both English and Spanish:

"You have the right to go to court to get an order called a temporary restraining order, also called a TRO, which may protect you from more abuse by your attacker. The officer who handed you this card can tell you how to get a TRO.

The kinds of things a judge can order in a TRO may include:

(1) That your attacker is temporarily forbidden from entering the home you live in;

(2) That your attacker is temporarily forbidden from having contact with you or your relatives;

(3) That your attacker is temporarily forbidden from bothering you at work;

(4) That your attacker has to pay temporary child support or support for you;

(5) That you be given temporary custody of your children; and,

(6) That your attacker pay you back any money you have to spend for medical treatment or repairs because of the violence. There are other things the court can order, and the court clerk will explain the procedure to you and will help you fill out the papers for a TRO.

You also have the right to file a criminal complaint against your attacker. The police officer who gave you this paper will tell you how to file a criminal complaint.

On weekends, holidays, and other times when the courts are closed, you still have a right to get a TRO. The police officer who gave you this paper can help you get in touch with a judge who can give you a TRO."

### N.J.S.A. 2C:25-24. Domestic violence offense report; contents; annual report by superintendent of state police

a. It shall be the duty of a law enforcement officer who responds to a domestic violence call to complete a domestic violence offense report. All information contained in the domestic violence offense report shall be forwarded to the appropriate county bureau of identification and to the State bureau of records and identification in the Division of State Police in the Department of Law and Public Safety. A copy of the domestic violence offense report shall be forwarded to the municipal court where the offense was committed unless the case has been transferred to the Superior Court.

b. The domestic violence offense report shall be on a form prescribed by the supervisor of the Stare bureau of records and identification which shall include, but not be limited to, the following information:

(1) The relationship of the parties;

(2) The sex of the parties;

(3) The time and date of the incident;

(4) The number of domestic violence calls investigated;

(5) Whether children were involved, or whether the alleged act of domestic violence had been committed in the presence of children;

(6) The type and extent of abuse;

(7) The number and type of weapons involved;

(8) The action taken by the law enforcement officer;

(9) The existence of any prior court orders issued pursuant to this act concerning the parties;

(10) The number of domestic violence calls alleging a violation of a domestic violence restraining order;

(11) The number of arrests for a violation of a domestic violence order; and,

(12) Any other data that may be necessary for a complete analysis of all circumstances leading to the alleged incident of domestic violence.

c. It shall be the duty of the Superintendent of State Police with the assistance of the Division of Systems and Communications in the Department of Law and Public Safety to compile and report annually to the Governor, the Legislature and the Advisory Council on Domestic Violence on the tabulated date from the domestic violence offense reports, classified by county.

## II. New Jersey Rules of Court
*cited in this book*

### R.1:6-2. Form of Motion; Hearing

a. Generally. An application to the court for an order shall be by motion, or in special cases, by order to show cause. A motion, other than for bail pursuant to R. 3:26-2 (d) or one made during trial or hearing, shall be by notice of motion in writing unless the court permits it to be made orally. Every motion shall state the time and place when it is to be presented to the court, the grounds upon which it is made and the nature of the relief sought and, as to motions filed in the Law Division-Civil Part only, the discovery end date or a statement that no such date has been assigned. The Motion shall be accompanied by a proposed form of order in accordance with R. 3:1-4 (a) or R. 4:42-1 (e), as applicable. The form of order shall note whether the motion was opposed or unopposed. If the motion or response thereto relies on facts not of record or not subject of judicial notice, it shall be supported by affidavit made in compliance with R. 1:6-6. The motion shall be deemed uncontested and there shall be no right to argue orally in opposition unless responsive papers are timely filed and served stating with particularity the basis of the opposition to the relief sought. If the motion is withdrawn or the matter settled, counsel shall forthwith inform the court.

b. Civil Motions in Chancery Division and Specially Assigned Cases. When a civil action, by reason of its complexity or other good cause, has ben specially assigned prior to trial to an individual judge for disposition of all pretrial and trial proceedings and in all cases pending in the Superior Court, Chancery Division, all motions therein shall be made directly to the judge assigned to the cause, who shall determine the mode and scheduling of their disposition. Except as provided in R. 5:5-4, motions filed in causes pending in the Superior Court, Chancery Division, Family Part, shall be governed by this paragraph.

c. Civil and Family Part Discovery and Calendar Motions. Every motion in a civil case or a case in the Chancery Division, Family Part, not governed by paragraph (b), involving any aspect of pretrial discovery or the calendar, shall be listed for disposition only if accompanied by a certification stating that he attorney for the moving party has either

(1) personally conferred orally or has made a specifically described good faith effort to confer orally with the attorney for the opposing party in order to resolve the issues raised by the motion by agreement or consent order and that such effort at resolution has been unsuccessful, or

(2) advised the attorney for the opposing party by letter, after the default has occurred, that continued noncompliance with a discovery obligation will result in an appropriate motion being made without further attempt to resolve the matter. The moving papers shall also set forth the date of any scheduled pretrial conference, arbitration proceeding scheduled pursuant to R. 4:21A, calendar call or trial, or state that no such dates have been fixed. Discovery and calendar motions shall be disposed of on the papers unless, on at least two days notice, the court specifically directs oral argument on its own motion or, in its discretion, on a party's request. A movant's request for oral argument shall be made either in the moving papers or reply; a respondent's request for oral argument shall be made in the answering papers.

d. Civil and Family Part Motions–Oral Argument. Except as is otherwise provided by R. 5:5-4 (family actions), no motion shall be listed for oral argument unless a party requests oral argument in the moving papers or in timely-filed answering or rely papers, or unless the court directs. A party requesting oral argument may, however, condition the request on the motion being contested. If the motion involves pretrial discovery or is directly addressed to the calendar, the request shall be considered only if accompanied by a statement of reasons and shall be deemed denied unless the court otherwise advises counsel prior to the return day. As to all other motions, the request shall be granted as of right.

e. Oral Argument–Mode. The court in civil matters, on its own motion or on a party's request, may direct argument of any motion by telephone conference without court appearance. A verbatim record shall be made of all such telephone arguments and the rulings thereon.

f. Order; Record Notation. If the court has made findings of fact and conclusions of law explaining its disposition of the motion, the order shall so note indicating whether the findings and conclusions were written or oral and the date on which they were rendered. If no such findings have been made, the court shall append to the order a statement of reasons for its disposition if it concludes that explanation is either necessary or appropriate. If the order directs a plenary or other evidential hearing, it shall specifically describe the issues to be so tried. A written order or record notation shall be entered by the court memorializing the disposition made on a telephone motion.

### R. 1:13-2. Proceedings by Indigents

a. Waiver of Fees. Except when otherwise specifically provided by these rules, whenever any person by reason of poverty seeks relief from the payment of any fees provided for by law which are payable to any court or clerk of court including the office of the surrogate or any public officer of this State, any court upon the verified application of such person, which application may be filed without fee, may in its discretion order the payment of such fees waived. In any case in which a person is represented by a legal aid society, a Legal Services project, private counsel representing indigents in cooperation with any of the preceding entities, the Office of the Public Defender, or counsel assigned in accordance with these rules, all such fees and any charges of public officers of this State for service of process shall be waived without the necessity of a court order.

b. Compensation of Attorneys. Except as provided by any order of the court, no attorney assigned to represent a person by reason of poverty shall take or agree to take or seek to obtain from the client, payment of any fee, profit, or reward for the conduct of such proceedings for office or other expenses; but no attorney shall be required to expend any personal funds in the prosecution of the cause.

### R. 5:1-4. Differentiated Case Management in Civil Family Actions

a. Case Management Tracks; Standards for Assignment. Except for summary actions, every civil family action shall be assigned, subject to reassignment as provided by paragraph (c) of this rule, to the following tracks as follows:

(1) Priority Track. The action shall be assigned to the priority track if it involves contested custody or parenting time issues.

(2) Complex Track. The action shall be assigned to the complex track for judicial management if it appears likely that it will require a disproportionate expenditure of court and litigant resources in preparation for trial and at trial because of the number of parties involved, the number of claims and defenses raised, the legal difficulty of the issues presented, the factual difficulty of the subject matter, the length and complexity of discovery, or a combination of these or other factors.

(3) Expedited Track. The action shall be assigned to the expedited track if it appears that it can be promptly tried with minimal pretrial proceedings, including discovery. Subject to reassignment as provided by paragraph (c) of this rule, a dissolution action shall be assigned to the expedited track if

(a) there is no dispute as to either the income of the parties or the identifiable value of the marital assets and no issue of custody or parenting time has been raised;

(b) the parties have been married less than five years and have no children;

(c) the parties have entered into a property settlement agreement; or,

(d) the action is uncontested.

(4) Standard Track. Any action not qualifying for assignment to the priority track, complex track, or expedited track shall be assigned to the standard track.

b. Procedure for Track Assignment. The Family Presiding Judge or a judge designated by the Family Presiding Judge shall make the track assignment as soon as practicable after all parties have filed case Information Statements required by R. 5:5-2 or after the case management conference required by R. 5:5-6, whichever is earlier. The track assignment shall not, however, precede the filing of the first responsive pleading in the action. In making the track assignment, due consideration shall be given to an attorney's request for track assignment. If all the attorneys agree on a track assignment, the case shall not be assigned to a different track except for good cause shown and after giving all attorneys the opportunity to be heard, in writing or orally. If it is not clear from an examination of the information provided by the parties which track assignment is most appropriate, the case shall be assigned to the track that affords the greatest degree of management. The parties shall be promptly advised by the court of the track assignment.

c. Track Reassignment. An action may be reassigned to a track other than that specified in the original notice to the parties either on the court's own motion or on application of a party. Unless the court otherwise directs, such application may be made informally to the family Presiding Judge or to a judge designated by the Family Presiding Judge and shall state with specificity the reasons therefore.

### R. 5:5-2. Case Information Statement

a. Applicability. The case information statement required by this rule shall be filed and served in all contested family actions, except summary actions, in which there is any issue as to custody, support, alimony, or equitable distribution. In all other family actions, a case information statement may be required by order on motion of the court or a party.

b. Time and Filing. Except as otherwise provided in R. 5:7-2, a Case Information Statement or certification that no such statement is required under subparagraph (a) shall be filed by each party with the clerk in the county of venue within 20 days after the filing of an Answer or Appearance. The Case Information Statement shall be filed in the form set forth in Appendix V of these rules. The court on either its own or a party's motion may, on notice to all parties, dismiss a party's pleadings for failure to have filed a Case Information Statement. If dismissed, said pleadings shall be subject to reinstatement upon such conditions as the court may deem just.

c. Amendments. Parties are under a continuing duty to inform the court of any changes in the information supplied on the Case Information Statement. All amendments to the statement shall be filed with the court no later than 20 days before the final hearing. The court may prohibit a party from introducing into evidence any information not disclosed or it may enter such other order as it deems appropriate.

d. Income Tax Returns. Following the entry of a final judgment, the court shall order the return to the parties of any income tax returns filed with a Case Information Statement under this rule.

e. Default; Notice for Equitable Distribution, Alimony, Child Support, and Other Relief. In those cases where equitable distribution, alimony, child support, and other relief are sought and a default has been entered, the plaintiff shall file and serve upon the defaulting party, in accordance with R. 1:5-2, A Notice of Application for Equitable Distribution, Alimony, Child Support, and Other Relief, not less than 20 days prior to the hearing date. The notice shall include the proposed trial date, a statement of the value of each asset and the amount of each debt sought to be distributed, a proposal for distribution, and a statement whether plaintiff is seeking alimony and/or child support and, if so, in what amount and a statement as to all other relief sought. Plaintiff shall annex to the notice a completed and filed Case Information Statement in the form set forth in Appendix V of these Rules.

Where a written property settlement agreement has been executed, plaintiff shall not be obligated to file such a notice. When the summons and complaint have been served on the defendant by substituted service pursuant to R. 4:4-4, a copy of the Notice of Application for Equitable Distribution, Alimony, Child Support and Other Relief Sought shall be filed with the County Clerk of the county of venue and notice thereof shall be served upon the defendant in the same manner as the summons or complaint or in any other manner permitted by the court, at least twenty (20) days prior to the date set for hearing. The notice shall state that such a notice has been filed with the County Clerk and can be examined by the defendant during normal business hours at the Family Division Manager's officer in the county in which the notice was filed. The notice shall provide the address of the county courthouse where the notice has been filed.

### R. 5:5-3. Financial Support in Summary Support Actions

In any summary action in which support of a child is in issue, each party shall, prior to commencement of any hearing, serve upon the other party and furnish the court with an affidavit or certification in the form set forth in Appendix XIV of these Rules. The court shall use the information provided on the affidavit or certification and any other relevant facts to set an adequate level of child support in accordance with R. 5:6A. In summary actions to determine the support of spouse, each party shall, prior to the commencement of any hearing, provide the opposing party and the court with an affidavit or certification of income, assets, needs, expenses, liabilities, and other relevant facts to assist the court in determining the issue of support. Such affidavit or certification shall be preserved for appellate review but shall not be filed. Pursuant to R. 5:4-2(g) complaints filed in the Family Part that contain requests for alimony, maintenance or child support must include a completed Confidential Litigant Information Sheet in the form set forth in Appendix XXIV of these Rules.

### R. 5:5-4. Motions in Family Actions

a. Motions. Motions in family actions shall be governed by R. 1:6-2 (b) except that, in exercising its discretion as to the mode and scheduling of disposition on motions, the court shall ordinarily grant requests for oral argument on substantive and nonroutine discovery motions and ordinarily deny requests for oral argument on calendar and routine discovery motions. When a motion is brought for enforcement or modification of a prior order or judgment, a copy of the order or judgment sought to be enforced or modified shall be appended to the pleading filed in support of the motion. When a motion is brought for the modification of an order or judgment for alimony or child support, the pleading filed in support of the motion shall have appended to it a copy of the prior Case Information Statement or Statements files before entry of the order or judgment sought to be modified and a copy of the current Case Information Statement.

b. Page Limits. Unless the court otherwise permits for good cause shown and except for the certification required by R. 4:42-9 (b) (affidavit of service), a certification in support of a motion shall not exceed fifteen pages. A certification in opposition to a motion or in support of a cross-motion or both shall not exceed twenty-five pages. A reply certification to opposing pleadings shall not exceed ten pages.

c. Time for Service and Filing. A notice of motion, except for motions brought pursuant to R. 1:10-3 and motions involving the status of a child, filed more than 45 days after the entry of the written judgment of divorce annulment, other than an ex parte motion, shall be served and filed, together with supporting affidavits and briefs, when necessary, not later than 29 days before the time specified for the return date. For example, a motion must be served and filed on the Thursday for a motion date falling on a Friday 29 days later. Any opposing affidavits, cross-motions, or objections shall be served and filed not later than 15 days before the return date. For example, a response must be served and filed on a Thursday for a motion date falling on a Friday 15 days later. Answers or responses to any opposing affidavits and cross-motions shall be served and filed not later than 8 days before the return date. For example, such papers would have to be served and filed on a Thursday for a motion date falling on the Friday of the following week. If service is made by mail, 3 days should be added to the above time periods.

d. Advance Notice. Every motion shall include the following language: **NOTICE TO LITIGANTS: IF YOU WANT TO RESPOND TO THIS MOTION YOU MUST DO SO IN WRITING.** This written response shall be by affidavit or certification. (Affidavits and certifications are documents filed with the court. In either document the person signing it swears to its truth and acknowledges that they are aware that they can be punished for not filing a true statement with the court. Affidavits are notarized and certifications are not.) If you would like to submit your own separate requests in a motion to the judge you can do so by filing a cross-motion. Your response and/or cross-motion may ask for oral argument. That means you can ask to appear before the court to explain your position. However, you must submit a written response even if you request oral argument. Any papers you send to the court must be sent to the opposing side, either to the attorney if the opposing party is represented by one, or to the other party if they represent themselves.

The response and/or cross-motion must be submitted to the court by a certain date. All predivorce motions, all enforcement motions (also known as motions for enforcement of litigants' rights, R. 1:10-3), or motions that deal with the status of children must be filed 16 days before the return date. (Since most motion days are on a Friday, motion papers must be filed on the Wednesday 16 days before.) A response and/or cross-motion must be filed eight days (Thursday) before the return date. Answers or responses to any opposing affidavits and cross-motions shall be served and filed not later than four days (Monday) before the return date. No other response is per-

mitted without permission of the court. All postjudgment motions, including all motions for modification of alimony, child support, custody, or parenting time/visitation must be filed 29 days (Thursday) before the (Friday) return date. A response and/or cross-motion must be filed 15 days (Thursday) before the return date. Answers or responses to any opposing affidavits and cross-motions shall be served and filed not later than eight days (Thursday) before the return date. No other response is permitted without permission of the court. If you mail in your papers you must add three days to the above time periods.

Response to motion papers sent to the court are to be sent to the following address: [address of court where motion is filed]. Call the Family Division Manager's office [see Appendix C] if you have any questions on how to file a motion, cross-motion or any response papers. Please note that the Family Division Manager's office cannot give you legal advice.

e. Tentative Decisions. In any Family Part motion scheduled for oral argument pursuant to this rule, the motion judge prior to the motion date may tentatively decide the matter on the basis of the motion papers, posting the tentative decision and making it available to the parties. After such tentative decision has been made, unless either party renews the request for oral argument, that request shall be deemed withdrawn and the tentative decision shall become final and shall be set forth in an appropriate order. If, however, either party renews the request for oral argument, the motion shall be argued as scheduled. This tentative motion decision process shall be subject to the general supervision of the Family Presiding Judge of the vicinage.

f. Orders on Family Part Motions. Absent good cause to the contrary, a written order shall be entered at the conclusion of each motion hearing.

g. Exhibits. Exhibits attached to certifications shall not be counted in determining compliance with the page limits contained in this Rule. Certified statements not previously filed with the court shall be included in page limit calculation.

## R. 5:6A. Child Support Guidelines

The guidelines set forth in Appendix IX of these Rules shall be applied when an application to establish or modify child support is considered by the court. The guidelines may be modified or disregarded by the court only where good cause is shown. Good cause shall consist of a) the considerations set forth in Appendix IX-A [omitted], or the presence of other relevant factors which may make the guidelines inapplicable or subject to modification, and b) the fact that injustice would result from application of the guidelines. In all cases, the determination of good cause shall be within the sound discretion of the court.

A completed child support guidelines worksheet in the form prescribed in Appendix IX of these Rules shall be filed with any order or judgment that includes child support that is submitted for the approval of the court. If a proposed child support award differs from the award calculated under the child support guidelines, the worksheet shall state the reason for the deviation and the amount of the award calculated under the child support guidelines.

## R. 5:7-2. Application *Pendente Lite*

a. Support *Pendente Lite*. Applications for support, counsel fees and costs *pendente lite*, whether made with the complaint or by notice of motion thereafter, shall be accompanied by a completed Case Information Statement in the form set forth in Appendix V to these rules pursuant to R. 5:5-2. If this form has previously been submitted, amendments thereto must be filed with the court no later than eight days prior to the motion hearing date. A completed Case Information Statement shall accompany the response to the application *pendente lite*. If previously submitted, amendments thereto must be filed with the court no later than eight days prior to the hearing date.

b. Restraints; Contempt. If *pendente lite* relief is sought, by way of preliminary restraint or to hold a party in contempt, the application shall be on petition and order to show cause.

## R. 5:7-4. Alimony and Child Support Payments

a. Allocation of Support. In awarding alimony, maintenance, or child support, the court shall separate the amounts awarded for alimony or maintenance and the amounts awarded for child support, unless for good cause shown the court determines that the amounts should be unallocated. In awarding child support, payments for health care, child care, and other expenses necessary to maintain the child and children shall be designated as part of the child support award unless good cause is shown why such amounts should be separated.

b. Payments Administered by the Probation Division. The responsibility for the administration and enforcement of the judgment or order, including the transfer of responsibility, shall be governed by the policies established by the Administrative Director of the Courts. Alimony, maintenance, or child support payments not presently administered by the Probation Division shall be so made on application of either party to the court unless the other party, on application to the court, shows good cause to the contrary. In nondissolution support proceedings, the court shall record its decision using the Uniform Order for Summary Support shown in Appendix XVI of these Rules. On the signing of any order that includes alimony, maintenance, child support, or medical support provisions to be administered by the Probation Division, the court shall, immediately after the hearing, send to the appropriate judicial staff one copy of the order which shall include a Confidential Litigant Information Sheet in the form prescribed in Appendix XXIV prepared by the parties or their attorneys providing the names, dates of birth, Social Security numbers, and mailing addresses of the parents and the children; the occupation and driver's license number of the parent who is ordered to pay support; the policy number and name of the health insurance provider of the parent who is ordered to insure the children; and, if income withholding is ordered, the name and address of the obligor's employer. When a party or attorney must prepare a formal written judgment or order pursuant to a judicial decision that includes alimony, maintenance, or child or medical support provisions to be administered by the Probation Division, the court shall, on the date of the hearing, record the support and health insurance provisions on a Temporary Support Order using the form prescribed in Appendix XVII of these Rules and shall immediately have such order and a Confidential Litigant Information Sheet in the form prescribed in Appendix XXIV (if it has not yet been provided to parties or counsel) delivered to the appropriate judicial staff so that a support account can be established on the Automated Child Support Enforcement System (ACSES). A probation account shall be established on ACSES within eight business days of the date the court order was signed. Demographic information provided on the Confidential Litigant Information Sheet shall be required to establish a probation account and send case initiation documents to the parties and the obligor's employer. The Temporary Support Order shall remain in effect until a copy of the final judgment or order is received by the Probation Division. Judgments or orders amending the amounts to be paid through the Probation Division shall be treated in the same manner.

c. Payments to the New Jersey Family Support Payment Center. A Judgment or order for payment of any support administered by the Probation Division shall be deemed to provide that payments are payable to the New Jersey Family Support Payment Center.

d. Income Withholding. All Complaints, notices, pleadings, orders, and judgments which include child support filed or entered on or after October 1, 1990 shall comply with the income withholding provisions of R. 5:7-5.

e. All Notices Applicable to All Orders and Judgments That Include Child Support Provisions. The judgment or order shall include notices stating:

(1) that, if support is not paid through immediate income withholding, the child support provisions of an order or judgment are subject to income withholding when a child support arrearage has accrued in an amount equal to or in excess of the amount of support payable for 14 days. The withholding is effective against the obligor's current and future income from all sources authorized by law;

(2) that any payment or installment of an order for child support or those portions of an order that are allocated for child support shall be fully enforceable and entitled to full faith and credit and shall be a judgment by operation of law on or after the date it is due;

(3) that no payment or installment of an order for child support or those portions of an order that are allocated for child support shall be retroactively modified by the court except for the period during which the party seeking relief has pending an application for modification as provided in N.J.S.A. 2A:17-56.23a;

(4) that the occupational, recreational, and professional licenses, including a license to practice law, held or applied for by the obligor may be denied, suspended, or revoked if: 1) a child support arrearage accumulates that is equal to or exceeds the amount of child support payable for six months, or 2) the obligor fails to provide health care coverage for the child as ordered by the court within six months, or 3) a warrant for the obligor's arrest has been issued by the court for obligor's failure to pay child support as ordered, or for obligor's failure to appear at a hearing to establish paternity or child support, or for obligor's failure to appear at a child support hearing to enforce a child support order and said warrant remains outstanding;

(5) that the driver's license held or applied for by the obligor may be denied, suspended or revoked if 1) a child support arrearage accumulates that is equal to or exceeds the amount of child support payable for six months, or 2) the obligor fails to provide health care coverage for the child as ordered by the court within six months;

(6) that the driver's license held or applied for by the obligor shall be denied, suspended, or revoked if the court issues a warrant for the obligor's arrest for failure to pay child support as ordered, or for failure to appear at a hearing to establish paternity or child support, or for failure to appear at a child support hearing to enforce a child support order and said warrant remains outstanding;

(7) that the amount of child support and/or the addition of a health care coverage provision in Title IV-D cases shall be subject to review, at least once every three years, on written request by either party to the Division of Family Development, P.O. Box 716, Trenton, NJ 08625-0716 and adjusted by the court, as appropriate, or upon application to the court;

(8) that the parties are required to notify the appropriate Probation Division of any change of employer, address or health care coverage provider within 10 days of the change and that failure to provide such information shall be considered a violation of the order;

(9) that, in accordance with N.J.S.A. 2A:34-23b, the custodial parent may require the non-custodial parent's health care coverage provider to make payments directly to the health care provider by submitting a copy of the relevant sections of the order to the insurer;

(10) that Social Security numbers are collected and used in accordance with section 205 of the Social Security Act (42 U.S.C. 405), that disclosure of an individual's Social Security number for Title IV-D purposes is mandatory, that Social Security numbers are used to obtain income, employment, and benefit information on individuals through computer matching programs with federal and state agencies, and that such information is used to establish and enforce child support under Title IV-D of the Social Security Act (42 U.S.C. 651 et seq.); and

(11) that after a judgment or order is entered and a probation support has been established, the obligee and obligor shall notify the appropriate Probation Division of any change of employer, health insurance provider, or address and the obligee and obligor shall notify the Probation Division of a change of address or a change in the status of the children as may be required in the order or judgment within ten days of the change, and any judgment or order that includes alimony, maintenance or child support shall so provide. Failure to provide information as to change of employer, health insurance provider, address, or status of the children shall be considered a violation of the order.

## R. 5:8-1. Investigation Before Award

In family actions in which the court finds that either the custody of children or parenting time issues, or both, are a genuine and substantial issue, the court shall refer the case to mediation in accordance with the provisions of R. 1:40-5. During the mediation process, the parties shall not be required to participate in custody evaluations with any expert. The parties may, however, agree to do so. The mediation process shall last no longer than two months from the date it commences or is ordered to commence, whichever is sooner. As set forth in R. 5:8-6, the court, on good cause shown, may extend the time period. The date for conclusion of mediation shall be set forth in any Case Management Order(s). If the mediation is not successful in resolving custody issues, the court may before final judgment or order require an investigation to be made by the Family Division of the character and fitness of the parties, the economic condition of the family, the financial ability of the party to pay alimony or support or both, and the parties' homes, which shall be limited to a factual description of the home where the child will reside or visit, appropriate child safety precautions in the home, number of household members and their relationship to the child, and criminal record checks for both parties. Any recommendations as to character and fitness of the parties must be made by mental health professionals qualified by licensure, experience, and training. In other family actions the court may, if the public interest so requires, order such an investigation.

The court may continue any family action for the purpose of such investigation, but shall not withhold the granting of any temporary relief by way of alimony, support, or pendente lite orders pertaining to parenting issues under R. 5:5-4 and R. 5:7-2 where the circumstances require. Such investigation of the parties shall be conducted by the Family Division, which shall file its report with the court no more than 45 days after its receipt of the judgment or order requiring the investigation, unless the court otherwise provides. If one of the parties lives outside the county of venue but still within New Jersey, then the Family Division in the county of residence shall conduct the investigation of that party and forward the report to the Family Division in the county of venue within the time frame set forth above.

### R. 5:8-5. Custody and Parenting Time/Visitation Plans, Recital in Judgment or Order

a. In any family action in which the parties cannot agree to a custody or parenting time/visitation arrangement, the parties must each submit a Custody and Parenting Time/Visitation Plan to the court no later than seventy-five (75) days after the last responsive pleading, which the court shall consider in awarding custody and fixing a parenting time or visitation schedule.

Contents of Plan. The Custody and Parenting Time/Visitation Plan shall include but not be limited to the following factors:

(1) Address of the parties;

(2) Employment of the parties;

(3) Type of custody requested with the reasons for selecting the type of custody;

(a) Joint legal custody with one parent having primary residential care;

(b) Joint physical custody;

(c) Sole custody to one parent, parenting time/visitation to the other; or,

(d) Other custodial arrangement;

(4) Specific schedule as top parenting time/visitation including, but not limited to, week nights, weekends, vacations, legal holidays, religious holidays, school vacations, birthdays, and special occasions (family outings, extracurricular activities, and religious services);

(5) Access to medical school records;

(6) Impact if there is to be a contemplated change of residence by a parent;

(7) Participation in making decisions regarding the child(ren); or,

(8) Any other pertinent information.

b. The court shall set out in its order or judgment fully and specifically all terms and conditions relating to the award of custody and proper support for the children.

c. Failure to comply with the provisions of the Custody and Parenting Time/Visitation Plan may result in the dismissal of the noncomplying party's pleadings or the imposition of other sanctions, or both. Dismissed pleadings shall be subject to reinstatement upon such conditions as the court may order.

# Local Courthouse Addresses

**Atlantic County Civil Court Building**
1201 Bacharach Boulevard
Atlantic City, NJ 08401
609-345-6700

**Atlantic County Criminal Court House**
4997 Unami Boulevard
Mays Landing, NJ 08330
609-909-8154

**Bergen County Justice Center**
10 Main Street
Hackensack, NJ 07601
201-527-2700

**Burlington County Courts Facility**
49 Rancocas Road
Mount Holly, NJ 08060
609-518-2500

**Camden County Hall of Justice**
101 South Fifth Street
Camden, NJ 08103
856-379-2200

**Cape May County Courthouse**
9 North Main Street
Cape May Court House, NJ 08210
609-465-1000

**Cumberland County Courthouse**
Broad & Fayette Streets
Bridgeton, NJ 08302
856-451-8000

**Essex County Courts Building**
50 West Market Street
Newark, NJ 07102
973-693-5701

**Gloucester County Courthouse**
I North Broad Street
Woodbury, NJ 08096
856-853-3200

**Hudson County Administration Building**
595 Newark Avenue
Jersey City, NJ 07306
201-795-6600

**Hunterdon County Justice Center**
65 Park Avenue
Flemington, NJ 08822
908-237-5800

**Mercer County Courthouse**
209 South Broad Street
Trenton, NJ 08650-0068
609-571-4000

**Middlesex County Courthouse**
1 Kennedy Square
New Brunswick, NJ 08903-0964
732-981-3200

**Monmouth County Courthouse**
71 Monument Park
Freehold, NJ 07728-1266
732-677-4210

**Morris County Courthouse**
Washington & Court Streets
Morristown, NJ 07963-0910
973-656-4000

**Ocean County Courthouse**
118 Washington Street
Toms River, NJ 08754
732-244-2121

**Passaic County Court House**
77 Hamilton Street
Paterson, NJ 07505-2017
973-247-8000

**Salem County Courthouse**
92 Market Street
Salem, NJ 08079
856-935-7510

**Somerset County Courthouse**
20 North Bridge Street
Somerville, NJ 08876-1262
908-231-7191

**Sussex County Judicial Center**
43-4 7 High Street
Newton, NJ 07860
973-579-0675

**Union County Courthouse**
2 Broad Street
Elizabeth, NJ 07207
908-659-4100

**Warren County Courthouse**
Second & Hardwick Streets
Belvidere, NJ 07823
908-475-6161

# Family Practice Division Family Division Managers and Telephone Numbers

**1. Atlantic/Cape May**
Florine Alexander
609-345-6700 x3446

**2. Bergen**
Johanna Antonacci
201-527-2501

**3. Burlington**
Barbara Sopronyi
609-518-2645

**4. Camden**
Joseph Gunn
856-379-2331

**5. Cumberland/Gloucester/Salem**
Paul Montana
856-853-3665

**6. Essex**
Bernadette Fiore
973-693-6667

**7. Hudson**
Joseph Mollica
201-795-6779

**8. Mercer**
Alfred Federico
609-571-4379

**9. Middlesex**
Charles C. Hager
732-981-3295

**10. Monmouth**
Mary McGevna
732-677-4050

**11. Morris/Sussex**
Greg Lambard
973-656-4305

**12. Ocean**
Brendon Toner
732-929-2042

**13. Passaic**
Cindy Thomson
973-247-8458

**14. Somerset/Hunterdon/Warren**
Amelia Wachter
908-231-7048

**15. Union**
Bruce Colandrea
908-659-3331

# New Jersey Child Support Customer Service Hotlines

The Administrative Office of the Courts (AOC) has established a Customer Service Bureau to ensure that child support customers receive timely responses to questions and complaints. The first step for you to get help is to call the toll-free hotline number.

If you need information beyond that provided by the hotline, contact your *probation worker,* who is generally assigned by the probation division in the county where you live. (In limited instances, child support may be paid through the probation division in the county where your spouse resides.) If more help is needed, you should call the Customer Service Bureau representative in the probation division handling your case. Probation Child Support staff will assist you with your requests.

All complaints or inquiries must be submitted in writing to your local probation Customer Service Bureau. Your letter will help explain your problem, give you a written record, and make it easier for the staff to follow developments on your case.

The following information should be included in your letter:

- ✪ your name, address, and daytime phone number;

- ✪ case number;

- ✪ a description of the nature of the complaint, issue, or question to be answered;

- ✪ the name or names of the individuals who are the subject of the complaint (if applicable); and,

- ✪ any other information such as dates of prior communication or documentation that may assist probation staff.

**Atlantic**
609-345-6700

**Bergen**
201-646-3510

**Burlington**
609-518-2750

**Camden**
856-379-2055

**Cape May**
609-456-1090

**Cumberland**
856-453-4600

**Essex**
973-693-6667

**Gloucester**
856-686-7411

**Hudson**
201-217-5474

**Hunterdon**
908-788-1145

**Mercer**
609-989-6741

**Middlesex**
732-981-2401

**Monmouth**
732-677-4800

**Morris**
973-656-4346

**Ocean**
732-929-2062

**Passaic**
973-247-8823

**Salem**
856-935-7510

**Somerset**
908-231-7675

**Sussex**
973-579-0620

**Union**
908-659-3311

**Warren**
908-475-6935

# New Jersey Child Support Guidelines

New Jersey courts use the following worksheets in determining the amount of child support awarded. Child support is awarded based on such factors as a parent's net income, time spent with the child, and the number of children involved. Worksheets organize these factors and produce the resulting award. Guidelines for both sole parenting and shared parenting situations are included since the criteria is different with each.

## APPENDIX IX-C

| CHILD SUPPORT GUIDELINES - SOLE PARENTING WORKSHEET | | | |
|---|---|---|---|
| Case Name: | County: | | |
| *VS*<br>*Plaintiff        Defendant*<br>Custodial Parent is the ❑ Plaintiff<br>❑ Defendant | Docket No.: | | |
| | Number of Children: | | |
| **All amounts must be weekly.** | CUSTODIAL | NON-CUSTODIAL | COMBINED |
| 1. Gross Taxable Income | $ | $ | |
| 1a. Mandatory Retirement Contributions (*non-taxable*) | −$ | −$ | |
| 1b. Alimony Paid (*Current and/or Past Relationships*) | −$ | −$ | |
| 1c. Alimony Received (*Current and/or Past Relationships*) | +$ | +$ | |
| 2. Adjusted Gross Taxable Income ((L1-L1a-L1b)+L1c) | $ | $ | |
| 2a. Federal, State and Local Income Tax Withholding | −$ | −$ | |
| 2b. Prior Child Support Orders (*Past Relationships*) | −$ | −$ | |
| 2c. Mandatory Union Dues | −$ | −$ | |
| 2d. Other Dependent Deduction (from L14 of a separate worksheet) | −$ | −$ | |
| 3. Net Taxable Income (L2-L2a-L2b-L2c-L2d) | $ | $ | |
| 4. Non-Taxable Income (*source:        *) | +$ | +$ | |
| 5. Net Income (L3+L4) | $ | $ | $ |
| 6. Percentage Share of Income (L5 Each Parent ÷ L5 Combined) | | | 100% |
| 7. Basic Child Support Amount (from Appendix IX-F Schedules) | | | $ |

## SOLE PARENTING WORKSHEET

| | | | |
|---|---|---|---|
| 8. Net Work-Related Child Care (from Appendix IX-E Worksheet) | | | +$ |
| 9. Child's Share of Health Insurance Premium | | | +$ |
| 10. Unreimbursed Health Care Expenses over $250 per child per year | | | +$ |
| 11. Court-Approved Extraordinary Expenses | | | +$ |
| 12. Government Benefits for the Child | | | −$ |
| 13. Total Child Support Amount ((L7+L8+L9+L10+L11)-L12) | | | $ |
| *if line 13 total support amount is zero, STOP - benefit apportionment is substituted for support order* | | | |
| 14. Each Parent's Share of the Support Obligation (L6 × L13) | $ | $ | |
| 15. Net Work-Related Child Care Paid | | −$ | |
| 16. Health Insurance Premium for the Child Paid | | −$ | |
| 17. Unreimbursed Health Care Expenses Paid (>$250/child/year) | | −$ | |
| 18. Court-Approved Extraordinary Expenses Paid | | −$ | |
| 19. Adjustment for Parenting Time Expenses (L7 × %time × 0.37). *Note: Not presumptive in some low income situations - see* App. IX-A., ¶13). | | - $ | |
| 20. Net Child Support Obligation (L14-L15-L16-L17-L18-L19) | | $ | |
| *If neither parent is requesting the other-dependent adjustment, go to line 24* | | | |
| 21. Child Support Order WITH Other-Dependent Deduction | | $ | |
| 22. Child Support Order WITHOUT Other-Dependent Deduction | | $ | |
| 23. Adjusted Child Support Order ((L21+L22)÷2) | | $ | |
| + Continued on Page 2 + | | | |

**APPENDIX IX-C**

| CHILD SUPPORT GUIDELINES - SOLE PARENTING WORKSHEET - PAGE 2 | | |
|---|---|---|
| 24. Self-Support Reserve Test (L5 - L20 or L23 for NCP; L5 for CP). If NCP result is greater than 105% of the poverty guideline for one person (*pg*) or CP net income is less than the *pg*, enter L20 or L23 amount on L26. If NCP L24 income is less than the *pg* and CP income is greater than the *pg*, go to L25. | $ | $ |
| 25. Obligor Parent's Maximum Child Support Obligation (L5 NCP income - 105% of poverty guideline for one person). Enter result here and on Line 26. | | $ |
| 26. Child Support Order | | $ |
| COMMENTS, REBUTTALS, AND JUSTIFICATION FOR DEVIATIONS | | |

1. THE CHILD SUPPORT ORDER FOR THIS CASE ❑ WAS ❑ WAS NOT BASED ON THE CHILD SUPPORT GUIDELINES AWARD.

2. IF DIFFERENT FROM THE CHILD SUPPORT GUIDELINES AWARD (LINE 26), ENTER AMOUNT ORDERED: $

3. THE CHILD SUPPORT GUIDELINES WERE NOT USED OR THE GUIDELINES AWARD WAS ADJUSTED BECAUSE:

(❑ additional pages attached)

4. The following court-approved extraordinary expenses were added to the basic support obligation:

5. Parenting Time: Custodial Parent_____% Non-custodial Parent _____%

6. Custodial Taxes: ❑ App. IX-H ❑ Circ.E ❑ Other:____ #Allowances:___ Marital: S M H
Non-Custodial Taxes: ❑ App. IX-H ❑ Circ.E ❑ Other:____ #Allowances:___ Marital: S M H

| PREPARED BY: | TITLE | DATE |
|---|---|---|
| | | |

# APPENDIX IX-D

## CHILD SUPPORT GUIDELINES - SHARED PARENTING WORKSHEET

| Case Name: | County: |
| --- | --- |
| *vs*<br>*Plaintiff*          *Defendant*<br>PPR is the ❑ Plaintiff ❑ Defendant | Docket No.:<br><br>Number of Children: |

| *All amounts must be weekly.* | Parent of Primary Residence (PPR) | Parent of Alternate Residence (PAR) | Combined |
| --- | --- | --- | --- |
| 1. Gross Taxable Income | $ | $ | |
| 1a. Mandatory Retirement Contributions (*non-taxable*) | −$ | −$ | |
| 1b. Alimony Paid (*Current and/or Past Relationships*) | −$ | −$ | |
| 1c. Alimony Received (*Current and/ or Past Relationships*) | +$ | +$ | |
| 2. Adjusted Gross Taxable Income ((L1 - L1a-L1b)+L1c) | $ | $ | |
| 2a. Federal, State and Local Income Tax Withholding | −$ | −$ | |
| 2b. Prior Child Support Orders (*Past Relationships*) | −$ | −$ | |
| 2c. Mandatory Union Dues | −$ | −$ | |
| 2d. Other Dependent Deduction (L14 of a Sole Parenting worksheet) | −$ | −$ | |
| 3. Net Taxable Income (L2-L2a-L2b-L2c-L2d) | $ | $ | |
| 4. Non-Taxable Income (*source:*          ) | +$ | +$ | |
| 5. Net Income (L3+L4) | $ | $ | $ |
| 6. Percent Share of Income (L5 Each Parent ÷ L5 Combined) | | | 1.00 |
| 7. Number of Overnights With Each Parent | | | |

**APPENDIX IX-D**

| | | | |
|---|---|---|---|
| 8. Percent of Overnights With Parent (L7 Parent ÷ L7 Combined) | | | 1.00 |
| **If PAR time sharing is less than the equivalent of two overnights per week (28%), use Sole Custody Worksheet** | | | |
| 9. Basic Child Support Amount (from Appendix IX-F Schedules) | | | $ |
| 10. PAR Shared Parenting Fixed Expenses (PAR L8×L9×0.38 ×2) | | $ | |
| 11. Government Benefits for the Child | | | $ |
| 12. Shared Parenting Basic Child Support Amount ((L9 + L10) - L11) | | | $ |
| 13. PAR Share of SP Basic Child Support Amount (PAR L6 × L12) | | $ | |
| 14 PAR Shared Parenting Variable Expenses (PAR L8 × L9 × 0.37) | | $ | |
| 15. PAR Adjusted SP Basic Child Support Amount (L13 - L10 - L14) | | $ | |
| 16. Net Work-Related Child Care (from Appendix IX-E Worksheet) | | | $ |
| 17. Child's Share of Health Insurance Premium | | | +$ |
| 18. Unreimbursed Health Care Expenses over $250 per child per year | | | +$ |
| 19. Court-Approved Extraordinary Expenses | | | +$ |
| 20. Total Supplemental Expenses (L16+L17+L18+L19) | | | $ |
| + Continued on Page 2 + | | | |

**SHARED PARENTING WORKSHEET**

| CHILD SUPPORT GUIDELINES - SHARED PARENTING WORKSHEET - PAGE 2 | | | |
|---|---|---|---|
| *All amounts must be weekly.* | Parent of Primary Residence (PPR) | Parent of Alternate Residence (PAR) | Combined |
| 20. Total Supplemental Expenses (from reverse side) | | | $ |
| 21. PAR's Share of Total Supplemental Expenses (PAR L6 × L20) | | $ | |
| 22. PAR Net Work-Related Child Care PAID | | $ | |
| 23. PAR Health Insurance Premium for the Child PAID | | +$ | |
| 24. PAR Unreimbursed Health Care Expenses (>$250/child /year) PAID | | +$ | |
| 25. PAR Court-Approved Extraordinary Expenses PAID | | +$ | |
| 26. PAR Total Payments/Supplemental Expenses (L22+L23+L24+L25) | | $ | |
| 27. PAR Net Supplemental Expenses (L21 - L26) | | $ | |
| 28. PAR Net Child Support Obligation (L15 + L27) | | $ | |
| *If neither parent is requesting the other-dependent adjustment, go to Line 32* | | | |
| 29. Line 28 PAR CS Oblig WITH Other-Dependent Deduction | | $ | |
| 30. Line 28 PAR CS Oblig WITHOUT Other-Dependent Deduction | | $ | |
| 31. Adjusted PAR CS Obligation ((L29+L30)÷2) | | $ | |
| 32. Self-Support Reserve Test (PAR L5 - PAR L28 or L31 if any). If PAR amount is greater than 105% of the poverty guideline for one person (*pg*) *or* the PPR L32 income is less than the *pg*, enter the L28 or L31 amount on the PAR L34. If PAR L32 amount is less than the *pg* and the PPR's L32 income is greater than the *pg*, go to Line 33. If L28 or L31 is negative, see App. IX-B (shared-parenting worksheet) for instructions. | $ | $ | |

**APPENDIX IX-D**

| | | |
|---|---|---|
| 33. Maximum CS Obligation (Obligor Parent's L5 net income - 105% of the poverty guideline for one person). Enter result here and on Line 34. | $ | $ |
| 34. Child Support Order (negative L28 or L31 denotes PPR obligation) | $ | $ |

*If the PAR is the Obligor, Continue to Line 35*

| | |
|---|---|
| 35. PPR Household Income Test - (L5 PPR net income from all sources + net income of other household members +L34 order) If less than the PPR household income threshold (see App. IX-A, ¶14(c)), the SOLE-CUSTODY WORKSHEET must be used. | $ |

**Comments, Rebuttals, and Justification for Deviations**

1. The child support order for this case ❑ was ❑ was not based on the child support guidelines award.

2. If different from the child support guidelines award (Line 34), enter amount ordered: $

3. The child support guidelines were not used or the guidelines award was adjusted because:



( ❑ additional pages attached)

4. The following extraordinary expenses were added to the basic support obligation:

5. Custodial Taxes:  ❑ App. IX-H ❑ Circ.E ❑ Other:____ #Allowances:___ Marital: S M H
Non-Custodial Taxes: ❑ App. IX-H ❑ Circ.E ❑ Other:____ #Allowances:___ Marital: S M H

| Prepared by: | Title | Date |
|---|---|---|
| | | |

| Child Support Guidelines Net Child Care Cost Worksheet | |
|---|---|
| 1. Parent's Adjusted Gross Income (IRS Definition - See Appendix IX-B) | $ |
| 2. **Annual** work-related child care cost | $ |
| 3. Maximum child care subject to federal tax credit. (Enter the **lesser** of the annual child care cost **or** $3,000 for one child/ $6,000 for two or more children). | $ |
| 4. If the annual child care cost is less than $3,000 for one child or $6,000 for two or more children, enter the child care tax credit percentage from the Column 2 of the Tax Credit Table here. If the child care costs are greater than these amounts, enter the maximum dollar credit from Column 3 of the Tax Credit Table on Line 5. | % |
| 5. Tax Credit (Line 3 ×Line 4 **or** enter the Column 3 maximum dollar tax credit). | $ |
| 6. Net annual child care expense (Line 2 - Line 5). | $ |
| 7. Net weekly child care cost (Line 6 ÷ 52).   Enter this amount on the Child Support Guidelines Sole Custody Worksheet, Line 8 or the Shared Custody Worksheet, Line 16. | $ |

| Federal Child Care Tax Credit Table | | | | |
|---|---|---|---|---|
| Column 1 | | Column 2 | Column 3 | |
| INCOME | | PARTIAL CREDIT LINE 3 AMOUNT: | MAXIMUM CREDIT LINE 4 AMOUNT: | |
| PARENT'S ADJUSTED GROSS INCOME (IRS Definition) | | COST <u>LESS</u> THAN $3,000/YR ($58/wk) for 1 CHILD <u>OR</u> $6,000/YR ($115/wk) for 2 OR MORE CHILDREN | COST <u>MORE</u> THAN $3.000/YR ($58/WK) for 1 CHILD <u>OR</u> $6.000/YR ($115/WK) for 2 OR MORE CHILDREN | |
| ANNUAL | WEEKLY | TAX CREDIT PERCENTAGE | 1 CHILD CC >$58/WK | 2 OR MORE CHILDREN CC > $115/WK |
| 0 - 15,000 | 0 - 288 | 35% (.35) | 1,050 | 2,100 |
| 15,001 - 17,000 | 289 - 326 | 34% (.34) | 1,020 | 2,040 |
| 17,001 - 19,000 | 327 - 365 | 33% (.33) | 990 | 1,980 |
| 19,001 - 21,000 | 366 - 403 | 32% (.32) | 960 | 1,920 |
| 21,001 - 23,000 | 404 - 442 | 31% (.31) | 930 | 1,860 |
| 23,001 - 25,000 | 443 - 480 | 30% (.30) | 900 | 1,800 |
| 25,001 - 27,000 | 481 - 519 | 29% (.29) | 870 | 1,740 |
| 27,001 - 29,000 | 520 - 557 | 28% (.28) | 840 | 1,680 |
| 29,001 - 31,000 | 558 - 596 | 27% (.27) | 810 | 1,620 |
| 31,001 - 33,000 | 597 - 634 | 26% (.26) | 780 | 1,560 |
| 33,001 - 35,000 | 635 - 673 | 25% (.25) | 750 | 1,500 |
| 35,001 - 37,000 | 674 - 711 | 24% (.24) | 720 | 1,440 |
| 37,001 - 39,000 | 712 - 750 | 23% (.23) | 690 | 1,380 |

| 39,001 - 41,000 | 751 - 788 | 22% (.22) | 660 | 1,320 |
| 41,001 - 43,000 | 789 - 826 | 21% (.21) | 630 | 1,260 |
| 43,001 - 45,000 | 827 - 865 | 20% (.20) | 600 | 1,200 |
| 45,001 + | 866 + | 20% (.20) | 600 | 1,200 |

## APPENDIX IX-F

## SCHEDULE OF CHILD SUPPORT AWARDS

| COMBINED NET WEEKLY INCOME | | ONE CHILD | TWO CHILDREN | THREE CHILDREN | FOUR CHILDREN | FIVE CHILDREN | SIX CHILDREN |
|---|---|---|---|---|---|---|---|
| 0 | | | | | | | |
| 50 | | *For combined net incomes that are less than $170 per week, the court shall establish a child support award based on the obligor's net income and living expenses and the needs of the child. In these circumstances, the support award should be between $5.00 per week and the support amount at $170 combined net weekly income as shown on this schedule.* | | | | | |
| 100 | | | | | | | |
| 150 | | | | | | | |
| 160 | | | | | | | |
| 170 | | 42 | 61 | 72 | 80 | 87 | 93 |
| 180 | | 44 | 65 | 77 | 85 | 92 | 98 |
| 190 | | 47 | 68 | 81 | 89 | 97 | 104 |
| 200 | | 49 | 72 | 85 | 94 | 102 | 109 |
| 210 | | 52 | 75 | 89 | 99 | 107 | 114 |
| 220 | | 54 | 79 | 93 | 103 | 112 | 120 |
| 230 | | 56 | 82 | 98 | 108 | 117 | 125 |
| 240 | | 59 | 86 | 102 | 113 | 122 | 131 |
| 250 | | 61 | 89 | 106 | 117 | 127 | 136 |
| 260 | | 64 | 93 | 110 | 122 | 132 | 141 |
| 270 | | 66 | 97 | 115 | 127 | 137 | 147 |
| 280 | | 69 | 100 | 119 | 131 | 142 | 152 |
| 290 | | 71 | 104 | 123 | 136 | 147 | 158 |
| 300 | | 73 | 107 | 127 | 140 | 152 | 163 |
| 310 | | 76 | 111 | 131 | 145 | 157 | 168 |
| 320 | | 78 | 114 | 136 | 150 | 162 | 174 |
| 330 | | 81 | 118 | 140 | 154 | 167 | 179 |
| 340 | | 83 | 121 | 144 | 159 | 172 | 184 |

**APPENDIX IX-F**

| | | | | | | |
|---|---|---|---|---|---|---|
| **350** | | 86 | 125 | 148 | 163 | 177 | 190 |
| **360** | | 88 | 128 | 152 | 168 | 182 | 195 |
| **370** | | 90 | 132 | 156 | 172 | 187 | 200 |
| **380** | | 93 | 135 | 160 | 177 | 192 | 205 |
| **390** | | 95 | 138 | 164 | 181 | 196 | 210 |
| **400** | | 97 | 142 | 168 | 186 | 201 | 215 |
| **410** | | 100 | 145 | 172 | 190 | 206 | 221 |
| **420** | | 102 | 149 | 176 | 195 | 211 | 226 |
| **430** | | 104 | 152 | 180 | 199 | 216 | 231 |
| **440** | | 107 | 155 | 184 | 203 | 220 | 236 |
| **450** | | 109 | 159 | 188 | 207 | 225 | 241 |
| **460** | | 111 | 162 | 191 | 212 | 229 | 245 |
| **470** | | 113 | 165 | 195 | 216 | 234 | 250 |
| **480** | | 116 | 168 | 199 | 220 | 238 | 255 |
| **490** | | 118 | 171 | 203 | 224 | 243 | 260 |
| **500** | | 120 | 175 | 206 | 228 | 247 | 265 |
| **510** | | 122 | 178 | 210 | 232 | 252 | 269 |
| **520** | | 124 | 181 | 214 | 236 | 256 | 274 |
| **530** | | 127 | 184 | 218 | 241 | 261 | 279 |
| **540** | | 129 | 187 | 221 | 245 | 265 | 284 |
| **550** | | 131 | 191 | 225 | 249 | 270 | 289 |
| **560** | | 133 | 194 | 229 | 253 | 274 | 294 |
| **570** | | 136 | 197 | 233 | 257 | 279 | 298 |
| **580** | | 138 | 200 | 237 | 261 | 283 | 303 |
| **590** | | 140 | 204 | 240 | 265 | 288 | 308 |
| **600** | | 142 | 207 | 244 | 270 | 292 | 313 |
| **610** | | 145 | 210 | 248 | 274 | 297 | 317 |
| **620** | | 147 | 213 | 251 | 278 | 301 | 322 |
| **630** | | 149 | 216 | 255 | 282 | 306 | 327 |

**SCHEDULE OF CHILD SUPPORT AWARDS**

| | | | | | | |
|---|---|---|---|---|---|---|
| **640** | | 151 | 220 | 259 | 286 | 310 | 332 |
| **650** | | 154 | 223 | 263 | 290 | 314 | 336 |
| **660** | | 156 | 226 | 266 | 294 | 319 | 341 |
| **670** | | 158 | 229 | 270 | 298 | 323 | 346 |
| **680** | | 160 | 232 | 274 | 302 | 328 | 351 |
| **690** | | 163 | 235 | 277 | 307 | 332 | 356 |
| **700** | | 165 | 239 | 281 | 311 | 337 | 360 |
| **710** | | 167 | 242 | 285 | 315 | 341 | 365 |
| **720** | | 169 | 245 | 289 | 319 | 346 | 370 |
| **730** | | 171 | 248 | 292 | 323 | 350 | 375 |
| **740** | | 174 | 251 | 296 | 327 | 355 | 379 |
| **750** | | 176 | 255 | 300 | 331 | 359 | 384 |
| **760** | | 178 | 258 | 303 | 335 | 363 | 389 |
| **770** | | 180 | 261 | 307 | 339 | 368 | 394 |
| **780** | | 182 | 264 | 310 | 343 | 372 | 398 |
| **790** | | 184 | 266 | 313 | 346 | 375 | 401 |
| **800** | | 186 | 269 | 316 | 349 | 379 | 405 |
| **810** | | 187 | 271 | 319 | 352 | 382 | 409 |
| **820** | | 189 | 273 | 322 | 356 | 386 | 413 |
| **830** | | 190 | 276 | 325 | 359 | 389 | 416 |
| **840** | | 192 | 278 | 328 | 362 | 392 | 420 |
| **850** | | 194 | 281 | 331 | 365 | 396 | 424 |
| **860** | | 195 | 283 | 333 | 368 | 399 | 427 |
| **870** | | 197 | 286 | 336 | 372 | 403 | 431 |
| **880** | | 199 | 288 | 339 | 375 | 406 | 435 |
| **890** | | 200 | 290 | 342 | 378 | 410 | 439 |
| **900** | | 202 | 293 | 345 | 381 | 413 | 442 |
| **910** | | 204 | 295 | 348 | 384 | 417 | 446 |
| **920** | | 205 | 297 | 350 | 387 | 419 | 449 |

**APPENDIX IX-F**

| | | | | | | |
|---|---|---|---|---|---|---|
| **930** | | 206 | 299 | 352 | 389 | 421 | 451 |
| **940** | | 207 | 300 | 353 | 390 | 423 | 453 |
| **950** | | 208 | 302 | 355 | 392 | 425 | 455 |
| **960** | | 209 | 303 | 357 | 394 | 427 | 457 |
| **970** | | 210 | 305 | 358 | 396 | 429 | 459 |
| **980** | | 212 | 306 | 360 | 398 | 431 | 461 |
| **990** | | 213 | 308 | 362 | 400 | 433 | 463 |
| **1,000** | | 214 | 309 | 363 | 401 | 435 | 466 |
| **1,010** | | 215 | 311 | 365 | 403 | 437 | 468 |
| **1,020** | | 216 | 312 | 367 | 405 | 439 | 470 |
| **1,030** | | 217 | 314 | 368 | 407 | 441 | 472 |
| **1,040** | | 218 | 315 | 370 | 409 | 443 | 474 |
| **1,050** | | 219 | 317 | 372 | 411 | 445 | 476 |
| **1,060** | | 220 | 318 | 373 | 412 | 447 | 478 |
| **1,070** | | 222 | 320 | 375 | 415 | 450 | 481 |
| **1,080** | | 223 | 322 | 377 | 417 | 452 | 484 |
| **1,090** | | 224 | 323 | 379 | 419 | 455 | 486 |
| **1,100** | | 226 | 325 | 382 | 422 | 457 | 489 |
| **1,110** | | 227 | 327 | 384 | 424 | 459 | 492 |
| **1,120** | | 228 | 329 | 386 | 426 | 462 | 494 |
| **1,130** | | 229 | 331 | 388 | 428 | 464 | 497 |
| **1,140** | | 231 | 332 | 390 | 431 | 467 | 500 |
| **1,150** | | 232 | 334 | 392 | 433 | 469 | 502 |
| **1,160** | | 233 | 336 | 394 | 435 | 472 | 505 |
| **1,170** | | 234 | 338 | 396 | 438 | 474 | 508 |
| **1,180** | | 236 | 339 | 398 | 440 | 477 | 510 |
| **1,190** | | 237 | 341 | 400 | 442 | 479 | 513 |
| **1,200** | | 238 | 343 | 402 | 444 | 482 | 515 |
| **1,210** | | 239 | 345 | 404 | 447 | 484 | 518 |

## SCHEDULE OF CHILD SUPPORT AWARDS

| | | | | | | |
|---|---|---|---|---|---|---|
| **1,220** | | 241 | 347 | 406 | 449 | 487 | 521 |
| **1,230** | | 242 | 348 | 408 | 451 | 489 | 523 |
| **1,240** | | 243 | 350 | 410 | 454 | 492 | 526 |
| **1,250** | | 244 | 352 | 413 | 456 | 494 | 529 |
| **1,260** | | 246 | 354 | 415 | 458 | 497 | 532 |
| **1,270** | | 247 | 356 | 417 | 461 | 499 | 534 |
| **1,280** | | 248 | 358 | 419 | 463 | 502 | 537 |
| **1,290** | | 250 | 360 | 421 | 466 | 505 | 540 |
| **1,300** | | 251 | 361 | 424 | 468 | 507 | 543 |
| **1,310** | | 252 | 363 | 426 | 471 | 510 | 546 |
| **1,320** | | 254 | 365 | 428 | 473 | 513 | 549 |
| **1,330** | | 255 | 367 | 430 | 475 | 515 | 552 |
| **1,340** | | 256 | 369 | 433 | 478 | 518 | 554 |
| **1,350** | | 257 | 371 | 435 | 480 | 521 | 557 |
| **1,360** | | 259 | 373 | 437 | 483 | 523 | 560 |
| **1,370** | | 260 | 375 | 439 | 485 | 526 | 563 |
| **1,380** | | 261 | 377 | 441 | 488 | 529 | 566 |
| **1,390** | | 263 | 378 | 444 | 490 | 531 | 569 |
| **1,400** | | 264 | 380 | 446 | 493 | 534 | 571 |
| **1,410** | | 265 | 382 | 448 | 495 | 537 | 574 |
| **1,420** | | 267 | 384 | 450 | 498 | 539 | 577 |
| **1,430** | | 268 | 386 | 453 | 500 | 542 | 580 |
| **1,440** | | 269 | 388 | 455 | 503 | 545 | 583 |
| **1,450** | | 271 | 390 | 457 | 505 | 547 | 586 |
| **1,460** | | 272 | 392 | 459 | 507 | 550 | 588 |
| **1,470** | | 273 | 394 | 461 | 510 | 552 | 591 |
| **1,480** | | 275 | 396 | 463 | 512 | 555 | 594 |
| **1,490** | | 276 | 398 | 466 | 514 | 558 | 597 |
| **1,500** | | 278 | 400 | 468 | 517 | 560 | 599 |

**APPENDIX IX-F**

| | | | | | | |
|---|---|---|---|---|---|---|
| **1,510** | | 279 | 401 | 470 | 519 | 563 | 602 |
| **1,520** | | 280 | 403 | 472 | 521 | 565 | 605 |
| **1,530** | | 282 | 405 | 474 | 524 | 568 | 608 |
| **1,540** | | 283 | 407 | 476 | 526 | 570 | 610 |
| **1,550** | | 284 | 409 | 478 | 529 | 573 | 613 |
| **1,560** | | 286 | 411 | 480 | 531 | 576 | 616 |
| **1,570** | | 287 | 413 | 483 | 533 | 578 | 619 |
| **1,580** | | 289 | 415 | 485 | 536 | 581 | 621 |
| **1,590** | | 290 | 417 | 487 | 538 | 583 | 624 |
| **1,600** | | 291 | 419 | 489 | 540 | 586 | 627 |
| **1,610** | | 293 | 421 | 491 | 543 | 588 | 630 |
| **1,620** | | 294 | 423 | 493 | 545 | 591 | 632 |
| **1,630** | | 295 | 425 | 495 | 547 | 593 | 635 |
| **1,640** | | 297 | 427 | 498 | 550 | 596 | 638 |
| **1,650** | | 299 | 429 | 501 | 553 | 600 | 642 |
| **1,660** | | 300 | 431 | 504 | 557 | 603 | 646 |
| **1,670** | | 302 | 434 | 507 | 560 | 607 | 649 |
| **1,680** | | 303 | 436 | 509 | 563 | 610 | 653 |
| **1,690** | | 305 | 438 | 512 | 566 | 614 | 657 |
| **1,700** | | 307 | 441 | 515 | 569 | 617 | 660 |
| **1,710** | | 308 | 443 | 518 | 572 | 620 | 664 |
| **1,720** | | 310 | 446 | 521 | 575 | 624 | 667 |
| **1,730** | | 311 | 448 | 524 | 579 | 627 | 671 |
| **1,740** | | 313 | 450 | 527 | 582 | 631 | 675 |
| **1,750** | | 315 | 453 | 529 | 585 | 634 | 678 |
| **1,760** | | 316 | 455 | 532 | 588 | 637 | 682 |
| **1,770** | | 318 | 457 | 535 | 591 | 641 | 686 |
| **1,780** | | 319 | 460 | 538 | 594 | 644 | 689 |
| **1,790** | | 321 | 462 | 541 | 598 | 648 | 693 |

## SCHEDULE OF CHILD SUPPORT AWARDS

| | | | | | | |
|---|---|---|---|---|---|---|
| **1,800** | | 323 | 464 | 544 | 601 | 651 | 697 |
| **1,810** | | 324 | 467 | 546 | 604 | 655 | 700 |
| **1,820** | | 326 | 469 | 549 | 607 | 658 | 704 |
| **1,830** | | 327 | 471 | 552 | 610 | 661 | 707 |
| **1,840** | | 328 | 473 | 554 | 612 | 663 | 710 |
| **1,850** | | 330 | 474 | 556 | 614 | 666 | 712 |
| **1,860** | | 331 | 476 | 558 | 616 | 668 | 715 |
| **1,870** | | 332 | 478 | 560 | 618 | 670 | 717 |
| **1,880** | | 333 | 479 | 562 | 621 | 673 | 720 |
| **1,890** | | 334 | 481 | 564 | 623 | 675 | 722 |
| **1,900** | | 335 | 483 | 566 | 625 | 677 | 725 |
| **1,910** | | 336 | 484 | 567 | 627 | 680 | 727 |
| **1,920** | | 337 | 486 | 569 | 629 | 682 | 730 |
| **1,930** | | 338 | 487 | 571 | 631 | 684 | 732 |
| **1,940** | | 340 | 489 | 573 | 634 | 687 | 735 |
| **1,950** | | 341 | 491 | 575 | 636 | 689 | 737 |
| **1,960** | | 342 | 492 | 577 | 638 | 691 | 740 |
| **1,970** | | 343 | 494 | 579 | 640 | 694 | 742 |
| **1,980** | | 344 | 496 | 581 | 642 | 696 | 745 |
| **1,990** | | 345 | 497 | 583 | 644 | 698 | 747 |
| **2,000** | | 346 | 499 | 585 | 646 | 701 | 750 |
| **2,010** | | 347 | 501 | 587 | 649 | 703 | 752 |
| **2,020** | | 349 | 502 | 589 | 651 | 705 | 755 |
| **2,030** | | 350 | 504 | 591 | 653 | 708 | 757 |
| **2,040** | | 351 | 505 | 593 | 655 | 710 | 760 |
| **2,050** | | 352 | 507 | 595 | 657 | 712 | 762 |
| **2,060** | | 353 | 509 | 597 | 659 | 715 | 765 |
| **2,070** | | 354 | 510 | 599 | 662 | 717 | 767 |
| **2,080** | | 355 | 512 | 601 | 664 | 719 | 770 |

**REPRINTED WITH THE PERMISSION OF GANN LAW BOOKS**

**APPENDIX IX-F**

| | | | | | | | |
|---|---|---|---|---|---|---|---|
| **2,090** | | 356 | 514 | 603 | 666 | 722 | 772 |
| **2,100** | | 357 | 515 | 605 | 668 | 724 | 775 |
| **2,110** | | 359 | 517 | 607 | 670 | 726 | 777 |
| **2,120** | | 360 | 519 | 608 | 672 | 729 | 780 |
| **2,130** | | 361 | 520 | 610 | 674 | 731 | 782 |
| **2,140** | | 362 | 522 | 612 | 677 | 733 | 785 |
| **2,150** | | 363 | 524 | 614 | 679 | 736 | 787 |
| **2,160** | | 364 | 525 | 616 | 681 | 738 | 790 |
| **2,170** | | 365 | 527 | 618 | 683 | 741 | 793 |
| **2,180** | | 367 | 529 | 621 | 686 | 744 | 796 |
| **2,190** | | 368 | 531 | 623 | 689 | 746 | 799 |
| **2,200** | | 369 | 533 | 626 | 691 | 749 | 802 |
| **2,210** | | 371 | 535 | 628 | 694 | 752 | 805 |
| **2,220** | | 372 | 537 | 630 | 696 | 755 | 808 |
| **2,230** | | 373 | 539 | 633 | 699 | 758 | 811 |
| **2,240** | | 375 | 541 | 635 | 702 | 760 | 814 |
| **2,250** | | 376 | 543 | 637 | 704 | 763 | 817 |
| **2,260** | | 377 | 544 | 640 | 707 | 766 | 820 |
| **2,270** | | 379 | 546 | 642 | 709 | 769 | 823 |
| **2,280** | | 380 | 548 | 644 | 712 | 772 | 826 |
| **2,290** | | 381 | 550 | 647 | 715 | 775 | 829 |
| **2,300** | | 382 | 552 | 649 | 717 | 777 | 832 |
| **2,310** | | 384 | 554 | 651 | 720 | 780 | 835 |
| **2,320** | | 385 | 556 | 654 | 722 | 783 | 838 |
| **2,330** | | 386 | 558 | 656 | 725 | 786 | 841 |
| **2,340** | | 388 | 560 | 658 | 728 | 789 | 844 |
| **2,350** | | 389 | 562 | 661 | 730 | 791 | 847 |
| **2,360** | | 390 | 564 | 663 | 733 | 794 | 850 |
| **2,370** | | 392 | 566 | 665 | 735 | 797 | 853 |

## SCHEDULE OF CHILD SUPPORT AWARDS

| | | | | | | |
|---|---|---|---|---|---|---|
| **2,380** | | 393 | 568 | 668 | 738 | 800 | 856 |
| **2,390** | | 394 | 570 | 670 | 740 | 803 | 859 |
| **2,400** | | 396 | 572 | 672 | 743 | 805 | 862 |
| **2,410** | | 397 | 574 | 675 | 746 | 808 | 865 |
| **2,420** | | 398 | 576 | 677 | 748 | 811 | 868 |
| **2,430** | | 400 | 577 | 680 | 751 | 814 | 871 |
| **2,440** | | 401 | 579 | 682 | 753 | 817 | 874 |
| **2,450** | | 402 | 581 | 684 | 756 | 820 | 877 |
| **2,460** | | 403 | 583 | 687 | 759 | 822 | 880 |
| **2,470** | | 405 | 585 | 689 | 761 | 825 | 883 |
| **2,480** | | 406 | 587 | 691 | 764 | 828 | 886 |
| **2,490** | | 407 | 589 | 694 | 766 | 831 | 889 |
| **2,500** | | 409 | 591 | 696 | 769 | 834 | 892 |
| **2,510** | | 410 | 593 | 698 | 772 | 836 | 895 |
| **2,520** | | 411 | 595 | 701 | 774 | 839 | 898 |
| **2,530** | | 413 | 597 | 703 | 777 | 842 | 901 |
| **2,540** | | 414 | 599 | 705 | 779 | 845 | 904 |
| **2,550** | | 415 | 601 | 708 | 782 | 848 | 907 |
| **2,560** | | 417 | 603 | 710 | 785 | 850 | 910 |
| **2,570** | | 418 | 605 | 712 | 787 | 853 | 913 |
| **2,580** | | 419 | 607 | 715 | 790 | 856 | 916 |
| **2,590** | | 420 | 609 | 717 | 792 | 859 | 919 |
| **2,600** | | 422 | 610 | 719 | 795 | 862 | 922 |
| **2,610** | | 423 | 612 | 722 | 798 | 865 | 925 |
| **2,620** | | 424 | 614 | 724 | 800 | 867 | 928 |
| **2,630** | | 426 | 616 | 726 | 803 | 870 | 931 |
| **2,640** | | 427 | 618 | 729 | 805 | 873 | 934 |
| **2,650** | | 428 | 620 | 731 | 807 | 875 | 937 |
| **2,660** | | 429 | 621 | 732 | 809 | 877 | 939 |

**REPRINTED WITH THE PERMISSION OF GANN LAW BOOKS**

## APPENDIX IX-F

| | | | | | | |
|---|---|---|---|---|---|---|
| **2,670** | | 430 | 623 | 734 | 811 | 879 | 941 |
| **2,680** | | 431 | 624 | 735 | 813 | 881 | 943 |
| **2,690** | | 432 | 625 | 737 | 814 | 883 | 945 |
| **2,700** | | 433 | 627 | 739 | 816 | 885 | 947 |
| **2,710** | | 434 | 628 | 740 | 818 | 887 | 949 |
| **2,720** | | 435 | 629 | 742 | 820 | 889 | 951 |
| **2,730** | | 436 | 631 | 743 | 822 | 891 | 953 |
| **2,740** | | 437 | 632 | 745 | 823 | 892 | 955 |
| **2,750** | | 438 | 634 | 747 | 825 | 894 | 957 |
| **2,760** | | 439 | 635 | 748 | 827 | 896 | 959 |
| **2,770** | | 440 | 636 | 750 | 829 | 898 | 961 |
| **2,780** | | 441 | 638 | 751 | 830 | 900 | 963 |
| **2,790** | | 442 | 639 | 753 | 832 | 902 | 965 |
| **2,800** | | 443 | 640 | 755 | 834 | 904 | 967 |
| **2,810** | | 444 | 642 | 756 | 836 | 906 | 969 |
| **2,820** | | 445 | 643 | 758 | 837 | 908 | 971 |
| **2,830** | | 446 | 645 | 759 | 839 | 910 | 973 |
| **2,840** | | 446 | 646 | 761 | 841 | 911 | 975 |
| **2,850** | | 447 | 647 | 763 | 843 | 913 | 977 |
| **2,860** | | 448 | 649 | 764 | 844 | 915 | 979 |
| **2,870** | | 449 | 650 | 766 | 846 | 917 | 981 |
| **2,880** | | 450 | 651 | 767 | 848 | 919 | 983 |
| **2,890** | | 451 | 653 | 769 | 850 | 921 | 985 |
| **2,900** | | 452 | 654 | 771 | 851 | 923 | 988 |

For cases in which the combined net income of the parents is more than $2,900 per week, the child support award at $2,900 represents the minimum basic support award. The court must add a discretionary amount of child support to the minimum basic award based on the factors specified in N.J.S.A. 2A:34-23. See Appendix IX-A, Extreme Income Situations, for additional information.

*DO NOT EXTRAPOLATE THESE SCHEDULES BEYOND $2,900 COMBINED WEEKLY NET INCOME*

# Blank Forms

appendix f

## TABLE OF FORMS

# Matrimonial Case Information Statement
## Appendix V
### FAMILY PART CASE INFORMATION STATEMENT

Attorney(s):
Office Address
Tel. No./Fax No.
Attorney(s) for:

|  | | |
|---|---|---|
| | Plaintiff, | |
| vs. | | |
| | Defendant. | |

SUPERIOR COURT OF NEW JERSEY
CHANCERY DIVISION, FAMILY PART
COUNTY

DOCKET NO.
CASE INFORMATION STATEMENT
OF _____

NOTICE:     This statement must be fully completed, filed and served, with all required attachments, in accordance with Court Rule 5:5-2 based upon the information available. In those cases where the Case Information Statement is required, it shall be filed within 20 days after the filing of the Answer or Appearance. Failure to file a Case Information Statement may result in the dismissal of a party's pleadings.

## PART A - CASE INFORMATION:

Date of Statement_____
Date of Divorce (post-Judgment matters)_____
Date(s) of Prior Statement(s)_____
_____
Your Birthdate_____
Birthdate of Other Party_____
Date of Marriage_____
Date of Separation_____
Date of Complaint_____
Does an agreement exist between parties relative to any issue?     [  ] Yes   [  ] No.    If Yes, ATTACH a copy (if written) or a summary (if oral).

### ISSUES IN DISPUTE:

Cause of Action_____
Custody_____
Parenting Time_____
Alimony_____
Child Support_____
Equitable Distribution_____
Counsel Fees_____
Other issues [be specific]_____
_____

1. Name and Addresses of Parties:
Your Name _____
Street Address _____  City_____  State/Zip_____
Other Party's Name _____
Street Address _____  City_____  State/Zip_____

2. Name, Address, Birthdate and Person with whom children reside:
*a. Child(ren) From This Relationship*

| Child's Full Name | Address | Birthdate | Person's Name |
|---|---|---|---|
| _____ | _____ | _____ | _____ |
| _____ | _____ | _____ | _____ |
| _____ | _____ | _____ | _____ |
| _____ | _____ | _____ | _____ |

*b. Child(ren) From Other Relationships*

| Child's Full Name | Address | Birthdate | Person's Name |
|---|---|---|---|
| _____ | _____ | _____ | _____ |
| _____ | _____ | _____ | _____ |
| _____ | _____ | _____ | _____ |

*Reprinted with the permission of Gann Law Books*

## PART B - MISCELLANEOUS INFORMATION:

1. Information about Employment (Provide Name & Address of Business, if Self-employed)

Name of Employer/Business _____ Address _____

Name of Employer/Business _____ Address _____

2. Do you have Insurance obtained through Employment/Business? [ ] Yes [ ] No. Type of Insurance:
Medical [ ]Yes [ ]No; Dental [ ]Yes [ ]No; Prescription Drug [ ]Yes [ ]No; Life [ ]Yes [ ]No; Disability [ ]Yes [ ]No
Other (explain) _____
Is Insurance available through Employment/Business? [ ] Yes [ ] No Explain:_____
_____

3. ATTACH Affidavit of Insurance Coverage as required by Court Rule *5:4-2* (f) (See Part G)

4. Additional Identification:
Confidential Litigant Information Sheet: Filed [ ]Yes [ ] No

5. ATTACH a list of all prior/pending family actions involving support, custody or Domestic Violence, with the Docket
   Number, County, State and the disposition reached. Attach copies of all existing Orders in effect.

## PART C. - INCOME INFORMATION:      Complete this section for self and (if known) for spouse.

### 1. LAST YEAR'S INCOME

|  | Yours | Joint | Spouse or Former Spouse |
|---|---|---|---|
| 1. Gross earned income last calendar (year) | $_____ | $_____ | $_____ |
| 2. Unearned income (same year) | $_____ | $_____ | $_____ |
| 3. Total Income Taxes paid on income (Fed., State, F.I.C.A., and S.U.I.). If Joint Return, use middle column. | $_____ | $_____ | $_____ |
| 4. Net income (1 + 2-3) | $_____ | $_____ | $_____ |

ATTACH to this form a corporate benefits statement as well as a statement of all fringe benefits of employment. (See Part G)

ATTACH a full and complete copy of last year's Federal and State Income Tax Returns. ATTACH W-2 statements, 1099's,
Schedule C's, etc., to show total income plus a copy of the most recently filed Tax Returns. (See Part G)
Check if attached: Federal Tax Return [ ]      State Tax Return [ ]      W-2 [ ] Other [ ]

### 2. PRESENT EARNED INCOME AND EXPENSES

|  | Yours | Other Party (if known) |
|---|---|---|
| 1. Average gross weekly income (based on last 3 pay periods – ATTACH pay stubs)  Commissions and bonuses, etc., are: [ ] included  [ ] not included*  [ ] not paid to you. | $_____ | $_____ |

*ATTACH details of basis thereof, including, but not limited to, percentage overrides, timing of payments, etc.
  ATTACH copies of last three statements of such bonuses, commissions, etc.

|  | Yours | Other Party |
|---|---|---|
| 2. Deductions per week (check all types of withholdings): [ ] Federal [ ] State [ ] F.I.C.A. [ ] S.U.I. [ ] Other | $_____ | $_____ |
| 3. Net average weekly income (1 - 2) | $_____ | $_____ |

### 3. YOUR CURRENT YEAR-TO-DATE EARNED INCOME
Provide Dates: From _____      To _____

1. GROSS EARNED INCOME: $_____      Number of Weeks_____
2. TAX DEDUCTIONS: (Number of Dependents:      )

Adopted 7/28/04 to be Effective 9/1/04                      2

a. Federal Income Taxes     a. $_____

b. N.J. Income Taxes     b. $_____

c. Other State Income Taxes     c. $_____

d. FICA     d. $_____

e. Medicare     e. $_____

f. S.U.I. / S.D.I.     f. $_____

g. Estimated tax payments in excess of withholding     g. $_____

h.     h. $_____

i.     i. $_____

TOTAL     $_____

3. GROSS INCOME NET OF TAXES   $     $_____

4. OTHER DEDUCTIONS              If mandatory, check box

   a. Hospitalization/Medical Insurance     a. $_____    [ ]

   b. Life Insurance     b. $_____    [ ]

   c. Union Dues     c. $_____    [ ]

   d. 401(k) Plans     d. $_____    [ ]

   e. Pension/Retirement Plans     e. $_____    [ ]

   f. Other Plans—specify     f. $_____    [ ]

   g. Charity     g. $_____    [ ]

   h. Wage Execution     h. $_____    [ ]

   i. Medical Reimbursement (flex fund)     i. $_____    [ ]

   j. Other:     j. $_____    [ ]

TOTAL     $_____

5. NET YEAR-TO-DATE EARNED INCOME:     $_____

NET AVERAGE EARNED INCOME PER MONTH:     $_____

NET AVERAGE EARNED INCOME PER WEEK     $_____

4. YOUR YEAR-TO-DATE GROSS UNEARNED INCOME FROM ALL SOURCES
(including, but not limited to, income from unemployment, disability and/or social
security payments, interest, dividends, rental income and any other miscellaneous
unearned income)

| Source | How often paid | Year to date amount |
|---|---|---|
| _____ | _____ | $_____ |
| _____ | _____ | $_____ |
| _____ | _____ | $_____ |
| _____ | _____ | $_____ |
| _____ | _____ | $_____ |
| _____ | _____ | $_____ |
| _____ | _____ | $_____ |
| _____ | _____ | $_____ |
| _____ | _____ | $_____ |

TOTAL GROSS UNEARNED INCOME YEAR TO DATE     $_____

## 5. ADDITIONAL INFORMATION:

1. How often are you paid? _____

2. What is your annual salary?    $ _____

3. Have you received any raises in the current year? [ ]Yes [ ]No.  If yes, provide the date and the gross/net amount.
_____

4. Do you receive bonuses, commissions, or other compensation, including distributions, taxable or non-taxable, in addition to your regular salary? [ ]Yes [ ]No. If yes, explain:_____
_____

5. Did you receive a bonuses, commissions, or other compensation, including distributions, taxable or non-taxable, in addition to your regular salary during the current or immediate past calendar year? [ ] Yes [ ] No If yes, explain and state the date(s) of receipt and set forth the gross and net amounts received: _____
_____

6. Do you receive cash or distributions not otherwise listed? [ ] Yes [ ] No If yes, explain. _____
_____

7. Have you received income from overtime work during either the current or immediate past calendar year? [ ]Yes [ ]No  If yes, explain. _____

8. Have you been awarded or granted stock options, restricted stock or any other non-cash compensation or entitlement during the current or immediate past calendar year? [ ]Yes  [ ]No  If yes, explain. _____
_____

9. Have you received any other supplemental compensation during either the current or immediate past calendar year? [ ]Yes  [ ]No. If yes, state the date(s) of receipt and set forth the gross and net amounts received. Also describe the nature of any supplemental compensation received._____
_____

10. Have you received income from unemployment, disability and/or social security during either the current or immediate past calendar year? [ ]Yes  [ ]No. If yes, state the date(s) of receipt and set forth the gross and net amounts received._____

11. List the names of the dependents you claim:_____

12. Are you paying or receiving any alimony? [ ]Yes [ ]No. If yes, how much and to whom paid or from whom received?   _____

13. Are you paying or receiving any child support? [ ]Yes [ ]No. If yes, list names of the children, the amount paid or received for each child and to whom paid or from whom received. _____
_____

14. Is there a wage execution in connection with support? [ ]Yes [ ]No If yes explain._____
_____

15. Has a dependent child of yours received income from social security, SSI or other government program during either the current or immediate past calendar year? [ ]Yes [ ]No. If yes, explain the basis and state the date(s) of receipt and set forth the gross and net amounts received _____
_____

16. Explanation of Income or Other Information:

_____
_____
_____
_____
_____
_____
_____
_____

## PART D - MONTHLY EXPENSES (computed at 4.3 wks/mo.)

Joint Marital Life Style should reflect standard of living established during marriage.  Current expenses should reflect the current life style.  Do not repeat those income deductions listed in Part C – 3.

| | Joint Marital Life Style<br>Family, including<br>_____ children | Current Life Style<br>Yours and<br>_____ children |
|---|---|---|
| **SCHEDULE A:  SHELTER** | | |
| *If Tenant:* | | |
| Rent…………………………………………………… | $_____ | $_____ |
| Heat (if not furnished)…………………………………. | $_____ | $_____ |
| Electric & Gas (if not furnished)…………………………. | $_____ | $_____ |
| Renter's Insurance…………………………………….. | $_____ | $_____ |
| Parking (at Apartment)…………………………………. | $_____ | $_____ |
| Other charges (Itemize)………………………………... | $_____ | $_____ |
| | | |
| *If Homeowner:* | | |
| Mortgage ………………………………………….…. | $_____ | $_____ |
| Real Estate Taxes (if not included w/mortgage payment)… | $_____ | $_____ |
| Homeowners Ins  (if not included w/mortgage payment)… | $_____ | $_____ |
| Other Mortgages or Home Equity Loans …………………. | $_____ | $_____ |
| Heat (unless Electric or Gas)………………………….… | $_____ | $_____ |
| Electric & Gas…………………………………………. | $_____ | $_____ |
| Water & Sewer………………………………………… | $_____ | $_____ |
| Garbage Removal……………………………………… | $_____ | $_____ |
| Snow Removal………………………………………… | $_____ | $_____ |
| Lawn Care……………………………………………. | $_____ | $_____ |
| Maintenance…………………………………………… | $_____ | $_____ |
| Repairs………………………………………………. | $_____ | $_____ |
| Other Charges (Itemize)………………………………… | $_____ | $_____ |
| | | |
| *Tenant or Homeowner:* | | |
| Telephone…………………………………………….… | $_____ | $_____ |
| Mobile/Cellular Telephone…………………………….… | $_____ | $_____ |
| Service Contracts on Equipment…………………………. | $_____ | $_____ |
| Cable TV……………………………………………… | $_____ | $_____ |
| Plumber/Electrician…………………………………….. | $_____ | $_____ |
| Equipment & Furnishings……………………………….. | $_____ | $_____ |
| Internet Charges………………………………………. | $_____ | $_____ |
| Other (itemize)……………………………………….… | $_____ | $_____ |
| TOTAL | $_____ | $_____ |
| | | |
| **SCHEDULE B:  TRANSPORTATION** | | |
| Auto Payment…………………………………………... | $_____ | $_____ |
| Auto Insurance (number of vehicles:  )……………………... | $_____ | $_____ |
| Registration, License…………………………………… | $_____ | $_____ |
| Maintenance…………………………………………… | $_____ | $_____ |
| Fuel and Oil…………………………………………… | $_____ | $_____ |
| Commuting Expenses…………………………………… | $_____ | $_____ |
| Other Charges (Itemize)………………………………… | $_____ | $_____ |
| TOTAL | $_____ | $_____ |

| SCHEDULE C: PERSONAL............................................... | Joint Marital Life Style Family, including _____ children | Current Life Style Yours and _____ children |
|---|---|---|
| Food at Home & household supplies............................... | $_____ | $_____ |
| Prescription Drugs.................................................. | $_____ | $_____ |
| Non-prescription drugs, cosmetics, toiletries & sundries...... | $_____ | $_____ |
| School Lunch........................................................ | $_____ | $_____ |
| Restaurants......................................................... | $_____ | $_____ |
| Clothing............................................................. | $_____ | $_____ |
| Dry Cleaning, Commercial Laundry............................. | $_____ | $_____ |
| Hair Care............................................................ | $_____ | $_____ |
| Domestic Help...................................................... | $_____ | $_____ |
| Medical (exclusive of psychiatric)*............................. | $_____ | $_____ |
| Eye Care*........................................................... | $_____ | $_____ |
| Psychiatric/psychological/counseling*.......................... | $_____ | $_____ |
| Dental (exclusive of Orthodontic)*............................. | $_____ | $_____ |
| Orthodontic*........................................................ | $_____ | $_____ |
| Medical Insurance (hospital, etc.)*............................. | $_____ | $_____ |
| Club Dues and Memberships..................................... | $_____ | $_____ |
| Sports and Hobbies................................................ | $_____ | $_____ |
| Camps................................................................ | $_____ | $_____ |
| Vacations............................................................ | $_____ | $_____ |
| Children's Private School Costs................................. | $_____ | $_____ |
| Parent's Educational Costs....................................... | $_____ | $_____ |
| Children's Lessons (dancing, music, sports, etc.).............. | $_____ | $_____ |
| Baby-sitting......................................................... | $_____ | $_____ |
| Day-Care Expenses................................................ | $_____ | $_____ |
| Entertainment...................................................... | $_____ | $_____ |
| Alcohol and Tobacco.............................................. | $_____ | $_____ |
| Newspapers and Periodicals..................................... | $_____ | $_____ |
| Gifts.................................................................. | $_____ | $_____ |
| Contributions....................................................... | $_____ | $_____ |
| Payments to Non-Child Dependents............................ | $_____ | $_____ |
| Prior Existing Support Obligations this family/other families (specify).................................................... | $_____ | $_____ |
| Tax Reserve (not listed elsewhere)............................. | $_____ | $_____ |
| Life Insurance...................................................... | $_____ | $_____ |
| Savings/Investment................................................ | $_____ | $_____ |
| Debt Service (from page 7) (not listed elsewhere)............ | $_____ | $_____ |
| Parenting Time Expenses......................................... | $_____ | $_____ |
| Professional Expenses (other than this proceeding)........... | $_____ | $_____ |
| Other (specify)..................................................... | $_____ | $_____ |

*unreimbursed only..............................................

| | | |
|---|---|---|
| TOTAL | $_____ | $_____ |

Please Note: If you are paying expenses for a spouse and/or children not reflected in this budget, attach a schedule of such payments.

| | | |
|---|---|---|
| Schedule A: Shelter.................................................. | $_____ | $_____ |
| Schedule B: Transportation........................................ | $_____ | $_____ |
| Schedule C: Personal............................................... | $_____ | $_____ |
| Grand Totals.......................................................... | $_____ | $_____ |

## PART E - BALANCE SHEET OF ALL FAMILY ASSETS AND LIABILITIES

### STATEMENT OF ASSETS

| Description | Title to Property (H, W, J) | Date of purchase/acquisition. If claim that asset is exempt, state reason and value of what is claimed to be exempt | Value $ Put * after exempt | Date of Evaluation Mo./Day/ Yr. |
|---|---|---|---|---|

**1. Real Property**

**2. Bank Accounts, CD's**

**3. Vehicles**

**4. Tangible Personal Property**

**5. Stocks and Bonds**

**6. Pension, Profit Sharing, Retirement Plan(s) 401(k)s, etc. [list each employer]**

**7. IRAs**

**8. Businesses, Partnerships, Professional Practices**

**9. Life Insurance (cash surrender value)**

**10. Loans Receivable**

**11. Other (specify)**

TOTAL GROSS ASSETS: $_____

TOTAL SUBJECT TO EQUITABLE DISTRIBUTION: $_____

TOTAL NOT SUBJECT TO EQUITABLE DISTRIBUTION: $_____

## STATEMENT OF LIABILITIES

| Description | Name of Responsible Party (H, W, J) | If you contend liability should not be considered in equitable distribution, state reason | Monthly Payment | Total Owed | Date |
|---|---|---|---|---|---|

**1. Real Estate Mortgages**

| | | | | | |
|---|---|---|---|---|---|
| | | | | | |
| | | | | | |
| | | | | | |

**2. Other Long Term Debts**

| | | | | | |
|---|---|---|---|---|---|
| | | | | | |
| | | | | | |
| | | | | | |

**3. Revolving Charges**

| | | | | | |
|---|---|---|---|---|---|
| | | | | | |
| | | | | | |
| | | | | | |
| | | | | | |
| | | | | | |
| | | | | | |
| | | | | | |
| | | | | | |
| | | | | | |

**4. Other Short Term Debts**

| | | | | | |
|---|---|---|---|---|---|
| | | | | | |
| | | | | | |
| | | | | | |

**5. Contingent Liabilities**

| | | | | | |
|---|---|---|---|---|---|
| | | | | | |
| | | | | | |

TOTAL GROSS LIABILITIES:  $_____
(excluding contingent liabilities)

NET WORTH:                $_____
(subject to equitable distribution)

Adopted 7/28/04 to be Effective 9/1/04

*Reprinted with the permission of Gann Law Books*

## PART F - STATEMENT OF SPECIAL PROBLEMS

Provide a Brief Narrative Statement of Any Special Problems Involving This Case: As example, state if the matter involves complex valuation problems (such as for a closely held business) or special medical problems of any family member etc.

I certify that the foregoing information contained herein is true. I am aware that if any of the foregoing information contained therein is willfully false, I am subject to punishment.

DATED: SIGNED: _____

## PART G - REQUIRED ATTACHMENTS

### CHECK IF YOU HAVE ATTACHED THE FOLLOWING REQUIRED DOCUMENTS

1. A full and complete copy of your last federal and state income tax returns
   with all schedules and attachments. (Part C-1) _____

2. Your last calendar year's W-2 statements, 1099's, K-1 statements. _____

3. Your three most recent pay stubs. _____

4. Bonus information including, but not limited to, percentage overrides, timing of payments, etc.;
   the last three statements of such bonuses, commissions, etc. (Part C) _____

5. Your most recent corporate benefit statement or a summary thereof showing the nature, amount
   and status of retirement plans, savings plans, income deferral plans, insurance benefits, etc. (Part C) _____

6. Affidavit of Insurance Coverage as required by Court Rule 5:4-2(f) (Part B-3) _____

7. List of all prior/pending family actions involving support, custody or Domestic Violence, with the
   Docket Number, County, State and the disposition reached. Attach copies of all existing Orders in
   effect. (Part B-5) _____

8. Attach details of each wage execution (Part C-5)

9. Schedule of payments made for a spouse and/or children not reflected in Part D. _____

10. Any agreements between the parties. _____

11. An Appendix IX Child Support Guideline Worksheet, as applicable, based upon available information. _____

*This page intentionally blank.*

# Property Division Worksheet

| Item of Property | Estimated Value | Husband or Wife | Notes |
|---|---|---|---|
| 1. | | | |
| 2. | | | |
| 3. | | | |
| 4. | | | |
| 5. | | | |
| 6. | | | |
| 7. | | | |
| 8. | | | |
| 9. | | | |
| 10. | | | |
| 11. | | | |
| 12. | | | |
| 13. | | | |
| 14. | | | |
| 15. | | | |
| 16. | | | |
| 17. | | | |
| 18. | | | |
| 19. | | | |
| 20. | | | |

*(Use as many entries as necessary to inventory property to be divided)*

*This page intentionally blank.*

# Debt Division Worksheet

| Creditor | Amount of Debt | Husband or Wife | Notes |
|---|---|---|---|
| 1. | | | |
| 2. | | | |
| 3. | | | |
| 4. | | | |
| 5. | | | |
| 6. | | | |
| 7. | | | |
| 8. | | | |
| 9. | | | |
| 10. | | | |
| 11. | | | |
| 12. | | | |
| 13. | | | |
| 14. | | | |
| 15. | | | |
| 16. | | | |
| 17. | | | |
| 18. | | | |
| 19. | | | |
| 20. | | | |

*(Use as many entries as necessary to inventory debts to be divided)*

*This page intentionally blank.*

## Verified Complaint for Divorce (Separation)

|  |  |
|---|---|
| Plaintiff, | NEW JERSEY SUPERIOR COURT |
|  | CHANCERY DIVISION |
|  | FAMILY PART |
|  | _____ COUNTY |
| v. | Docket No. |
|  | CIVIL ACTION |
| Defendant | VERIFIED COMPLAINT FOR DIVORCE |

Plaintiff, _____, residing at _____
in the _____ of _____, County of _____, and State
of New Jersey, by way of complaint against Defendant says:

    1.    He/She was lawfully married to _____, Defendant herein,
on or about the _____ day of _____, _____, in a _____ ceremony.

    2.    Plaintiff was a bona fide resident of the state of New Jersey when this cause of action
arose, and has ever since and for more than one year next preceding the commencement of this
action, continued to be such bona fide resident.

    3.    Defendant resides at _____, in the _____
of _____, County of _____, and State of New Jersey.

    4.    Defendant and Plaintiff separated in or about the month of _____,
and have lived separate and apart since that time.

    5.    _____ children were born of the marriage, to wit; _____, age _____,
_____, age _____, _____, age _____, _____,
age _____, and _____, age _____, all of whom are presently in the custody of
Plaintiff.

    6.    There have been no previous proceedings between Plaintiff and Defendant respecting the marriage or its dissolution or respecting maintenance of Plaintiff in any court.

WHEREFORE, Plaintiff demands judgment:

    A.    Dissolving the marriage between the parties;

    B.    Awarding Plaintiff custody of the minor children born of the marriage;

    C.    Compelling the Defendant to support Plaintiff and said minor children;

D.      Equally distributing all property, both real and personal, owned or acquired by the parties during the course of the marriage;

E.      For counsel fees and costs;

F.      Allowing Plaintiff/Defendant to resume use of her maiden name;

G.      For such relief as the Court may deem equitable and just.

Dated: _____


_____, Plaintiff

## R. 4:5-1 CERTIFICATION

1.      I am the Plaintiff in this matter.  In that capacity, I am fully familiar with the facts of this case.

2.      To the best of my knowledge, information, and belief, I am not aware of any other action or arbitration proceeding pending or contemplated concerning the subject matter of this Complaint in any court, nor am I aware of any other persons who should be joined in this matter.

I certify that the foregoing statements made by me are true.  I am aware that if any of the foregoing statements made by me are willfully false, I am subject to punishment.

Dated: _____


_____, Plaintiff

## CERTIFICATION OF NON-COLLUSION

_____ hereby certifies as follows:

1.      I am the Plaintiff in the foregoing Complaint for Divorce.  The allegations of the Complaint are true to the best of my knowledge, information, and belief; and the Complaint is made in good faith, and without collusion, for the causes set forth in it.

I certify that the foregoing statements made by me are true.  I am aware that if any of the foregoing statements made by me are willfully false, I am subject to punishment.

Dated: _____


_____, Plaintiff

### Verified Complaint for Divorce (Extreme Cruelty)

|  |  |
|---|---|
| Plaintiff, | NEW JERSEY SUPERIOR COURT<br>CHANCERY DIVISION<br>FAMILY PART<br>_____ COUNTY |
| v. | Docket No.<br>CIVIL ACTION |
| Defendant | VERIFIED COMPLAINT FOR DIVORCE |

Plaintiff, _____, residing at _____ in the _____ of _____, County of _____, and State of New Jersey, by way of complaint against Defendant says:

1.    He/She was lawfully married to _____, Defendant herein, on or about the _____ day of _____, _____, in a _____ ceremony.

2.    Plaintiff was a bona fide resident of the state of New Jersey when this cause of action arose, and has ever since and for more than one year next preceding the commencement of this action, continued to be such bona fide resident.

3.    Defendant resides at _____, in the _____ of _____, County of _____, and State of New Jersey.

4.    Defendant has been guilty of extreme cruelty toward Plaintiff, beginning on or about _____, _____, and continuing to date.

5.    Plaintiff sets forth the particular acts of extreme cruelty committed by Defendant as follows:

(a)

(b)

(c)

(d)

6.    The above-described acts of extreme cruelty have made it improper and unreasonable to expect the Plaintiff to continue to live in matrimony with the Defendant.

7.    More than three months have passed since the occurrence of the last act of extreme cruelty complained of and forming the basis for the Plaintiff's cause of action. The acts of extreme cruelty committed by Defendant within a period of three months prior to the filing of the within Complaint, as set forth herein, are alleged not as comprising the entire basis for Plaintiff's cause of action, but as relating back to describe, confirm and, as necessary, qualify those acts which constitute said cause of action.

8.    Defendant vacated the marital premises on or about _____, _____.

9.    _____ children were born of the marriage, to wit; _____, age _____, and _____, age _____ , all of whom are presently in the custody of Plaintiff.

10. There have been no previous proceedings between the Plaintiff and the Defendant respecting the marriage or its dissolution or respecting maintenance of the Plaintiff in any court.

WHEREFORE, Plaintiff demands judgment:

A. Dissolving the marriage between the parties;

B. Awarding Plaintiff custody of the minor children born of the marriage;

C. Compelling the Defendant to support Plaintiff and said minor children;

D. Equally distributing all property, both real and personal, owned or acquired by the parties during the course of the marriage;

E. For counsel fees and costs;

F. Allowing Plaintiff/Defendant to resume use of her maiden name;

G. For such relief as the Court may deem equitable and just.

Dated: _____

_____, Plaintiff

### R. 4:5-1 CERTIFICATION

1. I am the Plaintiff in this matter. In that capacity, I am fully familiar with the facts of this case.

2. To the best of my knowledge, information, and belief, I am not aware of any other action or arbitration proceeding pending or contemplated concerning the subject matter of this Complaint in any court, nor am I aware of any other persons who should be joined in this matter.

I certify that the foregoing statements made by me are true. I am aware that if any of the foregoing statements made by me are willfully false, I am subject to punishment.

Dated: _____

_____, Plaintiff

### CERTIFICATION OF NON-COLLUSION

hereby certifies as follows:

_____ hereby certifies as follows:

1. I am the Plaintiff in the foregoing Complaint for Divorce. The allegations of the Complaint are true to the best of my knowledge, information, and belief; and the Complaint is made in good faith, and without collusion, for the causes set forth in it.

I certify that the foregoing statements made by me are true. I am aware that if any of the foregoing statements made by me are willfully false, I am subject to punishment.

Dated: _____

_____, Plaintiff

## Certification of Insurance Coverage

|  | NEW JERSEY SUPERIOR COURT |
| :-- | :-- |
|  | CHANCERY DIVISION |
| Plaintiff, | FAMILY PART |
|  | _____ COUNTY |
| v. | Docket No. |
|  | CIVIL ACTION |
| Defendant | CERTIFICATION OF INSURANCE |
|  | COVERAGE |

_____ hereby certifies as follows:

    1.    I am the Plaintiff in the captioned matter. I am fully familiar with the facts stated herein.

    2.    At present, the following insurance policies are in existence regarding Defendant, Plaintiff and the child of the marriage:

(a) Insurance carrier:

Policy number:

Named insured(s):

Person(s) covered by the policy:

Description of the coverage and term of the policy:

If Life Insurance, named beneficiaries:


(b) Insurance carrier:

Policy Number:

Named insured(s):

Person(s) covered by the policy:

Description of coverage and term of the policy:

If Life Insurance, named beneficiaries:

(c)  Insurance carrier:

Policy Number:

Named insured(s):

Persons covered by the policy:

Description of coverage and term of the policy:

If Life Insurance, named beneficiaries:


3.      To the best of my knowledge, information, and belief, there have been no policies of insurance which have been canceled or modified within the past 90 days. (NOTE: If policies have been canceled or modified, add "except as follows" and list these policies.)




I hereby certify that the foregoing statements made by me are true.  I am aware that if the foregoing statements made by me are willfully false, I am subject to punishment.

Dated: _____

_____, Plaintiff

## Sample Letter For Filing Complaint, Other Pleadings

[Date]

Clerk

_____ County Superior Court

Chancery Division

[Address]

Re: _____ v. _____

Dear Sir or Madam:

You will find enclosed and original and two copies of Complaint, Case Information Statement, and Certificate of Insurance Coverage in the referenced Family Part matter. Please file the enclosed materials and return a copy marked "filed" to me in the stamped, self-addressed envelope which is enclosed for your convenience. My check in the amount of $250 is enclosed.

Thank you.

Very truly yours,

_____

Enc.

*This page intentionally blank.*

# CIVIL CASE INFORMATION STATEMENT

## (CIS)

Use for initial Law Division – Civil Part pleadings (not motions) under Rule 4:5-1.

**Pleading will be rejected for filing, under Rule 1:5-6(c), if information above the black bar is not completed or if attorney's signature is not affixed.**

| FOR USE BY CLERK'S OFFICE ONLY |
| --- |
| PAYMENT TYPE:    CK    CG    CA |
| CHG/CK NO. |
| AMOUNT: |
| OVERPAYMENT: |
| BATCH NUMBER: |

| ATTORNEY/PRO SE NAME | TELEPHONE NUMBER (    ) | COUNTY OF VENUE |
| --- | --- | --- |
| FIRM NAME (If applicable) | | DOCKET NUMBER (When available) |
| OFFICE ADDRESS | | DOCUMENT TYPE |
| | | JURY DEMAND  ☐ YES  ☐ NO |

| NAME OF PARTY (e.g., John Doe, Plaintiff) | CAPTION |
| --- | --- |
| | |

| CASE TYPE NUMBER (See reverse side for listing) | IS THIS A PROFESSIONAL MALPRACTICE CASE?  ☐ YES  ☐ NO  IF YOU HAVE CHECKED "YES," SEE N.J.S.A. 2A:53A-27 AND APPLICABLE CASE LAW REGARDING YOUR OBLIGATION TO FILE AN AFFIDAVIT OF MERIT. |
| --- | --- |

| RELATED CASES PENDING?  ☐ YES ☐ NO | IF YES, LIST DOCKET NUMBERS |
| --- | --- |

| DO YOU ANTICIPATE ADDING ANY PARTIES (arising out of same transaction or occurrence)?  ☐ YES ☐ NO | NAME OF DEFENDANT'S PRIMARY INSURANCE COMPANY, IF KNOWN  ☐ NONE  ☐ UNKNOWN |
| --- | --- |

## THE INFORMATION PROVIDED ON THIS FORM CANNOT BE INTRODUCED INTO EVIDENCE.

CASE CHARACTERISTICS FOR PURPOSES OF DETERMINING IF CASE IS APPROPRIATE FOR MEDIATION

| A.  DO PARTIES HAVE A CURRENT, PAST OR RECURRENT RELATIONSHIP?  ☐ YES ☐ NO | IF YES, IS THAT RELATIONSHIP | ☐ EMPLOYER-EMPLOYEE  ☐ FRIEND/NEIGHBOR  ☐ OTHER (explain) _____  ☐ FAMILIAL  ☐ BUSINESS  _____ |
| --- | --- | --- |

B.  DOES THE STATUTE GOVERNING THIS CASE PROVIDE FOR PAYMENT OF FEES BY THE LOSING PARTY?  ☐ YES  ☐ NO

USE THIS SPACE TO ALERT THE COURT TO ANY SPECIAL CASE CHARACTERISTICS THAT MAY WARRANT INDIVIDUAL MANAGEMENT OR ACCELERATED DISPOSITION:

| ♿ | DO YOU OR YOUR CLIENT NEED ANY DISABILITY ACCOMMODATIONS?  ☐ YES  ☐ NO | IF YES, PLEASE IDENTIFY THE REQUESTED ACCOMMODATION: _____ |
| --- | --- | --- |

WILL AN INTERPRETER BE NEEDED?  ☐ YES  ☐ NO    IF YES, FOR WHAT LANGUAGE: _____

ATTORNEY SIGNATURE

Revised effective 4/1/05

**SIDE 2**

# CIVIL CASE INFORMATION STATEMENT
## (CIS)
Use for initial pleadings (not motions) under *Rule* 4:5-1

**CASE TYPES** (Choose one and enter number of case type in appropriate space on the reverse side.)

### Track I — 150 days' discovery
| | |
|---|---|
| 151 | NAME CHANGE |
| 175 | FORFEITURE |
| 302 | TENANCY |
| 399 | REAL PROPERTY (other than Tenancy, Contract, Condemnation, Complex Commercial or Construction) |
| 502 | BOOK ACCOUNT |
| 505 | OTHER INSURANCE CLAIM (INCLUDING DECLARATORY JUDGMENT ACTIONS) |
| 506 | PIP COVERAGE |
| 510 | UM or UIM CLAIM |
| 511 | ACTION ON NEGOTIABLE INSTRUMENT |
| 512 | LEMON LAW |
| 599 | CONTRACT/COMMERCIAL TRANSACTION |
| 801 | SUMMARY ACTION |
| 802 | OPEN PUBLIC RECORDS ACT (SUMMARY ACTION) |

### Track II — 300 days' discovery
| | |
|---|---|
| 305 | CONSTRUCTION |
| 509 | EMPLOYMENT (other than CEPA or LAD) |
| 602 | ASSAULT AND BATTERY |
| 603 | AUTO NEGLIGENCE – PERSONAL INJURY |
| 605 | PERSONAL INJURY |
| 610 | AUTO NEGLIGENCE – PROPERTY DAMAGE |
| 699 | TORT – OTHER |

### Track III — 450 days' discovery
| | |
|---|---|
| 005 | CIVIL RIGHTS |
| 301 | CONDEMNATION |
| 604 | MEDICAL MALPRACTICE |
| 606 | PRODUCT LIABILITY |
| 607 | PROFESSIONAL MALPRACTICE |
| 608 | TOXIC TORT |
| 609 | DEFAMATION |
| 616 | WHISTLEBLOWER / CONSCIENTIOUS EMPLOYEE PROTECTION ACT (CEPA) CASES |
| 617 | INVERSE CONDEMNATION |
| 618 | LAW AGAINST DISCRIMINATION (LAD) CASES |

### Track IV — Active Case Management by Individual Judge / 450 days' discovery
| | |
|---|---|
| 156 | ENVIRONMENTAL/ENVIRONMENTAL COVERAGE LITIGATION |
| 303 | MT. LAUREL |
| 508 | COMPLEX COMMERCIAL |
| 701 | ACTIONS IN LIEU OF PREROGATIVE WRITS |

#### Mass Tort (Track IV)
| | | | |
|---|---|---|---|
| 240 | REDUX/PHEN-FEN (formerly "DIET DRUG") | 601 | ASBESTOS |
| 248 | CIBA GEIGY | 619 | VIOXX |
| 264 | PPA | | |

999 OTHER (Briefly describe nature of action) _____

_____

**If you believe this case requires a track other than that provided above, please indicate the reason on Side 1, in the space under "Case Characteristics."**

Please check off each applicable category:

☐ Verbal Threshold    ☐ Putative Class Action    ☐ Title 59

**Summons**

NEW JERSEY SUPERIOR COURT
CHANCERY DIVISION
Plaintiff,                      FAMILY PART
_____ COUNTY

v.                              Docket No.
                                CIVIL ACTION
Defendant                       SUMMONS

TO: _____

### THE STATE OF NEW JERSEY, TO THE ABOVE NAMED DEFENDANT:

The Plaintiff, named above, has filed a lawsuit against you in the Superior Court of New Jersey. The Complaint attached to this Summons states the basis for this lawsuit. If you dispute this Complaint, you or your attorney must file a written answer or motion and proof of service with the deputy clerk of the Superior Court in the county listed above within 35 days from the date you received this Summons, not counting the date you received it. (The address of each deputy clerk of the Superior Court is provided). If the Complaint is one in foreclosure, you must file a written answer or motion and proof of service with the Clerk of the Superior Court, [Address]. A filing fee* payable to the Clerk of the Superior Court and a completed Case Information Statement must accompany your answer or motion when it is filed. You must also send a copy of your answer or motion to Plaintiff's attorney whose name and address appear above, or to Plaintiff, if no attorney is named above. A telephone call will not protect your rights; you must file and serve a written answer or motion (with fee and completed Case Information Statement) if you want the court to hear your defense.

If you do not file and serve a written answer or motion within 35 days, the court may enter a judgment against you for the relief Plaintiff demands, plus interest and costs of suit. If judgment is entered against you, the Sheriff may seize your money, wages or property to pay all or part of the judgment.

If you cannot afford an attorney, you may call the Legal Services office in the county where you live. A list of these offices is provided. If you do not have an attorney and are not eligible for free legal assistance, you may obtain a referral to an attorney by calling one of the Lawyer Referral Services. A list of these numbers is also provided.

Dated: _____

_____
[signature]
Clerk of the Superior Court

Name of Defendant to be served:_____

Address for service:_____

*$135 for Chancery Division and Law Division cases

*This page intentionally blank.*

**Appearance (Uncontested case)**

|  |  |
|---|---|
| Plaintiff, | NEW JERSEY SUPERIOR COURT<br>CHANCERY DIVISION<br>FAMILY PART<br>_____ COUNTY |
| v. | Docket No. |
| Defendant | CIVIL ACTION APPEARANCE |

Defendant, _____ (Defendant), residing at _____
_____ hereby enters Defendant's appearance in the captioned
matter to be heard solely on questions of custody, visitation, support, alimony, property division,
debt division, counsel fees, costs, and such other matters as the court may deem appropriate.

Dated: _____

_____, Defendant

CERTIFICATION OF SERVICE

I hereby certify that this Appearance was served on Plaintiff at Plaintiff's last known address,
_____, within the time permitted by R. 4:6-1.

Dated: _____

_____, Defendant

*This page intentionally blank.*

## Property Settlement Agreement

THIS IS AN AGREEMENT by and between _____ of _____,
_____, _____, County, New Jersey (Husband), and _____ of
_____, _____, _____, County, New Jersey (Wife).

## BACKGROUND

WHEREAS, Husband and Wife were married on _____ at _____; and

WHEREAS, there has been child(ren) of the marriage, _____, born
_____, (Child(ren)); and

WHEREAS, the parties desire to amicably settle and determine all matters relating to their respective
property interests arising out of the marriage relationship, the custody of the Child(ren), and the obligations of the parties toward the support and maintenance of the Child(ren); and

WHEREAS, the parties to this Agreement hereby mutually rescind all prior agreements of a similar
nature and declare this to be the sole agreement pertaining to the matters agreed upon herein; and

WHEREAS, Husband and Wife respectively acknowledge that before signing this Agreement each had
the opportunity to obtain the advice of his or her own counsel, independently selected, as to their
rights and obligations, [state what each party did regarding counsel such as: Husband having chosen
not to retain an attorney, although advised to do so, and Wife having been represented by
_____], and each being free from any duress or influence on the part of
the other; and

WHEREAS, there have been no previous proceedings between the parties in any court pertaining to the
marriage relationship, the dissolution of it, and the maintenance of the Husband, Wife, and Child; and

WHEREAS, the parties have carefully read and understood the terms of this Agreement and have
freely consented hereto, believing this Agreement to be fair, just, and reasonable.

NOW, THEREFORE, on this _____ day of _____, _____, in consideration of these
mutual promises, and intending to be legally bound hereby, the parties covenant and agree as follows:

## ARTICLE I.
## GENERAL

1.1 Parties Separate and Apart. The parties shall hereafter be free to live separate and apart from each
other without any form of restraint or control by the other fully as if he or she were unmarried. Neither
shall disturb, trouble, nor interfere in any way with the other or with any person associating with the
other. The parties shall not molest each other or endeavor to compel the other to cohabit with him or her.

1.2 Further Documents. Husband and Wife agree to execute all documents necessary to the furtherance and completion of the terms of this Agreement, at any time and from time to time hereafter.

1.3 Situs. This Agreement shall be interpreted under the laws of the State of New Jersey and shall comprise the entire understanding between the parties.

1.4 Survivorship. This Agreement shall inure to the benefit of and shall be binding upon the parties hereto, their heirs, executors, administrators, successors, and assigns. All obligations of the Husband and Wife under this agreement shall survive the death of the Parties and shall be binding and constitute a charge upon their estates.

1.5 Change of Residence. Throughout the life of this Agreement, each party shall keep the other informed of his or her residence and telephone number or such other place as he or she may readily receive communications, informing the other of any change of such residence or place of communication within seven days of the actual change thereof.

1.6 General Release. Except as otherwise provided herein, Husband and Wife hereby each release and forever discharge the other of and from all actions, causes of action, claims, rights, liabilities, or demands whatsoever in law or in equity, which either party ever had or now has, or may hereafter have against the other, arising out of or in connection with any matter or thing whatsoever up to the date of this Agreement, it being the intention of the parties that henceforth there shall be as between them only such rights and obligations as are specifically provided in this Agreement.

## ARTICLE II.
## CHILD

2.1 Custody and Visitation. Husband and Wife shall have joint custody of the Child(ren), with primary physical custody of the Child(ren) remaining with the Wife.

2.2 Liberal Visitation Schedule. A reasonable and liberal visitation schedule shall be worked out with the Husband. Both parties will cooperate with each other in effectuating the rights of each other to custody and visitation with the Child(ren), and the dates and times of visitation shall be agree upon by the parties after reference to school schedules, the needs of the Child(ren), and reasonable notice of such visitation on the part of the Husband.

2.3 Welfare of the Child(ren). Both parties shall conduct themselves in a manner consistent with the best interests of the Child(ren), and neither party shall do anything to diminish the natural affection that exists between each of them and the Child(ren). Each party agrees to communicate freely and openly with the other party concerning the health, education, and welfare of the Child(ren).

2.4 Geographical Limitations. In the event that the Wife wishes to relocate from the State of New Jersey, Wife shall cooperate fully with Husband to preserve Husband's rights of custody and visitation with the Child(ren).

2.5 Rights of Child(ren). Nothing contained herein shall limit the right of the Wife or Husband on behalf of the Child(ren) to pursue any remedy against the Husband or Wife or his or her estate with respect to any provision contained in this Agreement for the benefit of said Child(ren).

## ARTICLE III.
## CHILD SUPPORT

3.1 Support for Child. The Husband shall pay to the Wife as and for child support in the amount of $_____ per week due and payable by the first of each month commencing on _____, payable through the Probation Department of _____ County. These payments shall continue until the Child(ren) reach emancipation, which shall include graduation from college.

3.2 Cost of Medical and Dental Insurance and Noncovered Medical and Dental Expenses. Husband shall provide medical and dental coverage, both as to the insurance and as to reimbursed expenses for the unemancipated Child.

## ARTICLE IV.
## EQUITABLE DISTRIBUTION OF PROPERTY

4.1 Division of Property. The Husband and Wife agree to divide the real and personal property of the marriage as follows:

(a) Real Property.

(1) Husband and Wife now own the marital residence located at _____ _____ (Property). The _____ is hereby granted the exclusive right to use and occupy the Property without any interference from the _____. _____ agrees to pay the mortgage payments of principal and interest.

(2) The cost of any required municipal improvements which may be assessed against the premises, together with the real estate taxes and the homeowners insurance as required by the mortgage, shall be paid by the _____.

(3) The _____ shall pay all of the utility bills, including gas, electric, telephone, water, and sewer. _____ agrees to pay any and all repair bills with respect to the premises.

(4) In the event either the Husband or the Wife dies while this Agreement is in full force and effect, the survivor shall have the first right of refusal to purchase the interest of the decedent with respect to the Property, and the same will be paid for at the appraised or fair market value. It is understood that the interest of the decedent with respect to the Property shall pass under the intestate laws in the event of no Will, or in accordance with any Will of the decedent.

(b) Personal Property. Each of the parties hereto waives and relinquishes any right they may have to claim any interest in and to the furniture, appliances, and miscellaneous personal property now in the possession of the other, and this Agreement shall constitute a good and sufficient bill of sale each to the other with respect thereto. A more specific inventory of personal property being retained by the parties is attached hereto and made a part hereof.

(c) Pensions. Each of the parties hereto, by the execution of this Agreement waive and relinquish any and all claims which either could raise in and to the pension account of the other at any time.

(d) Bank Accounts.

(1) Husband and Wife hereby waive any and all interest they may have in any bank accounts retained by Wife or Husband, respectively, at the time of the separation of the parties.

(2) The joint savings account maintained by the parties at _____ Bank shall be closed and the funds contained therein distributed to the Wife.

(3) The joint checking account maintained by the parties at _____ Bank has been closed, with the funds therein being retained by the Husband and applied towards the payment of joint obligations of the Husband and Wife.

(e) Vehicles. Husband and Wife previously divided the vehicles to their mutual satisfaction.

(f) Life Insurance. Husband and Wife shall maintain the life insurance policies currently in existence on their respective lives, maintaining the current benefit level and paying the periodic premiums therefor. It is agreed by the parties that these policies shall name the child(ren) or a trustee for the benefit of the children as beneficiary, and shall be maintained until the youngest child has attained the age of twenty-five (25) years.

(g) Liabilities and Obligations.

(1) _____ agrees to assume and be responsible for the following obligations and to further indemnify and hold _____ harmless thereon:

(i) The mortgage against the marital residence located at the Property, having a current outstanding balance of approximately _____.

(ii) A line of credit from _____ Bank encumbering the marital residence located at the Property and having a current outstanding balance of approximately _____.

(2) Wife agrees to assume and be responsible for the following obligations and to further indemnify and hold Husband harmless thereon:

(i) An obligation to _____ Card bearing account number _____ and having an approximate outstanding balance of _____.

(ii) An obligation to _____ Card bearing account number _____ and having an approximate outstanding balance of _____.

4.2 Equitable Distribution of Property Acquired During Marriage. It is specifically understood and agreed that this Agreement constitutes an equitable distribution of property, both real and personal, which was largely and beneficially acquired by Husband and Wife or either of them during the marriage, as contemplated by Chapter 212, Laws of 1971, and any amendments thereto, of the State of New Jersey.

## ARTICLE V.
## ALIMONY AND EXPENSES

5.1 Release of Alimony and Expenses. Each of the parties hereto releases the other from subsequent claims for alimony, alimony pendente lite, or spousal support, except as follows:

## ARTICLE VI.
## MODIFICATION

6.1 Modification to be in Writing. No modification or waiver of any of the terms hereof shall be valid unless in writing and signed by both parties and no waiver of any breach hereof or default hereunder shall be deemed a waiver of any subsequent default of the same or similar nature.

## ARTICLE VII.
## MISCELLANEOUS PROVISIONS

7.1 Financial Disclosure. The parties confirm that each has relied on the substantial accuracy of the financial disclosure of the other as an inducement of the execution of this Agreement. The parties further agree that each has made full, complete, and accurate disclosure of assets, debts, and other information relevant to the negotiation and adjudication of alt aspects of the divorce action. The parties further agree that if specific values of property are not set forth in this Agreement, that each is personally aware of the value of all items and that each waives any requirement for written memorandum of value.

7.2 Integration. This Agreement constitutes the entire understanding of the parties and supersedes any and all prior agreement and negotiations between them. There are no representations or warranties other than those expressly set forth herein.

7.3 Severability. If any term, condition, clause, or provision of this Agreement shall be determined or declared to be void or invalid in law or otherwise, then only that term, condition, clause, or provision shall be stricken from this Agreement and in all other respects this Agreement shall be valid and continue in full force, effect, and operation. Likewise, the failure of any party to meet his or her obligations under any one or more of the paragraphs herein, with the exception of the satisfaction of the conditions precedent, shall in no way avoid or alter the remaining obligations of the parties.

7.4 Tax Consequences. The Husband and Wife acknowledge that they have been advised that there may be tax consequences relating to this Agreement. Each of the parties was advised to obtain independent tax advice from tax professionals or tax counsel before executing this Agreement. Husband did not seek the advice of an attorney or tax professional with respect to tax consequences, and Wife's attorney rendered no advice with respect to tax consequences.

7.5 Claim for Child(ren) as Dependent on Tax Return(s). Husband and Wife agree that Husband may claim the Child(ren) as a dependent for the tax year. Thereafter, Husband and Wife shall claim the Child(ren) as a dependent in alternating years.

7.6 After-Acquired Personal Property. Each of the parties shall hereafter own and enjoy, independently of any claim or right of the other, all items of personal property, tangible or intangible, hereafter acquired by him or her, with full power in him or her to dispose of the same as fully and effectively, in all respects and for all purposes, as though he or she were unmarried.

7.7 Warranty As to Existing Obligations. Husband and Wife represent that they have not heretofore incurred or contracted for any debt or liability or obligation for which the estate of the other party may be responsible or liable except as may be provided for in this Agreement. Each party agrees to indemnify or hold the other party harmless from and against any and all such debts, liabilities, or obligations of every kind which may have heretofore been incurred by them, including those for necessities, except for the obligations arising out of this Agreement.

7.8 Strict Performance. Failure on the part of either party to insist upon the strict performance of any of the provisions of this Agreement shall in no way constitute a waiver of any subsequent default of same or similar nature.

7.9 Attorney's Fees for Enforcement. In the event that either party breaches any provision of this Agreement, and the other party retains counsel to assist in enforcing the terms thereof, the parties hereby agree that the breaching party will pay all attorney's fees, court costs, and expenses incurred by the other party in enforcing the Agreement.

SIGNED, SEALED, AND DELIVERED
IN THE PRESENCE OF:

_____        _____
Witness                                                              , Wife

Date: _____

_____        _____
Witness                                                              , Husband

Date: _____

STATE OF NEW JERSEY            :
                                              :
COUNTY OF                              :

BE IT REMEMBERED, that on this _____ day of _____, _____, before me, the subscriber, a Notary Public of the State of New Jersey, personally appeared _____ who, I am satisfied, is the person named in the within Agreement, and thereupon she acknowledged that she signed, sealed, and delivered the same as her act and deed for the uses and purposes therein expressed.

_____
Notary Public of New Jersey

STATE OF NEW JERSEY            :
                                              :
COUNTY OF                              :

BE IT REMEMBERED, that on this _____ day of _____, _____, before me, the subscriber, a Notary Public of the State of New Jersey, personally appeared _____ who, I am satisfied, is the person named in the within Agreement, and thereupon acknowledged that he signed, sealed, and delivered the same as his act and deed for the uses and purposes therein expressed.

_____
Notary Public of New Jersey

*This page intentionally blank.*

**Certification of Service**

|                        |                                    |
|------------------------|------------------------------------|
|                        | NEW JERSEY SUPERIOR COURT          |
|                        | CHANCERY DIVISION                  |
| Plaintiff,             | FAMILY PART                        |
|                        | _____ COUNTY     |
| v.                     | Docket No.                         |
|                        |                                    |
| Defendant              | CIVIL ACTION                       |
|                        | CERTIFICATION OF SERVICE           |

_____ hereby certifies as follows:

1.    I am the Plaintiff in this matter.

2.    I hereby certify that the original and one copy of the a Notice of Motion, together with supporting papers and form of Order were forwarded this date to the Civil Motions Clerk, New Jersey Superior Court, Chancery Division, Family Part, _____, _____, New Jersey _____ via _____.

3.    I further certify that the copies of the within papers were forwarded this date to defense counsel, _____ Esq., _____ via Certified U.S. Mail, Return Receipt Requested. I certify that the foregoing statements made by me are true. I certify that if the foregoing statements made by me are willfully false, I am subject to punishment.

Dated: _____

_____, Plaintiff

*This page intentionally blank.*

**Sample Notice of Motion**
**(Delinquent Pendente Lite Child Support)**

|  |  |
|---|---|
| Plaintiff, | NEW JERSEY SUPERIOR COURT<br>CHANCERY DIVISION<br>FAMILY PART<br>_____ COUNTY |
| v. | Docket No.<br>CIVIL ACTION |
| Defendant | NOTICE OF MOTION |

To:

Attorney for Defendant

NOTICE: IF YOU WISH TO RESPOND TO THIS MOTION, YOU MUST DO SO IN WRITING. Your written response must be in the form of a certification or affidavit. That means that the person signing it swears to the truth of the statements in the certification or affidavit and is aware that the court can punish him or her if the statements are knowingly false. You may ask for oral argument, which means you can ask to appear before the court to explain your position. If the court grants oral argument, you will be notified of the time, date and place. Your response, if any, must be in writing even if you request oral argument. Any papers you send to the court must also be sent to the opposing party's attorney, or the opposing party if they are not represented by an attorney.

PLEASE TAKE NOTICE that on ___day, _____, at _____ (a.m./p.m.), or as soon thereafter as the parties can be heard, the undersigned Plaintiff, shall make application to the above named Court at the _____ County Courthouse, _____ New Jersey _____ for an Order compelling Defendant's immediate payment of delinquent pendente lite child support to the Plaintiff during the pendency of this matter. Plaintiff shall rely on the attached certification in support of this Motion. A proposed form of Order is likewise annexed hereto. Oral argument is requested.

Dated: _____

_____, Plaintiff

## CERTIFICATION OF FILING AND SERVICE

I hereby certify that the original and one copy of the foregoing Notice of Motion, together with supporting papers and form of Order were forwarded this date to the Civil Motions Clerk, New Jersey Superior Court, Chancery Division, Family Part, _____ County Courthouse, _____, _____, New Jersey _____ via hand delivery.

I further certify that the copies of the within papers were forwarded this date to defense counsel, _____, Esq., _____ via Certified U.S. Mail, Return Receipt Requested.

Dated: _____

_____, Plaintiff

**Sample Certification in Support of Motion**

|                        |                                              |
|------------------------|----------------------------------------------|
|                        | NEW JERSEY SUPERIOR COURT                    |
|                        | CHANCERY DIVISION                            |
| Plaintiff,             | FAMILY PART                                   |
|                        | _____ COUNTY           |
| v.                     | Docket No.                                   |
|                        | CIVIL ACTION                                 |
| Defendant              | CERTIFICATION OF PLAINTIFF                    |
|                        | _____, IN SUPPORT              |
|                        | OF MOTION TO COMPEL PAYMENT                  |
|                        | OF PENDENTE LITE CHILD SUPPORT               |

_____ hereby certifies as follows:

    1. I am the Plaintiff in the captioned matter. I am fully familiar with the facts stated herein.

    2. I submit this Certification in support of my Motion to compel Defendant's immediate payment of delinquent pendente lite child support to me on behalf of _____, the child of our marriage, during the pendency of this matter.

    3. I filed a Complaint for divorce on _____ and have filed my Case Information Statement, a copy of which is attached hereto as Exhibit "A." Defendant, _____, and I are presently living separate and apart. No trial, hearing, or Early Settlement Panel dates have yet been scheduled by the Court.

    4. Since I filed for divorce, Defendant has refused to make any payments toward the support of our child, who is in my custody at the marital residence, located at _____ _____. Defendant gives no reason for this refusal. At present, Defendant is providing only limited parenting time to our child.

    5. As the Case Information Statement indicates, I earn $ _____ on a weekly basis. Defendant earns $ _____. Under the R.5:6A Child Support Guidelines, I have calculated that I am entitled to $ _____ in weekly child support. My calculations for this figure were based upon the (Sole-Parenting/Shared-Parenting) Worksheet contained in Appendix IX-C of the New Jersey Rules of Court, a copy of which is attached as Exhibit "B."

6. As the amount of child support requested is that expressly called for in the applicable Child Support Guidelines, and since Defendant has not provided a legitimate basis of any kind that would preclude Defendant's payment of this amount, Plaintiff respectfully requests that the court enter an order directing Defendant to pay child support to me in the amount set forth in Paragraph 5 above.

7. I further request that the Court order Defendant to pay all child support payments ordered pursuant to this Motion through the Probation Department of _____ County.

I hereby certify that the foregoing statements made by me are true. I am aware that if the foregoing statements made by me are willfully false, I am subject to punishment.

Dated: _____

_____, Plaintiff

**Sample Form of Order**

NEW JERSEY SUPERIOR COURT
CHANCERY DIVISION
Plaintiff,                        FAMILY PART
_____ COUNTY

v.                                Docket No.

Defendant                         CIVIL ACTION
                                  ORDER

This matter having been opened to the Court on Motion by Plaintiff, pro se, in the presence of the Defendant, and the Court having considered the papers, exhibits, and oral argument submitted by the parties, and good cause appearing as set forth on the record;

It is on this _____ day of _____, _____,

ORDERED that:

  1. Defendant, _____, shall pay the amount of $ _____ per week in  child support to Plaintiff, effective immediately, pending further order of this Court; and

  2. All child support payments made by Defendant shall be paid through the Probation Department of _____ County in accordance with any and all rules and procedures applicable thereto; and

  3. Two copies of this order shall immediately be filed by Plaintiff with the aforesaid Probation Department; and

  4. A copy of this Order shall be served upon the Defendant within seven (7) days of the entry hereof.

_____
                                                          J.S.C.

*This page intentionally blank.*

**Notice of Equitable Distribution, Alimony, Child Support, and Other Relief**

|                          | NEW JERSEY SUPERIOR COURT |
|--------------------------|---------------------------|
|                          | CHANCERY DIVISION |
| Plaintiff,               | FAMILY PART |
|                          | _____ COUNTY |
| v.                       | Docket No. |
|                          | CIVIL ACTION |
| Defendant                | R. 5:5-2(e) NOTICE OF EQUITABLE |
|                          | DISTRIBUTION, ALIMONY, CHILD |
|                          | SUPPORT AND OTHER RELIEF |

Plaintiff, _____ ("Plaintiff"), pursuant to R. 5:5-2(e), hereby provides Defendant notice with regard to the following issues in the captioned matter:

1. Proposed trial date: _____

2. Assets and their value:

   (a) _____

   (b) _____

   (c) _____

   (d) _____

   (e) _____

   (f) _____

   (g) _____

   (h) _____

   (i) _____

3. Debts to be distributed:

   (a) _____

   (b) _____

   (c) _____

   (d) _____

(e) _____

(f) _____

4. Plaintiff's proposal for distribution of property, assets, and debts: _____
_____
_____

5. Alimony/Child Support:  Plaintiff seeks alimony from Defendant in the amount of $_____, based upon [Example: the income information set forth in Plaintiff's and Defendant's Case Information Statements]. Plaintiff seeks child support for the child of the marriage in the amount of $_____, based upon the Child Support Guidelines set forth in Appendix IX to R. 5:6A.

Dated: _____

_____, Plaintiff

## CERTIFICATION OF SERVICE

I hereby certify that this Appearance was served on Defendant within the time permitted by R. 5:5-2.

Dated: _____

_____, Plaintiff

## Financial Statement for Summary Support Actions

|  |  |
|---|---|
|  | NEW JERSEY SUPERIOR COURT |
|  | CHANCERY DIVISION |
| Plaintiff, | FAMILY PART |
|  | _____ COUNTY |
| v. | Docket No. |
|  |  |
| Defendant | FINANCIAL STATEMENT FOR |
|  | SUMMARY SUPPORT ACTIONS |
|  | PURSUANT TO R. 5:5-3 |

**PART A - PERSONAL INFORMATION:** Provide the following information about yourself.

Name (last, first, middle):                    Social Security No.:

Address:                                        Home Phone No.:

Employer:                                       Occupation:

**PART B - GROSS WEEKLY INCOME:** Report your weekly income. Divide monthly by 4.3; biweekly by 2.

1. Salary, wages, commissions, bonuses, and other payments
   for services performed:                                      $

2. Income from operating a business minus ordinary and
   necessary expenses:                                          $

3. Social Security Retirement (over 62, green check):           $

4. Social Security Disability (green check):                    $

5. Veterans' Administration pension:                            $

6. Worker's compensation:                                       $

7. Other pensions, disability, or retirement income:            $

8. Unemployment compensation:                                   $

9. Interest, dividends, annuities, or other investment income:  $

10. Income from the sale, trade, or conversion of capital assets:    $ _____

11. Income from an estate of a decedent (a will):    $ _____

12. Alimony or separate maintenance from a previous marriage:    $ _____

13. Income from Trusts:    $ _____

14. Other income (specify): _____ $ _____

15. Other income (specify): _____ $ _____

**Total Gross Income** (add lines 1 through 15):    $ _____


**PART C - WEEKLY EXEMPTIONS:** Report the following deductions from your weekly income.

1. Number of tax exemptions claimed: _____

2. Mandatory union dues:    $ _____

3. Mandatory retirement contributions:    $ _____

4. Health insurance premium:
   (you must include child(ren) named in the complaint)    $ _____

5. Alimony or child support orders paid:
   (State: _____) (Case No.: _____)    $ _____


**PART D - OTHER DEPENDENT DEDUCTION:** Complete this section only if (1) you are legally responsible for supporting a child or children other than those named in the support complaint or application; (2) the child or children are living with you; and, (3) you are requesting credit for the amount spent on raising the other child or children when the support award is calculated. You are legally responsible for all children that are yours by birth or adoption. Answer the questions about the other parent of the child or children for whom you are requesting the credit (for example, your current spouse who is the biological mother/father of at least one of your children).

1. Number of other legal dependents:
   (you must provide proof of the legal relationship) _____

2. Number of tax exemption(s) the parent of the other child(ren) claims: _____

3. Weekly gross income of the parent of the other child(ren): $ _____

4. Mandatory union dues of the parent of the other child(ren): $ _____

5. Mandatory retirement contributions of the parent
   of the other child(ren): $ _____

6. Health insurance premiums paid by the parent
   of the other child(ren): $ _____

7. Alimony or child support orders paid by the parent
   of the other child(ren): $ _____

**PART E - CREDIT FOR CHILD CARE EXPENSES:** (Complete this section only if (1) you pay for work related child care for a child or children for whom you and the other parent share a legal responsibility to support and (2) you are requesting a credit for those expenses when your support amount is calculated).

1. Annual child care cost:
   (if paid weekly, divide by 52; if monthly, divide by 4.3) $ _____

2. Child care provider: _____

**PART F - INCOME PAID TO YOUR CHILD(REN) IN YOUR NAME:** (Complete if your child(ren) receive(s) regular payment from a government source in your name, e.g., Social Security, black lung, or veteran's benefits.)

1. Source of benefit(s): _____

2. Weekly amount of benefits (attach verification): $ _____

**PART G - HEALTH INSURANCE BENEFITS:** Answer the following about your health insurance benefits.

1. Health insurance provider: _____    2. Includes Children: ( ) Yes ( ) No

3. Policy carrier: _____    4. Date coverage began: _____

## PART H - CERTIFICATION

I certify that the foregoing statements made by me are true to the best of my knowledge. I am aware that if any of the foregoing statements are willfully false, I am subject to punishment.

Dated: _____

_____
Signature

**IMPORTANT:** You must attach a copy of your last federal tax return or your three most recent pay stubs to verify your income. Self-employed persons and business owners must attach a copy of the most recent federal tax forms for their business. If you are requesting a deduction, you must attach proof of your expenses or obligations.

**Final Judgment of Divorce**

|  |  |
|---|---|
|  | NEW JERSEY SUPERIOR COURT |
|  | CHANCERY DIVISION |
| Plaintiff, | FAMILY PART |
|  | _____ COUNTY |
| v. | Docket No. |
|  | CIVIL ACTION |
| Defendant | FINAL JUDGMENT OF DIVORCE |

This matter coming on to be heard by the Court on _____, _____, and the Plaintiff appearing pro se, in the presence of the Defendant, and the Court having heard and considered the Complaint and proofs, the Plaintiff having been a bona fide resident of the State of New Jersey for more than one year next preceding the commencement of this action, the Court having acquired personal jurisdiction over each of the parties in accordance with the Rules of Court, and the Plaintiff, having pleaded and proved the cause of action for Divorce under the statutes made and provided; and it further appearing that the parties have entered into an agreement dated _____, _____, which Agreement was introduced into evidence, and it further appearing that the Plaintiff and Defendant testified that each had entered into that Agreement fully and voluntarily and that they understood all of the terms of that Agreement; and for good cause shown:

It is on this _____ day of _____, _____,

ORDERED and ADJUDGED that the marriage between the parties is hereby dissolved; and it is further

ORDERED and ADJUDGED that Plaintiff be and hereby is permitted to retake her maiden name of _____; and it is further

ORDERED and ADJUDGED that the Settlement Agreement dated _____, _____, and annexed to this Judgment is hereby made a part of this Final Judgment of Divorce and the same is incorporated herein and made a part hereof and it shall not merge with but shall survive this Final Judgment of Divorce.

_____
J.S.C.

*This page intentionally blank.*

Form **8332**
(Rev. December 2003)

Department of the Treasury
Internal Revenue Service

# Release of Claim to Exemption
# for Child of Divorced or Separated Parents

▶ **Attach** to noncustodial parent's return **each year** exemption is claimed.

OMB No. 1545-0915

Attachment
Sequence No. **115**

| Name of noncustodial parent claiming exemption | Noncustodial parent's social security number (SSN) ▶ | | |
|---|---|---|---|

**Part I**     **Release of Claim to Exemption for Current Year**

I agree not to claim an exemption for_____

Name(s) of child (or children)

for the tax year 20_____ .

_____     _____     _____

Signature of custodial parent releasing claim to exemption          Custodial parent's SSN               Date

**Note:** *If you choose not to claim an exemption for this child (or children) for future tax years, also complete Part II.*

**Part II**     **Release of Claim to Exemption for Future Years** (If completed, see **Noncustodial parent** below.)

I agree not to claim an exemption for_____

Name(s) of child (or children)

for the tax year(s)_____ .

(Specify. See instructions.)

_____     _____     _____

Signature of custodial parent releasing claim to exemption          Custodial parent's SSN               Date

## General Instructions

**Purpose of form.** If you are a **custodial parent,** you may use this form to release your claim to your child's exemption. To do so, complete this form (or a similar statement containing the same information required by this form) and give it to the noncustodial parent who will claim the child's exemption. The noncustodial parent must attach this form or similar statement to his or her tax return **each year** the exemption is claimed.

You are the **custodial parent** if you had custody of the child for most of the year. You are the **noncustodial parent** if you had custody for a shorter period of time or did not have custody at all. For the definition of custody, see **Pub. 501,** Exemptions, Standard Deduction, and Filing Information.

**Support test for children of divorced or separated parents.** Generally, the custodial parent is treated as having provided over half of the child's support if:

• The child received over half of his or her total support for the year from one or both of the parents **and**

• The child was in the custody of one or both of the parents for more than half of the year.

**Note:** *Public assistance payments, such as Temporary Assistance for Needy Families (TANF), are not support provided by the parents.*

For this support test to apply, the parents must be one of the following:

• Divorced or legally separated under a decree of divorce or separate maintenance,

• Separated under a written separation agreement, **or**

• Living apart at all times during the last 6 months of the year.

If the support test applies, and the other four dependency tests in your tax return instruction booklet are also met, the custodial parent can claim the child's exemption.

**Exception.** The custodial parent will not be treated as having provided over half of the child's support if **any** of the following apply.

• The custodial parent agrees not to claim the child's exemption by signing this form or similar statement.

• The child is treated as having received over half of his or her total support from a person under a multiple support agreement (**Form 2120,** Multiple Support Declaration).

• A pre-1985 divorce decree or written separation agreement states that the noncustodial parent can claim the child as a dependent. But the noncustodial parent must provide at least $600 for the child's support during the year. This rule does not apply if the decree or agreement was changed after 1984 to say that the noncustodial parent cannot claim the child as a dependent.

**Additional information.** For more details, see **Pub. 504,** Divorced or Separated Individuals.

## Specific Instructions

**Custodial parent.** You may agree to release your claim to the child's exemption for the current tax year or for future years, or both.

• Complete **Part I** if you agree to release your claim to the child's exemption for the current tax year.

• Complete **Part II** if you agree to release your claim to the child's exemption for any or all future years. If you do, write the specific future year(s) or "all future years" in the space provided in Part II.

To help ensure future support, you may not want to release your claim to the child's exemption for future years.

**Noncustodial parent.** Attach this form or similar statement to your tax return for **each year** you claim the child's exemption. You may claim the exemption **only** if the other four dependency tests in your tax return instruction booklet are met.

**Note:** *If the custodial parent released his or her claim to the child's exemption for any future year, you **must** attach a copy of this form or similar statement to your tax return for each future year that you claim the exemption. **Keep a copy for your records.***

**Paperwork Reduction Act Notice.** We ask for the information on this form to carry out the Internal Revenue laws of the United States. You are required to give us the information. We need it to ensure that you are complying with these laws and to allow us to figure and collect the right amount of tax.

You are not required to provide the information requested on a form that is subject to the Paperwork Reduction Act unless the form displays a valid OMB control number. Books or records relating to a form or its instructions must be retained as long as their contents may become material in the administration of any Internal Revenue law. Generally, tax returns and return information are confidential, as required by Internal Revenue Code section 6103.

The time needed to complete and file this form will vary depending on individual circumstances. The estimated average time is:

| | |
|---|---|
| **Recordkeeping** . . . . . . . | 6 min. |
| **Learning about the law or the form** . . . . . . . . | 5 min. |
| **Preparing the form** . . . . . | 7 min. |
| **Copying, assembling, and sending the form to the IRS** . . | 13 min. |

If you have comments concerning the accuracy of these time estimates or suggestions for making this form simpler, we would be happy to hear from you. You can write to the Tax Products Coordinating Committee, Western Area Distribution Center, Rancho Cordova, CA 95743-0001. **Do not** send the form to this address. Instead, see the Instructions for Form 1040 or Form 1040A.

Cat. No. 13910F          Form **8332** (Rev. 12-2003)

# Index

## A

abuse, 10, 33, 51, 53, 55, 96, 97, 99, 102, 107

Ad Dammum clause, 87, 92

addiction, 2, 3, 32, 96, 99, 107

adultery, 2, 3, 32, 96, 99

Affidavit of Service, 75

alimony, 2, 18, 20, 39, 41, 43, 45, 46, 47, 48, 51, 57, 58, 64, 82, 84, 87, 91, 92, 99, 108, 109

    factors, 47, 48

    types, 46

alternative dispute resolution (ADR), 95, 102

annotations, 20

annuities, 57

annulment, 5, 6

Answer, 98, 99

Appearance, 24, 85

Appellate Division, 15, 16, 21

Armed Forces, 60

arrearage, 69, 70

assault, 103

assets, 2, 8, 19, 20, 34, 35, 39, 40, 41, 47, 48, 68, 76, 89, 105, 109

    hiding, 34, 35

    nonmarital, 40

Atlantic Reporter, 21

attorneys, 3, 4, 5, 14, 16, 17, 18, 19, 23, 24, 25, 26, 27, 28, 29, 30, 33, 34, 37, 44, 53, 54, 55, 63, 71, 72, 73, 76, 78, 83, 84, 88, 95, 96, 97, 98, 99, 101, 102, 108, 110

    fees, 24

    hiring, 24, 98

    referral services, 26

    selecting, 26

    working with, 28

# SPHINX® PUBLISHING ORDER FORM

| BILL TO: | | | SHIP TO: | | |
|---|---|---|---|---|---|
| | | | | | |
| | | | | | |
| Phone # | | Terms | F.O.B. | Chicago, IL | Ship Date |

**Charge my:** ☐ VISA ☐ MasterCard ☐ American Express

☐ **Money Order or Personal Check**

Credit Card Number

Expiration Date

| Qty | ISBN | Title | Retail | Ext. | Qty | ISBN | Title | Retail | Ext. |
|---|---|---|---|---|---|---|---|---|---|
| | | **SPHINX PUBLISHING NATIONAL TITLES** | | | ____ | 1-57248-345-8 | How to Form Your Own Corporation (4E) | $26.95 | ____ |
| ____ | 1-57248-363-6 | 101 Complaint Letters That Get Results | $18.95 | ____ | ____ | 1-57248-520-5 | How to Make Money on Foreclosures | $16.95 | ____ |
| ____ | 1-57248-361-X | The 529 College Savings Plan (2E) | $18.95 | ____ | ____ | 1-57248-232-X | How to Make Your Own Simple Will (3E) | $18.95 | ____ |
| ____ | 1-57248-483-7 | The 529 College Savings Plan Made Simple | $7.95 | ____ | ____ | 1-57248-479-9 | How to Parent with Your Ex | $12.95 | ____ |
| ____ | 1-57248-460-8 | The Alternative Minimum Tax | $14.95 | ____ | ____ | 1-57248-379-2 | How to Register Your Own Copyright (5E) | $24.95 | ____ |
| ____ | 1-57248-349-0 | The Antique and Art Collector's Legal Guide | $24.95 | ____ | ____ | 1-57248-394-6 | How to Write Your Own Living Will (4E) | $18.95 | ____ |
| ____ | 1-57248-347-4 | Attorney Responsibilities & Client Rights | $19.95 | ____ | ____ | 1-57248-156-0 | How to Write Your Own Premarital Agreement (3E) | $24.95 | ____ |
| ____ | 1-57248-482-9 | The Childcare Answer Book | $12.95 | ____ | ____ | 1-57248-504-3 | HR for Small Business | $14.95 | ____ |
| ____ | 1-57248-382-2 | Child Support | $18.95 | ____ | ____ | 1-57248-230-3 | Incorporate in Delaware from Any State | $26.95 | ____ |
| ____ | 1-57248-487-X | Cómo Comprar su Primera Casa | $8.95 | ____ | ____ | 1-57248-158-7 | Incorporate in Nevada from Any State | $24.95 | ____ |
| ____ | 1-57248-488-8 | Cómo Conseguir Trabajo en los Estados Unidos | $8.95 | ____ | ____ | 1-57248-531-0 | The Infertility Answer Book | $16.95 | ____ |
| ____ | 1-57248-148-X | Cómo Hacer su Propio Testamento | $16.95 | ____ | ____ | 1-57248-474-8 | Inmigración a los EE.UU. Paso a Paso (2E) | $24.95 | ____ |
| ____ | 1-57248-532-9 | Cómo Iniciar su Propio Negocio | $8.95 | ____ | ____ | 1-57248-400-4 | Inmigración y Ciudadanía en los EE.UU. Preguntas y Respuestas | $16.95 | ____ |
| ____ | 1-57248-462-4 | Cómo Negociar su Crédito | $8.95 | ____ | ____ | 1-57248-453-5 | Law 101 | $16.95 | ____ |
| ____ | 1-57248-463-2 | Cómo Organizar un Presupuesto | $8.95 | ____ | ____ | 1-57248-374-1 | Law School 101 | $16.95 | ____ |
| ____ | 1-57248-147-1 | Cómo Solicitar su Propio Divorcio | $24.95 | ____ | ____ | 1-57248-377-6 | The Law (In Plain English)® for Small Business | $19.95 | ____ |
| ____ | 1-57248-507-8 | The Complete Book of Corporate Forms (2E) | $29.95 | ____ | ____ | 1-57248-476-4 | The Law (In Plain English)® for Writers | $14.95 | ____ |
| ____ | 1-57248-383-0 | The Complete Book of Insurance | $18.95 | ____ | ____ | 1-57248-223-0 | Legal Research Made Easy (3E) | $21.95 | ____ |
| ____ | 1-57248499-3 | The Complete Book of Personal Legal Forms | $24.95 | ____ | ____ | 1-57248-449-7 | The Living Trust Kit | $21.95 | ____ |
| ____ | 1-57248-528-0 | The Complete Book of Real Estate Contracts | $18.95 | ____ | ____ | 1-57248-165-X | Living Trusts and Other Ways to Avoid Probate (3E) | $24.95 | ____ |
| ____ | 1-57248-500-0 | The Complete Credit Repair Kit | $19.95 | ____ | ____ | 1-57248-486-1 | Making Music Your Business | $18.95 | ____ |
| ____ | 1-57248-458-6 | The Complete Hiring and Firing Handbook | $18.95 | ____ | ____ | 1-57248-186-2 | Manual de Beneficios para el Seguro Social | $18.95 | ____ |
| ____ | 1-57248-484-5 | The Complete Home-Based Business Kit | $16.95 | ____ | ____ | 1-57248-220-6 | Mastering the MBE | $16.95 | ____ |
| ____ | 1-57248-353-9 | The Complete Kit to Selling Your Own Home | $18.95 | ____ | ____ | 1-57248-455-1 | Minding Her Own Business, 4E | $14.95 | ____ |
| ____ | 1-57248-229-X | The Complete Legal Guide to Senior Care | $21.95 | ____ | ____ | 1-57248-480-2 | The Mortgage Answer Book | $14.95 | ____ |
| ____ | 1-57248-498-5 | The Complete Limited Liability Company Kit | $24.95 | ____ | ____ | 1-57248-167-6 | Most Val. Business Legal Forms You'll Ever Need (3E) | $21.95 | ____ |
| ____ | 1-57248-391-1 | The Complete Partnership Book | $24.95 | ____ | ____ | 1-57248-388-1 | The Power of Attorney Handbook (5E) | $22.95 | ____ |
| ____ | 1-57248-201-X | The Complete Patent Book | $26.95 | ____ | ____ | 1-57248-332-6 | Profit from Intellectual Property | $28.95 | ____ |
| ____ | 1-57248-514-0 | The Complete Patent Kit | $39.95 | ____ | ____ | 1-57248-329-6 | Protect Your Patent | $24.95 | ____ |
| ____ | 1-57248-480-2 | The Mortgage Answer Book | $14.95 | ____ | ____ | 1-57248-376-8 | Nursing Homes and Assisted Living Facilities | $19.95 | ____ |
| ____ | 1-57248-369-5 | Credit Smart | $18.95 | ____ | ____ | 1-57248-385-7 | Quick Cash | $14.95 | ____ |
| ____ | 1-57248-163-3 | Crime Victim's Guide to Justice (2E) | $21.95 | ____ | ____ | 1-57248-350-4 | El Seguro Social Preguntas y Respuestas | $16.95 | ____ |
| ____ | 1-57248-481-0 | The Easy Will and Living Will Kit | $16.95 | ____ | ____ | 1-57248386-5 | Seniors' Rights | $19.95 | ____ |
| ____ | 1-57248-251-6 | The Entrepreneur's Internet Handbook | $21.95 | ____ | ____ | 1-57248-217-6 | Sexual Harassment: Your Guide to Legal Action | $18.95 | ____ |
| ____ | 1-57248-235-4 | The Entrepreneur's Legal Guide | $26.95 | ____ | ____ | 1-57248-378-4 | Sisters-in-Law | $16.95 | ____ |
| ____ | 1-57248-160-9 | Essential Guide to Real Estate Leases | $18.95 | ____ | ____ | 1-57248-219-2 | The Small Business Owner's Guide to Bankruptcy | $21.95 | ____ |
| ____ | 1-57248-375-X | Fathers' Rights | $19.95 | ____ | ____ | 1-57248-395-4 | The Social Security Benefits Handbook (4E) | $18.95 | ____ |
| ____ | 1-57248-517-5 | File Your Own Divorce (6E) | $24.95 | ____ | ____ | 1-57248-216-8 | Social Security Q&A | $12.95 | ____ |
| ____ | 1-57248-450-0 | Financing Your Small Business | $17.95 | ____ | ____ | 1-57248-328-8 | Starting Out or Starting Over | $14.95 | ____ |
| ____ | 1-57248-459-4 | Fired, Laid Off or Forced Out | $14.95 | ____ | ____ | 1-57248-525-6 | Teen Rights (and Responsibilities) (2E) | $14.95 | ____ |
| ____ | 1-57248-502-7 | The Frequent Traveler's Guide | $14.95 | ____ | ____ | 1-57248-457-8 | Tax Power for the Self-Employed | $17.95 | ____ |
| ____ | 1-57248-331-8 | Gay & Lesbian Rights | $26.95 | ____ | ____ | 1-57248-366-0 | Tax Smarts for Small Business | $21.95 | ____ |
| ____ | 1-57248-139-0 | Grandparents' Rights (3E) | $24.95 | ____ | ____ | 1-57248-530-2 | Unmarried Parents' Rights (3E) | $16.95 | ____ |
| ____ | 1-57248-475-6 | Guía de Inmigración a Estados Unidos (4E) | $24.95 | ____ | ____ | 1-57248-362-8 | U.S. Immigration and Citizenship Q&A | $18.95 | ____ |
| ____ | 1-57248-187-0 | Guía de Justicia para Víctimas del Crimen | $21.95 | ____ | ____ | 1-57248-387-3 | U.S. Immigration Step by Step (2E) | $24.95 | ____ |
| ____ | 1-57248-253-2 | Guía Esencial para los Contratos de Arrendamiento de Bienes Raices | $22.95 | ____ | ____ | 1-57248-392-X | U.S.A. Immigration Guide (5E) | $26.95 | ____ |
| ____ | 1-57248-334-2 | Homeowner's Rights | $19.95 | ____ | ____ | 1-57248-178-0 | ¡Visas! ¡Visas! ¡Visas! | $9.95 | ____ |
| ____ | 1-57248-164-1 | How to Buy a Condominium or Townhome (2E) | $19.95 | ____ | ____ | 1-57248-177-2 | The Weekend Landlord | $16.95 | ____ |
| ____ | 1-57248-197-7 | How to Buy Your First Home (2E) | $14.95 | ____ | ____ | 1-57248-451-9 | What to Do — Before "I DO" | $14.95 | ____ |
| ____ | 1-57248-384-9 | How to Buy a Franchise | $19.95 | ____ | ____ | 1-57248-531-0 | What to Do When You Can't Get Pregnant | $16.95 | ____ |
| ____ | 1-57248-472-1 | How to File Your Own Bankruptcy (6E) | $21.95 | ____ | | | | | |
| ____ | 1-57248-390-3 | How to Form a Nonprofit Corporation (3E) | $24.95 | ____ | | | **(Form Continued on Following Page)** | **Subtotal** | ____ |

To order, call Sourcebooks at 1-800-432-7444 or FAX (630) 961-2168 (Bookstores, libraries, wholesalers—please call for discount)
*Prices are subject to change without notice.*
Find more legal information at: **www.SphinxLegal.com**

# SPHINX® PUBLISHING ORDER FORM

| Qty | ISBN | Title | Retail | Ext. |
|-----|------|-------|--------|------|
| ____ | 1-57248-225-7 | Win Your Unemployment Compensation Claim (2E) | $21.95 | ____ |
| ____ | 1-57248-330-X | The Wills, Estate Planning and Trusts Legal Kit | $26.95 | ____ |
| ____ | 1-57248-473-X | Winning Your Personal Injury Claim (3E) | $24.95 | ____ |
| ____ | 1-57248-333-4 | Working with Your Homeowners Association | $19.95 | ____ |
| ____ | 1-57248-380-6 | Your Right to Child Custody, Visitation and Support (3E) | $24.95 | ____ |
| ____ | 1-57248-505-1 | Your Rights at Work | $14.95 | ____ |

### CALIFORNIA TITLES

| Qty | ISBN | Title | Retail | Ext. |
|-----|------|-------|--------|------|
| ____ | 1-57248-489-6 | How to File for Divorce in CA (5E) | $26.95 | ____ |
| ____ | 1-57248-464-0 | How to Settle and Probate an Estate in CA (2E) | $28.95 | ____ |
| ____ | 1-57248-336-9 | How to Start a Business in CA (2E) | $21.95 | ____ |
| ____ | 1-57248-194-3 | How to Win in Small Claims Court in CA (2E) | $18.95 | ____ |
| ____ | 1-57248-246-X | Make Your Own CA Will | $18.95 | ____ |
| ____ | 1-57248-397-0 | Landlords' Legal Guide in CA (2E) | $24.95 | ____ |
| ____ | 1-57248-241-9 | Tenants' Rights in CA | $21.95 | ____ |

### FLORIDA TITLES

| Qty | ISBN | Title | Retail | Ext. |
|-----|------|-------|--------|------|
| ____ | 1-57248-396-2 | How to File for Divorce in FL (8E) | $28.95 | ____ |
| ____ | 1-57248-356-3 | How to Form a Corporation in FL (6E) | $24.95 | ____ |
| ____ | 1-57248-490-X | How to Form a Limited Liability Co. in FL (4E) | $24.95 | ____ |
| ____ | 1-57071-401-0 | How to Form a Partnership in FL | $22.95 | ____ |
| ____ | 1-57248-456-X | How to Make a FL Will (7E) | $16.95 | ____ |
| ____ | 1-57248-354-7 | How to Probate and Settle an Estate in FL (5E) | $26.95 | ____ |
| ____ | 1-57248-339-3 | How to Start a Business in FL (7E) | $21.95 | ____ |
| ____ | 1-57248-204-4 | How to Win in Small Claims Court in FL (7E) | $18.95 | ____ |
| ____ | 1-57248-381-4 | Land Trusts in Florida (7E) | $29.95 | ____ |
| ____ | 1-57248-491-8 | Landlords' Rights and Duties in FL (10E) | $22.95 | ____ |

### GEORGIA TITLES

| Qty | ISBN | Title | Retail | Ext. |
|-----|------|-------|--------|------|
| ____ | 1-57248-340-7 | How to File for Divorce in GA (5E) | $21.95 | ____ |
| ____ | 1-57248-493-4 | How to Start a Business in GA (4E) | $21.95 | ____ |

### ILLINOIS TITLES

| Qty | ISBN | Title | Retail | Ext. |
|-----|------|-------|--------|------|
| ____ | 1-57248-244-3 | Child Custody, Visitation, and Support in IL | $24.95 | ____ |
| ____ | 1-57248-206-0 | How to File for Divorce in IL (3E) | $24.95 | ____ |
| ____ | 1-57248-170-6 | How to Make an IL Will (3E) | $16.95 | ____ |
| ____ | 1-57248-265-9 | How to Start a Business in IL (4E) | $21.95 | ____ |
| ____ | 1-57248-252-4 | Landlords' Legal Guide in IL | $24.95 | ____ |

### MARYLAND, VIRGINIA AND THE DISTRICT OF COLUMBIA

| Qty | ISBN | Title | Retail | Ext. |
|-----|------|-------|--------|------|
| ____ | 1-57248-240-0 | How to File for Divorce in MD, VA, and DC | $28.95 | ____ |
| ____ | 1-57248-359-8 | How to Start a Business in MD, VA, or DC | $21.95 | ____ |

### MASSACHUSETTS TITLES

| Qty | ISBN | Title | Retail | Ext. |
|-----|------|-------|--------|------|
| ____ | 1-57248-115-3 | How to Form a Corporation in MA | $24.95 | ____ |
| ____ | 1-57248-466-7 | How to Start a Business in MA (4E) | $21.95 | ____ |
| ____ | 1-57248-398-9 | Landlords' Legal Guide in MA (2E) | $24.95 | ____ |

### MICHIGAN TITLES

| Qty | ISBN | Title | Retail | Ext. |
|-----|------|-------|--------|------|
| ____ | 1-57248-467-5 | How to File for Divorce in MI (4E) | $24.95 | ____ |
| ____ | 1-57248-182-X | How to Make a MI Will (3E) | $16.95 | ____ |
| ____ | 1-57248-468-3 | How to Start a Business in MI (4E) | $18.95 | ____ |

### MINNESOTA TITLES

| Qty | ISBN | Title | Retail | Ext. |
|-----|------|-------|--------|------|
| ____ | 1-57248-142-0 | How to File for Divorce in MN | $21.95 | ____ |
| ____ | 1-57248-179-X | How to Form a Corporation in MN | $24.95 | ____ |
| ____ | 1-57248-178-1 | How to Make a MN Will (2E) | $16.95 | ____ |

### NEW JERSEY TITLES

| Qty | ISBN | Title | Retail | Ext. |
|-----|------|-------|--------|------|
| ____ | 1-57248-512-4 | File for Divorce in NJ (2E) | $24.95 | ____ |
| ____ | 1-57248-448-9 | How to Start a Business in NJ | $21.95 | ____ |

### NEW YORK TITLES

| Qty | ISBN | Title | Retail | Ext. |
|-----|------|-------|--------|------|
| ____ | 1-57248-193-5 | Child Custody, Visitation and Support in NY | $26.95 | ____ |
| ____ | 1-57248-351-2 | File for Divorce in NY | $26.95 | ____ |
| ____ | 1-57248-249-4 | How to Form a Corporation in NY (2E) | $24.95 | ____ |
| ____ | 1-57248-401-2 | How to Make a NY Will (3E) | $16.95 | ____ |
| ____ | 1-57248-469-1 | How to Start a Business in NY (3E) | $21.95 | ____ |
| ____ | 1-57248-198-6 | How to Win in Small Claims Court in NY (2E) | $18.95 | ____ |
| ____ | 1-57248-122-6 | Tenants' Rights in NY | $21.95 | ____ |

### NORTH CAROLINA AND SOUTH CAROLINA TITLES

| Qty | ISBN | Title | Retail | Ext. |
|-----|------|-------|--------|------|
| ____ | 1-57248-185-4 | How to File for Divorce in NC (3E) | $22.95 | ____ |
| ____ | 1-57248-371-7 | How to Start a Business in NC or SC | $24.95 | ____ |
| ____ | 1-57248-091-2 | Landlords' Rights & Duties in NC | $21.95 | ____ |

### OHIO TITLES

| Qty | ISBN | Title | Retail | Ext. |
|-----|------|-------|--------|------|
| ____ | 1-57248-503-5 | How to File for Divorce in OH (3E) | $24.95 | ____ |
| ____ | 1-57248-174-9 | How to Form a Corporation in OH | $24.95 | ____ |
| ____ | 1-57248-173-0 | How to Make an OH Will | $16.95 | ____ |

### PENNSYLVANIA TITLES

| Qty | ISBN | Title | Retail | Ext. |
|-----|------|-------|--------|------|
| ____ | 1-57248-242-7 | Child Custody, Visitation and Support in PA | $26.95 | ____ |
| ____ | 1-57248-495-0 | How to File for Divorce in PA (4E) | $24.95 | ____ |
| ____ | 1-57248-358-X | How to Form a Corporation in PA | $24.95 | ____ |
| ____ | 1-57248-094-7 | How to Make a PA Will (2E) | $16.95 | ____ |
| ____ | 1-57248-357-1 | How to Start a Business in PA (3E) | $21.95 | ____ |
| ____ | 1-57248-245-1 | Landlords' Legal Guide in PA | $24.95 | ____ |

### TEXAS TITLES

| Qty | ISBN | Title | Retail | Ext. |
|-----|------|-------|--------|------|
| ____ | 1-57248-171-4 | Child Custody, Visitation, and Support in TX | $22.95 | ____ |
| ____ | 1-57248-399-7 | How to File for Divorce in TX (4E) | $24.95 | ____ |
| ____ | 1-57248-470-5 | How to Form a Corporation in TX (3E) | $24.95 | ____ |
| ____ | 1-57248-496-9 | How to Probate and Settle an Estate in TX (4E) | $26.95 | ____ |
| ____ | 1-57248-471-3 | How to Start a Business in TX (4E) | $21.95 | ____ |
| ____ | 1-57248-111-0 | How to Win in Small Claims Court in TX (2E) | $16.95 | ____ |
| ____ | 1-57248-355-5 | Landlords' Legal Guide in TX | $24.95 | ____ |
| ____ | 1-57248-513-2 | Write Your Own TX Will (4E) | $16.95 | ____ |

### WASHINGTON TITLES

| Qty | ISBN | Title | Retail | Ext. |
|-----|------|-------|--------|------|
| ____ | 1-57248-522-1 | File for Divorce in WA | $24.95 | ____ |

SubTotal This page ____

SubTotal previous page ____

Shipping— $5.00 for 1st book, $1.00 each additional ____

Illinois residents add 6.75% sales tax ____

Connecticut residents add 6.00% sales tax ____

**Total** ____

To order, call Sourcebooks at 1-800-432-7444 or FAX (630) 961-2168 (Bookstores, libraries, wholesalers—please call for discount)

*Prices are subject to change without notice.*

Find more legal information at: **www.SphinxLegal.com**